# Lame Stories from the Vet from Inglewood

# Lame Stories from the Vet from Inglewood

Sandra Chesterton

| Library of Congress Control Number: | | 2023905945 |
|---|---|---|
| ISBN: | Hardcover | 978-1-6698-8051-6 |
| | Softcover | 978-1-6698-8050-9 |
| | eBook | 978-1-6698-8049-3 |



Print information available on the last page.

Rev. date: 04/04/2023

**To order additional copies of this book, contact:**
Xlibris
NZ TFN: 0800 008 756 (Toll Free inside the NZ)
NZ Local: 9-801 1905 (+64 9801 1905 from outside New Zealand)
www.Xlibris.co.nz
Orders@Xlibris.co.nz
849990

# CONTENTS


Foreword ........ vii
Acknowledgements ........ ix

Chapter 1 Desperation (1983) ........ 1
Chapter 2 Beginnings (1950–1968) ........ 13
Chapter 3 Journeys on the Way (1969–1974) ........ 26
Chapter 4 New Vet, New Country (1974) ........ 36
Chapter 5 Settling In (1974–1980) ........ 46
Chapter 6 Learning Lameness Part 1 (1974–1980) ........ 56
Chapter 7 Learning Lameness Part 2 (1974–1980) ........ 66
Chapter 8 Real Live Data (1980s) ........ 76
Chapter 9 Right Place, Right Time, Right Friends (1985) ........ 83
Chapter 10 Cow CCTV (1986–) ........ 92
Chapter 11 Lame Vet (1990–1993) ........ 101
Chapter 12 Videoing Myself and Cows (1993–1999) ........ 117
Chapter 13 A Scientist in the Field (1997–2003) ........ 126
Chapter 14 Lameness Solutions: Making Tracks (–2008) ........ 140
Chapter 15 Ballroom Dancing (2002–2004) ........ 149
Chapter 16 From Vet on the Ground to Flying Vet (2004–2006) 158
Chapter 17 New Angles (2008–2010) ........ 171
Chapter 18 Patience Everywhere (2010–) ........ 184
Chapter 19 Enter Infection (2012) ........ 195
Chapter 20 Solving the Double Problem (2012–2015) ........ 205
Chapter 21 Old House, New House (2012–2016) ........ 216
Chapter 22 Data Addiction Carries On (2017–2022) ........ 226

Footnotes ........ 237

# FOREWORD

I AM NEIL CHESTERTON, the vet from Inglewood, and I am writing this foreword because this book is about me although I didn't actually write it.

I love teaching, especially about cows. I always use real life stories to get my points across. When I was travelling and doing a series of talks with a vet friend, Gonzalo, in Uruguay, he said I should make a book of the stories that I tell which come from around the world – "Call it 'Lame Stories' or something like that," he said. "Then everyone can enjoy them."

I am not good at writing things down, so my wife, Sandra, has done that instead of me. She decided to write the book in the first person and has made the stories sound just like me! She is the ghost writer.

Somehow on occasions in my life I have been the right person in the right place at the right time. Some things were waiting for the right moment to fit together or to be discovered. I just happened to be the data geek on the spot willing to write a record when some data needed to be collected. I just happened to be the person listening when a farmer had a story to tell.

Sandra has chosen some of my stories about becoming a vet and some of the interesting experiences I have been privileged to take part in. Many of these stories involve others who have crossed my path, and I want to thank them for their input into my journey. Some of the stories are more about cows than people. And many of the stories are ones that farmers told me and I remembered. Some of the people have been named and others have been called by pseudonyms, mostly because I don't know their real names.

If you are a dairy farmer reading this, I hope these little stories Sandra has collected give you a jumble of experiences that will enrich your understanding of lameness of cows and how to prevent it and hopefully on the way give you some lightbulb moments that change the way you see cows.

If you are not a farmer, I hope you will enjoy an insider view of farming cows. And if you are an animal lover – especially a cow lover – then you will enjoy learning that cows are not dumb animals. I hope that every reader will enjoy meeting people through these pages whom you may not have met otherwise.

So here are my "lame" stories as collected by Sandra.

Neil Chesterton,
*Inglewood 2023*

# ACKNOWLEDGEMENTS

THE BOOK IS about my family – so they are the first ones that I want to thank – for being their special interesting selves. A special thanks to my husband, Neil, who has allowed me to portray his enthusiastic data collecting self without complaining – except to forbid the word "cute" as a comment of his. It gets assigned to me instead. This book has been years in the making and you have had to endure "the book" or the "Lame Book" comments and questions for a long time. Thanks also to my writer son, Peter, who turned his skills on to my earlier manuscripts and thereby improved them greatly. Thanks also to friends who gave me advice. Thanks to Carol Pritchard who read the manuscript and gave valuable feedback. And finally to Gonzalo Tuñon who was the original instigator of the whole project.

# CHAPTER 1

# Desperation (1983)

IT WAS A fine spring day as I drove out in the early morning to meet up with a farmer named Colin on his farm near Inglewood. I was the vet for his cows. In Taranaki, New Zealand, the grass is somehow greener than green, if that is possible. However, darkness clouded Colin's spring morning. He could not see the blue sky. The black cloud this morning was lameness.[1]

He probably didn't really have time to look up. Spring[2] is a busy, almost frenetic time for farmers in the seasonal dairy system[3] that operates in New Zealand. "Spring" can start as early as July, just whenever the cows begin to have their calves. Usually, the farmer has timed the cows to all calve within as short a time frame as possible. This means that the cows will all be at the same stage of their milking season so that they all dry off together for a rest – and a holiday for the farmer. However, this does mean that the springtime, when they all calve together, is anything but a holiday.

Every day there are cows delivering their calves who must be checked; the newly born calves have to be collected from the paddocks and taken to shelter and fed the first milk. There may be a cow that has got into difficulty calving and needs to be helped, or a vet might have to be called. Then the cows that have already calved need to be milked, always checking for mastitis.[4] All this is before breakfast.

In the middle of the day, there are other regular jobs such as deciding which paddock the cows will spend the night in and general maintenance or fixing something such as a pump that has broken down. Then, just when the calving has finished and the cows are happily milking, it is time to think about next year's calves. Mating time. And that is only the farm work – there might be children to take to school or housework to be done as well.

Taranaki, where the town of Inglewood is to be found and where I live, is a central western province of the North Island of New Zealand. Looking at a map of New Zealand, you can see that Taranaki sticks out into the Tasman Sea as the volcanic mountain of the same name has made a sort of lump on the side of the island. Indeed, the province is dominated by that mountain. It is a good reason to live here if you like mountain walking and hiking. It juts out into the sea, so if you like surfing, you would come here as well. The climate is mild because of the sea being nearby, and the coastal towns make for ideal places to retire to. Also, Taranaki is covered with green. It used to be mostly thick forest, but now much of the land has been cleared and is growing grass for our thousands of dairy cows.

View of Taranaki

It is in spring that the grass grows at a seemingly impossible rate – luscious bundles that cows fairly stuff into their mouths. A perfect time to have calves and produce milk on this grass. A cow, upon arriving in the paddock, goes to the best-looking clumps of grass and seizes great mouthfuls of the stuff with her tongue and then swallows it nearly whole. In the spring weather, when the grass is growing very fast and is extra lush, the cows can sometimes get into trouble eating too much of it too fast. To eat enough grass to make milk, a cow has to cram in at least sixty kilos of it every day, needing to take a staggering thirty thousand bites, one a second.[5] It is almost like vacuuming the field. What she is doing is harvesting the sunshine.

Later, she sits down and gradually regurgitates the grass as small balls or cuds to chew and enjoy. Well, I am not sure whether cows actually do enjoy it, but they look like they are in a dream chewing away. We, as humans, also enjoy chewing something like a stalk of grass; whoever invented chewing gum possibly saw that people would be kept calm and patient if they had something to chew. Cows will spend about eight hours per day just chewing. Each cud gets chewed on average around forty times. With a purpose.

The cow has four stomachs to manage to extract the goodness from the grass to nourish itself and, if she has a calf, to also produce milk. The first, biggest stomach which receives the fresh grass is really a giant mixing bag and brewing pot where the grass, as it gets smashed into finer particles by all that chewing, also mixes with special bacteria which do the heavy work of digesting. Then as the brew moves along, all the cow's other stomachs need to do is to remove the liquid and soak up the goodies. A walking, milk-making miracle.

Some of these things I have learned by just watching cows and enjoying the lovely scenery. It is fun to watch cows and to learn trivial facts to amaze your friends – did you know some cows are left-hand rotating chewers and others right-handed; some may be both. Every time I think of this, I have a little try to see if I am a right-handed masticator or a left-handed one.

I did sometimes feel guilty getting paid to work here. And I was certainly working in a beautiful place but a place with problems to be solved by watching those same animals.

After I arrived in Inglewood, every day I was meeting people with problems with their animals. You meet the people first. For this, you need to have some people skills, trying to get along with as many people as possible. Some people might call this a sort of "bedside manner" for vets. This is before you can check out the cows – the actual patients. Sometimes, the relationships between myself and the people had a few bumps to start with.

When I first started out in Inglewood, I was always meeting new people. First, meeting the other New Zealand vets. Then Gunner, the vet from Denmark, who taught me lots of helpful hints and gave me good ideas. Then on my rounds, meeting farmers. I met Pete, a farmer with lots of lame cows to be treated, with whom I shared learning how to treat those cows and how to get them walking well again. I met Colin, the farmer I was visiting today, who provoked me to investigate the reasons why cows might get lame in the first place. All these had parts to play in my story before that day when I drove out to visit Colin's farm.

However, some people I met while doing my vet work taught me that it always pays to drop the bedside manner and be myself no matter what the circumstances – take Joe, for instance. He was another farmer I met early in my career.

The day I first met Joe, I was out at a farm just doing my ordinary veterinary work and enjoying the scenery, when I called in on the radio telephone to see what was next. It turned out that the office had been trying to contact me for a while to tell me that I was late for my next visit.

"Don't worry," the lady receptionist in the vet office said, "stay calm and it will be all right – just tell him that you had a difficult calving or something."

"Okay," I said, "ah, what is the call?"

"You are half an hour late for a vaccination at Joe's place – he might be a little angry." This was a real understatement.

Vaccinations were the only calls that had a time of appointment attached as usually there were quite a few cows to gather, and then they had to wait in a group in a yard. I had clean forgotten that I had this call booked in. I had not met Joe before this. I quickly got going and headed off to his farm. As I drove up towards the cattle yard, I was met by a rather flustered wife.

"Don't worry," she said quickly and added, "don't say anything. Tell him you were delayed."

I drove up to the shed, and there was a very tall farmer wearing a straw hat and with a very red face. He was obviously furious at my lateness and having to hold his cows back in the yard.

He began to shout at me.

"I am sorry," I said, and then I took a breath and admitted, "It is entirely my fault I am late. I forgot your call was waiting."

He stopped shouting in midsentence. Gruffly he said, "Well . . . well, let's get on with it . . ."

By the time we had finished, we were on good terms.

"Call me Joe," he said, and since then, we have always got on well – with my lateness now just a joke.

Studying at university in vet school in Sydney, we hadn't been taught how to deal with cantankerous farmers, but I had learned that you just need to be up front and that dealing with the people who own the cows is just as important as fixing their cows. If the cow has a problem, so does the farmer.

I was finding out that a problem that many cows had was a lameness problem. At university, we had not had much teaching on lameness problems or how to treat them. We had learned even less on how to prevent lameness. What a good start for a vet who was going to end up in New Zealand working in a dairy practice, meeting lame cows almost every day! In fact, as by then I had discovered, the university teachers knew as much as I did about the type of lameness that I was seeing on the farms that I visited – meaning very little. No one until then had really studied it or realised that there was a difference between lame cows on pastures and lame cows that had been housed all their lives.

The one thing that I did remember from my university days was something that didn't happen in a lecture room. It was a coincidence that happened one day as I and two other vet students were walking home for lunch after a morning of practical study out on the farm. We were passing the cattle yards of the university farm where we were staying during the final year of our veterinary studies. We happened to notice a Jersey cow in a crush or holding pen. The three of us strolled over to see what was happening. It looked like some action.

There was a visiting vet there who asked if we would like to see how he treated a lame cow. He happened to be a vet from New Zealand. Of course, we were enthusiastic to see something really practical, and with our very limited experience so far, anything would be a real treat. He showed us how to lift a foot, examine it, and treat it so that the cow could walk much better. This probably wasn't the only session on lameness, but this is the experience that I remember – a vet who enjoyed helping the cow and did a good job. We continued to the dining room for our lunch, and this event was stored in the back of my mind.

Now with university behind me and at work in New Zealand, I was finding that every day I was treating lame cows. Every day farmers would ask me what they should do to stop their cows from getting lame. And I didn't know! And neither did anyone else or any of the books I had read – written about cows that were housed. In New Zealand, where I was working, most of the cows live outside on green paddocks where they eat the grass where it grows.

In the Northern Hemisphere, it is quite the other way around – the cows live inside, and the farmer brings the feed to them. They have huge barns where they live, and the farmer spends lots of time cutting grass to make stored feed for them as well as buying in grains. Of course, there is a reason for this, as the weather there gets much colder, and in the winter, there is no grass to eat in the paddock anyway – it may even be covered with snow. In the warmer months, most of the cows will go outside to graze for some of the time, so they are not totally shut in. This makes for a completely different life for the cows and for the cows' feet. Maybe the lameness problem would just have to stay in the back of my mind until someone solved it.

Then I met Colin.

In North Taranaki, the landscape has the look of a green feather duvet or eiderdown that is lumpy, spreading out from the foothills of the mountain. Our resident volcano, Taranaki Maunga, otherwise known as "the mountain" because of its various eruptions, has seen to it that all the area around it has lumpy hills filled with (not feathers but) really rich well-draining volcanic soils, thick and deep. This soil grows lots of good eating grass for our dairy cows. Of course, all these bumps get in the way of travel, for vehicles as well as walking cows. This is most annoying when you have to go around a hill, not the shortest way across the farm. Or, worse still, when you need to go down a steep hill and then up the other side. But it means that the picture is always changing, and there is always the chance of a stunning view from the tops of the hills – if you don't get blown off, that is.

From some of the hills near Inglewood, you can get a 360-degree view with one single mountain cone on one side and on the opposite side a view of the bigger mountains that are at the centre of the North

Island. And if you are high enough and far enough north, you may even see the sea as well. These hills and winding roads also create a game of what-is-around-the-corner as you drive off to visit a farm – and you hope it isn't a milk tanker truck. The spin-off from all the heavy traffic of milk tankers needing to daily travel between farms to collect the white liquid gold produced by the cows, is that the roads are almost all well surfaced. In fact, the first rural roads in New Zealand to be surfaced with bitumen were in Taranaki.

Colin's farm was nestled among some of these bumps. His farm was on the side of a steep valley, one of the many which radiated out from the mountain. The road to the farm followed the ridge – where the milking shed was positioned close by it – so that the milk tanker could easily collect the milk. The paddocks were down the hill. Although Colin's farm was quite typical, Colin was not a typical farmer but an accountant who had decided to have a change and milk cows.

Many times, I find that people who don't start out as farmers but as something else, often end up becoming really great farmers. He had bought a farm near Inglewood with a herd of about 180 cows. The farm was operational when he bought it, so he just began milking cows – only to find that too many of his cows were getting lame far too often. I think that he had nearly a third of his cows go lame that season. And as his vet, I had no answers – yet. The plan to find some answers was about to get into action.

Being an accountant, he could calculate how much in plain money terms that the lameness was costing him, and it was lots of money. He knew how much he was losing on each lame cow and how soon he wouldn't be able to meet his mortgage payments. That is a lot of extra stress for a farmer, especially a new farmer, and at a time of the year when there was so much else going on.

In fact, we don't really know exactly how much a lame cow costs the farmer in dollars as it depends on when the cow gets lame, what sort of lameness it is, whether it gets better quickly and so on. Most people say that on average it probably costs the farmer about $250 in New Zealand terms per cow. If you have four cows get lame, that is around $1,000.

All costs that surely could be avoided. No wonder there were "clouds" over Colin's farm.

But there is another cost to the farmer that I learned that day on Colin's farm: the "cloud" of feeling helpless. This is how it all came about.

It was one day about eight years into my vet career and I was talking to Colin, again, along the same lines about lame cows.

"Why are my cows getting lame? What can I do about it?" he asked in desperation. The same question that all the other farmers were asking. Then and there I made a decision: If my Northern Hemisphere vet books can't give my farmers an answer, I will have to find one out for myself for the Southern Hemisphere.

I dropped the bedside manner, "Well, I really don't know," I said to Colin.

It was the truth.

"But I mean to find out. I will come to your farm and have a look around and watch what happens with the cows from the beginning of your day."

What did I already know? Well, very little. I did already know that here in New Zealand, lameness was different from what was described in the books that I had on my shelf. Here, something different was happening to the cows' feet. I knew this because I had been writing things down and collecting vet data for a few years already. And nothing was adding up.

To Colin, his animals were really important. They were his livelihood and also his responsibility. Watching cows get lame and have to limp along is hard on a farmer. His animals had a problem, and he felt it. I was, in a way, his only hope.

I arrived at the farm at five o'clock in the morning on the day appointed. It was still mostly dark, but I was ready to see what I could see. I didn't really know what I was looking for, but if keenness was part of the deal, at least I had that – or maybe you could call it desperation. I had to be back at the clinic for the rest of my calls by 8:00 a.m. This made a very small window of time in which to start to find out as much as I could about lameness. That window had just opened up its first crack as, little did I realise, that this was to be a turning point and, in a way, the real start of my vet career.

Colin's farm was a small farm typical of Taranaki, some green hilly pastures with cows dotted around one of the paddocks eating the grass and a "track" for the cows to walk along, which doubled as a roadway for the tractor or motorbike to get back and forth from the various farm paddocks to the place where the cows were milked – generally called "the shed."

As I arrived early in the morning on the day my lameness career was to start, Colin was about to go on his motor bike to fetch the cows from the paddock at the bottom of the hill. I hopped on the back, and we set off along the track. Halfway to the paddock he stopped and dropped me off so that I could watch how well the cows walked along the track.

My plan was to hide behind the hedge so that the cows would not notice me, and then I could see how the cows walked on the track and maybe spot some of the problems. I sat down in the paddock behind a hedge with my notebook ready to make some good observations, while Colin disappeared into the paddock where the cows had been grazing that night.

Five minutes later, it wasn't the cows coming out of the paddock – it was Colin himself coming back.

"Hop on the bike," he ordered. "I want to show you something."

I hesitated, "I am sure I can see better from here."

"No, you have to see this, and you will know why I need you."

We rode along the track back to the paddock, and there, lying on the grass, were three dead cows.

They had died of frothy bloat. This is a particular problem with ruminant animals with four stomachs. If a cow eats too much fresh, green grass too quickly and the first stomach (rumen) starts to ferment, it can quickly fill with bubbles or froth. If the cow cannot burp or belch enough of the air out because it is in tiny frothy bubbles, then the stomach just keeps filling up with bubbles until she can hardly breathe. If no one rescues her, she can die of suffocation.

"Oh no!" I said, thinking that the morning observation was off. "What can I do to help?"

"Nothing," said Colin in a blank tone. "This is a terrible loss, but I know what I did wrong – I didn't drench them last milking. My fault. But with lameness, that's worse, I don't know what I am doing wrong with that. My cows suffer for days before I can get them right. I feel like I have let them down. There must be something that I can do to prevent lameness, but I don't know what – please stay and help us find out."

Colin had said what many farmers feel, how stressed he was with something when he didn't understand what was going wrong or what to do about it.

What he said was true. We have known for a long time how to prevent bloat: give the cows a little drink of oil (drench) to prevent the bubbles from forming. And he was also right about the lameness problem. There was very little information about what might cause lameness for the New Zealand cow, let alone how to prevent it. For Colin, the dead cows, about which he could now do nothing, seemed a "minor problem" in comparison to the helplessness he felt watching cows get lame and not knowing what to do. If he felt like he was letting his cows down by not doing the right things, then I was letting Colin and my other farmers down by not getting to the bottom of the lameness problem.

Colin was as desperate as many farmers I have talked to since then. Lameness wears you down, is stressful and makes you feel helpless, not to mention the economic and welfare costs. I have had farmers tell me that the worst thing in their life on the farm is watching lame cows struggling along to get to the milking shed.

One farmer turned to me and said, "See that tree over there, if you come back and find me hanging there don't be surprised." This is HELP in capital letters.

If cows could talk, I think that they also would have been saying MOO (translation: HELP ME). I don't think there is any condition or disease of cows that is more debilitating or painful than lameness. Imagine what you would feel if you had to walk along with a stone stuck inside your shoe, and there was no way you could get it out!

This lameness problem was a hidden giant ogre, like a black cloud over our lovely farms. How could I find out what was feeding it?

My first question was – where to start? I needed information and ideas, but where to find them? These days, if you want to find some information about something or even how to do something, it appears easy – just ask Google – but what if you ask Google and Google doesn't know? Or worse still, as in those early days, what if there was no Google?

The old adage goes: When you don't know something – ask. Questions for myself. Questions for farmers, vets, and researchers. I decided to start with the farmers.

So I started collecting ideas from the farmers. I would ask, "Why do you think that (other) farmers get lots of lame cows?" Often the first, most obvious answer was "Well, you would get sore feet too if you walked along on that rough surface on that track." This was most likely true, but was this the only answer? This is what I set myself to find out.

So began my journey towards working out how lameness came about and then making lameness understandable and preventable, a journey I am still pursuing. The journey, which began that day at Colin's farm, became the story of the lightbulbs that my farmers turned on as I puzzled about each problem. Each lightbulb was a story or observation that I would write down and then set about verifying. Some of these things took me years to discern and prove, and many were things that my farmers could have easily told me if I had known what questions to ask.

Fortunately for me, I had arrived on the scene towards the end of the major one-hundred-year development of the dairy industry, just when there were new developments in technology. And at the same time the veterinary industry was also developing. The focus was now shifting from fixing one problem cow to looking at the wider health of the entire herd. I was the right person in the right place at the right time.

CHAPTER 2

# Beginnings (1950–1968)

I OFTEN MEET YOUNG people who have dreams of becoming a vet. When I was young, I had no such dream. Early memories may have been of farmland and open fields, but that was only when I was very young and became a faint memory. How I came to be a vet standing out in a paddock talking to Colin, the modern dairy farmer, is quite a journey – halfway around the world in fact. My journey towards helping farmers understand their lameness problems started unrecognised and well before that day. To be the right person, I needed to be in the right place with the right background and at the right time.

At the Rotolactor

In my photograph album, there are not very many pictures of me, but one that stands out is a photograph of myself and my sisters which was taken when I was about eleven years old. Obviously, I was going to be a vet or a farmer as you can see by the cows in the picture. My sisters and I are posing in front of a herd of cows about to milked in a very interesting dairy milking facility.

It was called the "Rotolactor,"[1] and nearly every school child in the eastern Australian state of New South Wales, during the 1950s and 1960s, visited it to watch cows being milked on the novel rotary milking platform. A merry-go-round for cows. Someone had come up with the idea that, instead of the milker walking to the cows, the cows and the milking machine would come to the milker by riding on a sort of carousel.

This sort of innovative facility marked about half a century of dairy technology development, and more was still to come. Much of it occurred as I grew up, as you can see by the photo, and then carried on during my watch as a vet. I used to be able to talk to people or their fathers who had milked their few cows by hand. Originally, for thousands of years, probably since the year dot, a milkmaid would carry a bucket and a stool to the cow in the paddock, sit beside her, and milk her by hand. Some people might think of Tess in *Tess of the D'Urbevilles*, the milkmaid in Thomas Hardy's novel.

A short history of the development of the modern dairy facilities that shaped the growth of the dairy industry is in order here to show how this was the perfect time for me to be a dairy vet. The industry's first big transition was from hand milking to the use of machines to milk the cows. A New Zealand second-generation farmer called Norman Daysh, who wanted to make life easier not only for the milkers but also for the cows,[2] invented a machine that used a vacuum pump to do the milking. This initial prototype was further developed by the big company DeLaval, which brought it out commercially to the farmer in 1917.

This was a revolution in dairying. Now there was no need to spend hours milking by hand – a machine could do it. And the machine could milk all four teats at once as it had four milking cups. So now instead of the milkmaid taking a bucket to the cow, the dairy farmer simply had to bring the cow to the machine. You could bring the machine to the cow, which would be much more difficult. This is sometimes done, of course, as farmers are very inventive when they are solving a problem. I have seen a portable milking machine with a milk storage vat pulled by a pair of bullocks on its way out to the cows to collect the milk. This was done whilst the new milking facility was being built. However, generally, the cow comes to the milking facility.

One machine by itself was not enough to milk a whole herd of cows, so the farmers would have several machines in a row with rails making little individual stalls in which the cows could stand whilst being milked. Each cow could choose one bail or cubicle to walk into in order to be milked. The milker would then attach the milking machine. When finished and the milk was all milked out, the farmer would take off the cups, and the cow would walk forwards straight out again via a door which opened in front of her at the far end of the stall. This was called a "walk-through" milking parlour.

In the walk-through, the farmer had to bend down to put the machines on the udders, so the next development was the idea of having a step up for the cows so that they would be higher up on a sort of a platform. Less bending down. The cows still walked through and out the far end of the bail. The Rotolactor, built in 1952 at Camden Park, Menangle, New South Wales, Australia, was a sort of modification of the walk-through idea. The platform instead of a straight row became a doughnut shape or a ring of milking stalls. The bails came to the cows instead of the cows choosing a bail for themselves.

Many different arrangements of the milking machine were tried. Instead of a walk-through milking set up, a "walk-past" milking parlour was thought of. The dividing rails were dispensed with, and the cows walked in from one end of the platform, which then was much longer. They would stand sideways to the milker and then proceed off the far end of the platform in a row when finished milking. Also, the platform could now be higher up with the milkers stepping down into a lower area beside the cows. This meant even less bending for the milker.

As farmers started keeping larger herds of cows, they needed to have more machines in the row, so someone thought of the idea of the cows turning back-on to the machine. The cows stood side by side. Then why not have two rows? This ended up with the milker in a deeper pit between the cows somewhat like the sort of pit you would see in a mechanic's repair shop. From the pit, the milker could attach the milking machines from the back of the cow between the back legs instead of from the side. Then, after the machine had taken the milk, the cows could turn again and continue walking out along the platform. Or a big gate could be lifted in front of them, and they could all walk out straight ahead without having to turn at all.

Another inventive New Zealand farmer, Ron Sharp from the Waikato, thought of the idea of letting the cows turn less so that they were kind of angle parked on the two platforms. Indeed, he said that this idea came to him when looking at angle-parked cars along a street in Hamilton.[3] He named it "herringbone" because from above it looked like a fish backbone. The cows now only had to make a slight turn to be back-on to the milking machine and another slight turn to walk out again. The modern "herringbone" milking system consists of just one row of milking machines spaced evenly over a lowered pit where a milker can stand out of the way of the cows and not have to bend down to attach the milking machines as he walks from one end of the pit to the other. When one row of cows is milked, the machines can be swung over pendulum-like to the other side to milk the next row of cows which would be standing in position waiting on the other side of the pit. The milking cups don't even need to be cleaned between cows as everything is above ground and away from the muck.

The Rotolactor, a mix of both the walk-through, with separate bails, and the herringbone, with milking from behind, was the precursor to the modern rotary milking facility. The platform was now circular and acted like a carousel. The cows entered an individual stall on a rotating platform; the milking machines were also on the platform and travelled with them around the circuit. The cows rode the platform whilst being milked. Then in the Rotolactor, having been rotated almost full circle and with the platform temporarily paused, the cows moved off forwards down an alleyway and out under the other side of the platform. Finally, another farmer in New Zealand, Merv Hicks of Taranaki, realised that the cows were clever enough to back out instead of just continuing forwards, and we had the birth of the turnstile rotary. This turned slowly enough for the cows to step off the platform without it even having to stop. Back in the 1960s, Merv must have known cows better and had again made life easier for cows and people including the builders, who no longer had to build a tunnel for the cows to use to exit from their bail. All this happened while I was still thousands of miles away from New Zealand and not even thinking about cows let alone becoming a vet.

I had already been a vet for some time when the most recent piece of the milking machine story, the invention of the robot milking machine, took place. In the robotic milking system, there is no person at all doing the actual milking. Instead, the cow, when she is ready to be milked, enters the milking box. Her tag is read by the scanner, and if it is time for her to be milked, a mechanised robot arm containing the milking machine cleans the udder and attaches the cups. At the same time, a feed tray in front of her is filled with grain or pellets. If it is not time for her to be milked, the front door of the box opens, and she walks right through without getting fed. In the 1960s this was a long way in the future, but today this system is in use in many indoor barns around the world and even in outdoor pasture-based systems.

The Rotolactor is now a piece of history, a stage in the development of dairy milking facilities. And so is that early picture of myself taken posing with my two sisters and the cows. This photo marked, appropriately enough, the end of the first stage in my journey and the beginning of the new one for myself and my family. I and my sisters, with our parents, had recently arrived from Zimbabwe, at that time called Rhodesia, to live in Sydney when we visited the Rotolactor on that lovely sunny Australian day. Since then, I have taken literally thousands of photos of dairy milking sheds of every type conceivable, with or without cows and with or without family members. My favourite ones have a view of Taranaki from the pit. I wonder if the cows enjoy the view too.

However, to start from further back in my story, the Rotolactor photo is not the oldest picture I have of myself. The first stage of my journey began well before then on another continent. I was born in Pretoria, South Africa, of an English-heritage father and an Afrikaans mother. However, before I was four years old, we moved to Zimbabwe and away from any close family, most of whom I have never met. We soon formed a new "family" with friends of my parents from the church and groups they belonged to. The only time we returned as a family to South Africa, where I born, was to go on a holiday to the beach at Durban. We travelled there in my father's 1953 Ford Consul.

I remember going on another holiday with a friend and his dad. We went to a waterfall and lake in a national park. All day long we played in the water – who needs clothes when there are only boys around? We paid for it the next day when neither of us could sit down as we were so badly sunburnt. My memories of growing up in Zimbabwe are those of a child and somewhat rose coloured. Simon, my best school friend, was the son of the headmaster of the little school that I attended. His memories are less rose tinted as his journey had him staying in Zimbabwe through a very difficult political time. His journey was completely different from the one I was going to travel, but we are still in touch as our paths crossed much later.

Riding my tricycle in Harare

When we first moved from South Africa to Zimbabwe, we lived in a farm cottage just outside the city of Harare. In an early photo of myself, I am riding a little trike around the farmhouse veranda. Many of my early memories of living in Zimbabwe are of farmland and running free in the fields – mostly tobacco fields. Maybe that is where I got to love the outdoors and making do. There were not many people who could afford fancy toys, so the local boys would get some old fence wire and twist it into a model car or truck with wheels on wire axles that really went around. Another longer piece of wire was used to make a steering wheel, which was tall enough to use as a handle and with which you could actually steer the car. My young friends knew how to make wire cars, and I must have learned enough from them as I made some for my children as they were growing up. When I was still at primary school near Harare, I would trade a peanut butter sandwich for the use of a car for the afternoon, and off we would go. I guess my mother may have been worried about me, but I was never worried.

The next house we lived in was right beside a railway line. Between us and the rails was just a foot path and the road. My mother had two little dogs, a Pekinese and a Maltese terrier. They were great friends. There was another much larger dog that roamed the neighbourhood that wasn't such a friend. He used to walk along the footpath outside our house every day about the same time. One day, the little Pekinese was out near the footpath and the bigger dog saw an opportunity to have some fun. He paused his walk and grabbed the little Pekinese. A high-pitched yelping rang out. At that point, the Maltese came running out of the house, raced up behind the bigger dog, and bit him squarely on the behind. The bigger dog, taken completely by surprise, didn't know what had hit him. He let out a lower pitched yelp, dropped the Pekinese, and ran off as fast as he could go. Ever after when walking along the footpath near our house he would cross over to the other side of the road and walk along beside the railway until he had passed by our house whereupon he crossed back again and continued on his way. I often recall this event when I am thinking about how animals remember events and behave differently because of something memorable.

Zimbabwe was a prosperous country, rich in minerals and with many farms producing crops for export. People had been living there for centuries. In the 1880s, diamonds were being mined there by a company owned by Cecil Rhodes. There were various underhand deals resulting in very unfair land acquisition. The country was called Rhodesia but was actually a combination of several countries. All those territories were nominally part of the British Commonwealth. But the situation was always changing. Black tribal nations tried to retake their lands and the government reacted. Independence was in the offing. The government was very biased, favouring the white people. In the background, as I got a little older, was always this precarious political situation, which was completely over my head. I would overhear serious conversations between my parents and their friends. Once I overheard them discussing moving to another country for a better future for their children. They were talking about a friend in Australia who could offer my father a job in hardware sales. A few days later, we were talking as a family around the dinner table when my parents asked us children to tell them where we would like to move to if we moved to another country. Immediately

I answered "Australia" (not even knowing where Australia was). My parents took this as a word from God – I never told them that I had heard the conversation that had occurred a few days earlier. A more concrete word from God was to come in the form of a gift, as we were given a large sum of money, about £1,000, by some Christian friends, which covered our expenses migrating to Australia in 1961.

We packed up, my parents virtually gave away their new house, and we set off on a steam train to Cape Town. You can imagine a boy of ten on a journey like this – a big adventure. Of course, this wasn't my first experience of steam trains as a train line had gone right by our home near Harare. There was a bit of a hill coming up to where our house was situated, so there was a lot of slow "I think I can" huffing to get up there. After the engine had gone past with the driver and his helpers, we young boys would grab a long stick and stand holding it out to clatter along the side of the carriages as they moved slowly past. Until one day, "Don't let me see you do that again!" said a gruff voice. The guard. We hadn't realised that were being watched. It was a sufficient fright for us kids, so, like the dog who was surprised by our Maltese terrier, we kept our distance when the train came up the hill. At least once though, I remember us children putting a coin on the tracks and after the train had gone by looking for the flattened remains. It was also fun to collect the black coal that had dropped off the coal wagon. But the long journey to the south to leave Zimbabwe to immigrate to Australia was the first time I had actually ridden on the train.

We arrived in Cape Town and stayed with some more of my parents' friends who lived on a hill overlooking the beach. There was no road to their beach house. Instead, their "street" was called Jacob's Ladder. You had to climb up 149 steps to get to the front gate. I remember counting the steps! Although we only stayed there around a week or two while we waited for our migrant ship to depart, I could still find the place some fifty-five years later when I visited South Africa again.

The first stage of the journey was on the steam train. Then from Cape Town, we boarded an ocean liner. We joined the *SS Waterman*, a little Dutch migrant ship travelling between the Netherlands and the Dutch East Indies (now Indonesia). This ship started out its life as a warship troop and cargo carrier in 1945 and was then converted to a cruise and passenger ship. Years later I met several Dutch farmers in Taranaki who had immigrated to New Zealand on one of its voyages to the Antipodes. This time the return voyage to the Netherlands of the *SS Waterman* after we disembarked in Sydney was not as a commercial passenger ship but, temporarily, as a troop carrier again. It had been commandeered by the Netherlands government to evacuate Dutch troops from Indonesia as the former Dutch East Indies had become independent. The *Waterman* continued until the early 1970s as a passenger ship.

This was my first ship experience and I loved it. My mother did not. She was seasick the entire journey. For us children, being aboard a ship for some weeks exploring and amusing ourselves was an adventure again. We were virtually free to go anywhere on the ship. My best friend was the cook, who always had spare custard for the kids! No wonder my favourite dessert became custard for a while. I still enjoy custard, but my favourite has now morphed into cheesecake, slightly different but still smooth and creamy, and mostly a dairy product!

We arrived in Fremantle, Western Australia, on my eleventh birthday and from there sailed to Sydney, which was to be our new home. We began to settle in. At first, we stayed with the friends who had offered my father a job. They had a small extra cottage at the back of their house and a big garden out the back with a guava tree – and guavas. Shortly we found a house to rent nearby. My mother took quite a while to adapt to her new life – it had been a huge upheaval. She wasn't working and so had limited opportunity to meet new friends. Being part of a local church family was her best connection. My father went to work in hardware stores, where he continued until he retired. I and my sisters went off to a local school. I have two sisters, one older and one younger – I am the meat in the sandwich. My older sister Christine was always the serious and wiser one, whilst myself and Ann got up to mischief.

Soon after my arrival at the suburban school in Lindfield, Sydney, I was to be faced with my biggest weakness – spelling. The teacher gave our class a spelling test and the next day handed out the results announcing each score. It seemed that she must have lost mine because my name and results were not called. At the next break, she called me to her desk.

"I know that English is your second language, so I can give you a little bit of help with your spelling if you like." I never enlightened her. I did mostly enjoy school, and although spelling has never been my strong point, I passed my other exams.

Imagine a boy with a strong British/South African accent starting as a new boy in school in Sydney. The first thing I did was to shed my accent, a feat accomplished fairly quickly and under pressure.

Although I am now a full-fledged Kiwi (New Zealander), a few fragments of my past accent and heritage remain, recognised by those who have lived in South Africa or have a good ear for it.

I was travelling in a car with a farmer and his wife in the South Island of New Zealand a good forty-five years later, and the wife mused, "You are not a Kiwi, are you?"

"Where do you think I am from?" I asked.

"Well, I think you are from Australia," returned the husband.

"No," said the wife, "you are from South Africa!"

"Well, you are both correct," and I happily explained.

My elder sister Christine remembers much more of the transition time from Zimbabwe to Sydney while my memories are just marked out by the photos. So the trip to the Rotolactor with school friends and family soon after we arrived in Sydney seemed to mark for me the start of the next stage in my journey.

It was also a time to meet new friends. It was during those early days in Sydney spent at Lindfield Primary School where I met Brett, the next of my best friends. Brett's father had a clock and watch shop just near our home in Lindfield, full of old and being-repaired clocks. I can still relive the memory of that shop every time I visit Brett's home – also full of large and old clocks, each with their own distinctive tick-tock. Growing up, I would visit Brett and we would make all sorts of things together, many of which resulted in explosions – well, he would make and I would help.

Brett and his family and the clock shop moved to another suburb, so we ended up attending different high schools. My high school had all sorts of new and exciting things to try. My new friends there encouraged me to do things I had never done before. Coming from the centre of a continent I had not had much to do with water or the sea, but here we were right next to a world-class harbour. Sports like rowing had never been available before, so with a couple of my friends, I joined the North Sydney Boys rowing team. This is where I first discovered that it was sometimes an advantage to be shorter than average! It was also good to learn to work as a team. We were a well-oiled team and took out some trophies, but we really enjoyed having fun and just being a team together. I was the one with a driver's licence, so I drove the team to regattas and practices. The last photo in my "early years" album has us all in our coxed four resting after having won a race. I am the one sitting just in front of the cox. Then all too soon we were to be moving on in life and the possibility of further studies.

The team resting after the race

This was back in the late 1960s when progress was speeding up, the Beatles hadn't found drugs yet, and folk music was still a big thing.

Flower power and hippies were around, and we wore wide trousers and Beatle haircuts. The Sydney Opera House was being built, and it seemed to us as if the world was just waking up and all washed and clean, you could say it "smells like Pears soap."[4] Near the end of our basic schooling, we all felt that the world was to be our oyster. My sisters were also planning their careers. Christine set out to study nursing and was to become a baby health nurse, whilst Ann chose a career in early childhood education. It is quite certain that had we stayed in Zimbabwe, the opportunities would have been very limited.

Although my sisters had obviously thought out their lives, as a young person leaving school, I didn't know what I wanted to do. I visited a careers advisor. The advisor gave me a questionnaire to fill out – just one page. I duly answered the few questions I saw on the page. All I really knew was that I didn't know. However, by some sort of alchemy the advisor had me summed up. "You like people, and you shouldn't work in an office. Maybe you could think of being a schoolteacher or a vet."

A vet – I had never thought of that! I didn't know very much about animals unless you called collecting bird skulls and other bones a premonition of an interest in animals!

"A good idea is to go and visit a vet to see what they do and if you might like it" was the advice of the careers advisor. The only vet I knew was the one that we had once visited with our pet fox terrier, Tosca, in order to get flea treatment or vaccinations.

Several weeks later, there I was at the vet clinic to see what I could see. What a disastrous experience! During the first operation that I observed, just a routine spay (surgical sterilisation), I fainted. And then same thing happened the next week with a castration. But then I visited a rural practice. I was hooked. Here were big, friendly animals living in the great outdoors, depending on the vet to keep them healthy and happy. Their owners were also friendly and had time to chat. So I applied for vet school. A city boy planning to become a country vet.

# CHAPTER 3

# Journeys on the Way (1969–1974)

THE APRICOTS LOOKED scrumptious, and they certainly were. To me they also had dollar signs on each piece. Fruit picking was hard work, but it did pay you well and made for an excellent job for someone preparing to be a student. Studying for five years at Sydney University Vet School would require money, and although the fees would be covered by the government and I had a small scholarship for a few living expenses, I was not going to be able to make ends meet without some sort of holiday job. My parents were not well off enough to continue to support me, so I found a holiday job fruit picking. For the holidays, I picked apricots down in the huge fruit-growing area of New South Wales and then found a job closer to home picking peaches where I could continue even though university had started.

Soon I was the proud owner of a small 75 cc motor scooter – my transport to university – ideal for Sydney traffic and very economical even if not great as a status symbol. I knew exactly how much it cost to fill the tank– 23 cents – and how many kilometres this would take me. By continuing with my fruit-picking job, I was also able to finance other expenses not actually connected with my studies, extra outings and the like.

Living in the northwest of Sydney, I was within motor bike range of the peach orchard, so I would ride out to the orchard every day in the holidays to pick delicious stone fruit. Any fruit that was not one hundred percent perfect would be just thrown away, or we could eat it. It was impossible to eat them all at the orchard, so I took some home as well. It seemed such a shame to waste them. The owner of the orchard had a brother who had a small vegetable patch to earn a bit of extra money over and above his allowance. He grew zucchini. He couldn't see the sense in picking them when they were only tiny; surely they would be worth much more "fully grown"? I got to take a few giant zucchini home as well for my mother to cook.

My motor scooter was my method of transport for all my university years. It travelled hundreds of kilometres around Sydney and then out of Sydney to the farms where I did practical work. Then during the last year of my studies, it took me to the university farm south of Sydney. It was also capable of taking two people to visit farms and other sights.

Now I had a holiday job and some transport. Having been brought up in a city and with the only animals around being our two pet dogs, I needed to find some sort of farm with large animals close by. This way I could get hands-on experience of larger animals.

Just to the north of where I lived was a more rural area, and there I found a little dairy farm only a relatively short drive from my home. Here was some handy farm animal experience, time to start to get to know how cows operated. It was run by a family who had a little four- or five-year-old son who, I am sure, was destined for a career as a stevedore, or a roughneck balancing on high girders and building skyscrapers. He would climb on top of everything to see what he could see. Even having his appendix removed and spending some time in hospital didn't slow him down. Within a week, despite the doctor's orders, there he was again on the roof of the shed inspecting our work and checking out the cows. It was interesting that the cows didn't seem to mind him up there, if indeed they noticed, and he certainly had a bird's-eye view of the whole operation – it was only those of us people down at ground level who were worried.

I would ride out to the dairy on weekends on my little scooter, leaving early in the morning to be on time for milking the cows. There were not many cows, only about fifty, and we milked them in an old "walk-through" milking parlour. This was the ideal way to get to know cows at close quarters. The cows would mill around in the small holding yard, and, one by one, with a little pat or coaxing, they would step into the stall that they chose with a door at the other end. Each cow seemed to have their favourite stall in which to be milked. They knew that this was the way out to the feeding troughs where they also knew we had previously put heaps of supplementary feed. While they stood in the bail, I would put the milking machine cups onto the cows' udders and try not to get kicked by the stroppy ones. When the cow was finished milking, I would open the door in front of her so she could walk out to the paddock via the barn where the extra food was waiting.

Cows, I discovered, were amazing. They knew how to get milked and whose turn it was. It was those cows that taught me the ropes. I got to know which ones were the friendly ones or the ones who could manage to get through to the feed the quickest, even opening the door for themselves if I had forgotten to latch it properly. One favourite cow, with tag number 103, used to turn around and try to lick my ear when I put the cups on. 103 was a number that I remembered as it was the number of the school bus that I had taken to high school. Now "Number 103" was the name for my friendly cow teacher.

After milking in the morning, we would all have breakfast together. This usually included toast cooked in an old-fashioned toaster where the sides opened out to turn the bread over. The toast very frequently got burned. I hated to see waste, so I would often eat the somewhat-burnt toast, so often, in fact, that I came to like it. Now whenever the cookies get burned, I make sure that they don't get thrown out. They are my special treat. Maybe it is nostalgia for the good old days!

Being a "poor" university student, I did have to make some economical food decisions similar to the burnt toast. I managed to live on canned baked beans and spaghetti for almost the entire three weeks of my practical experience on a big beef farm south of Sydney. The farm manager allowed me to stay in the workers' quarters. I could use the cooking facilities, but aside from the occasional piece of steak given to me by the farmer, I supplied my own food. This farm was on the very edge of my motor scooter range, but the rest of the large animal vet experience that I needed was much further afield, so I had to find some alternate cheap transport. In those days this was hitchhiking, standing by the side of the road with a thumb out waiting to see if someone would pick you up in their vehicle and take you a bit further along the road towards your destination.

Hitching was an experience in itself. I had finished some farm experience time at a farm near Goulburn, south of Sydney. I walked to the edge of the township to hitch a ride back to Sydney. An old car with a young driver pulled up and offered the first ride. We set off. Just a short way down the road he pulled up; it seemed that there was some problem with the steering. He dived under the car with a bit of what looked like old wire and did some repairs. He got in again and we started off.

"I sometimes have problems with the steering," he offhandedly said by way of explanation.

We turned off the main road to take a less travelled route, which soon turned out to be quite windy. As we wound from side to side, my driver spotted a friend up ahead. He put his foot down and started to overtake. We were on the wrong side of the road and racing along around bend after bend. I was terrified. This continued for what seemed ages, probably only five or ten minutes. Then, "Oh no, the steering," muttered the young guy, and he pulled off the road. Fortunately, whilst he and his friend tinkered with the steering, I was picked up by another passing car.

On another occasion, I had arrived in a township north of Sydney to do some practical observations at an abattoir, over our two-week break. After a short tour of the facility on the first day of my required experience, the vet in charge took me to his office. There he quietly said to me that the locals didn't appreciate outsiders in the works. Apparently, there was some sort of mafia thing going on. He signed me off for my two weeks "experience," and I was free to enjoy two weeks of leave. I decided to try and hitch to Darwin in the far north as I thought that it would be an interesting place to go. There was a local truck stop nearby which was on the route to the north. Checking with the workers there, I found there were no Darwin trucks due for at least five days, so I changed my destination and decided to go in the opposite direction, instead heading south to Adelaide nearly two thousand kilometres away, where I had some friends. I stayed there for a few days and then started out to hitch back home to Sydney. I was just walking out of the city when a car pulled up ahead of me. The driver asked if I needed a ride. In fact, he had driven past me, possibly to check me out, and then waited. When I got into the car, the driver asked whether I had a driver's licence. "Yes, I have my licence," I informed him.

"I have to get to Melbourne today, and I am too tired to drive that far."

So I drove the car and its owner to Melbourne, where the man dropped me off at a bushy roundabout. There I caught a few hours of sleep before getting on the road again to uneventfully hitch home to Sydney. Quite an interesting way to sightsee.

I also "hitched" a ride in another type of transport, this time a light plane. One of the vets with whom I was seeing practice and learning the practicalities of being a country vet in Australia was also a pilot. He had two clinics hundreds of kilometres apart – one in Murray Bridge on the border between New South Wales and Victoria and another clinic in Broken Hill, in western New South Wales. To travel the huge distances between farms, he had a small plane. He was the vet equivalent of the Flying Doctor Service.

One morning, we took off to visit several widely separated farms for tuberculosis (TB) testing of the stock. Animals can get TB and pass it on to people, so there is a government programme to check cows for the disease. Getting close to the first farm, we saw fog up ahead. The vet looked around for somewhere to land until the fog might clear enough to find the farm landing strip. He spotted an old salt pan that made a suitable runway. Just beyond the salt pan, we could see an old house and some sheds.

"Let's explore," he said. So we walked over to see what was there.

It was all totally deserted and looked as though the people had just walked out yesterday. There was no indication of why they might have left. We walked over to explore the sheds and barn. We were surprised to find inside the barn lots of equipment and harness for the horse-drawn implements which were all still parked right there. Maybe the exodus was quite some time ago. The farm was so isolated that no one had come past to see and loot. The fog lifted and we resumed our TB testing run and returned home but not before I had made an internal decision that when I was looking for a vet job I would try and find a location where farms were closer together.

I also made a second decision as a result of my experience as a student working with vets. I was staying with a country vet who was one of the two vets in the practice. He wasn't on duty for emergencies on this particular weekend when I was there. He and his family were all packed up and ready in the car to go for a swim and picnic at a nearby river, when there was a phone call just as we were leaving the house. The vet ran inside to answer the phone.

"Sorry everyone," he said as he emerged again. "We will have to go to the river another day. I have to go and see an animal. The other vet is busy with another emergency."

The family all climbed out of the car, and he and I headed off to the new emergency. This second decision was that I would try to find a job in a vet practice with more than one vet for emergencies. This was still in the future, so I just kept it for "future reference."

When I was in my last year of high school, my family moved to a different suburb of Sydney where a house was available for rent. The family had joined the lively little local church and had become part of the fellowship there. Until I finished the year at high school, I stayed with another family nearer to my high school and joined the rest of the family later when I started my university studies. I had only recently become a Christian like my parents and wanted to join in with a church nearby, and this one seemed really friendly. It was a good choice as it was here at the church youth group that I first met Sandra. Coincidentally, I discovered that my motor scooter route home from university went right past her home, so when I wanted really good food, I would call in to her home where there was always a good meal going – and good company. Well, that was my excuse.

Sandra and her twin sister were the eldest of a family of six children. There was always something happening there as the property was also a wholesale nursery and florist business. I had already begun my veterinary studies, and she and her sister were still at high school. Their route home from school also just so happened to be on that same road home from university. It was amazing how often I could time it right to be driving past just as they were walking home. Times, of course, were adjusted to fit into after school music lessons and sports practices.

As a church youth group, we went on fun outings. I had been on several canoeing expeditions with friends from school and had an old wooden canoe, so I organised a canoe day at a local river park. It is rather difficult to transport a canoe on a little scooter, so I enlisted the help of my friend Brett from primary school. He had a car and roof rack. The day after the canoe trip, he invited Sandra's sister, Anne, out on a date. So I followed his example and invited Sandra.

So now I had a girlfriend to transport on the back of my little scooter. We could travel quite a distance. I even took her out to visit the dairy farm at Dural where the little roof-climbing boy lived. The cows there were really friendly, and I thought that if Sandra was to remain my girlfriend, it would be good if she could also get to know cows. It wasn't just the cows to visit – there was a really nice little café on the route out there. I would take Sandra on the back of my scooter around the local area, but when I needed a more comfortable method of transport, I would borrow my father's green VW beetle and go out on a real date.

Both romances developed as we all studied for the next few years. Sandra took biological sciences with statistics and computing thrown in. Those were the days when computers took up whole rooms, and you had to type your programming onto punch cards. Her sister became an actuary, and Brett followed his father's footsteps and became a clockmaker. These four years of courtship must have been good for me as during that time I never failed an exam. From Sandra's perspective, it must have been a different sort of courtship too, including milking cows, visiting farms, and meeting other wild vet students.

The veterinary science course was five years long, so plenty of time to really get to know the others in our course. We started out with sixty of us, and only five of the sixty were girls. It is a different story now many years later; the numbers are reversed. Almost all vet students are young ladies with just a few young men. Some of us were brought up in the city, and some came from farms a varied bunch of us. Remarkably nearly all of us passed the course (at least in the end).

Since my university days, I have journeyed back to Australia for several vet school class reunions. It is interesting where we have all ended up. But mostly we get nostalgic about our years of study before responsibility hit. The most memorable year was the final year. During the semester, whilst we were studying, all the final year vet students lived in the student hostel on the university farm near Camden, south of Sydney. We all had our own rooms, and although there was a dining hall and common rooms, we could also make a cup of coffee in our rooms. My cup was a bit cracked, but with the constant use of powdered milk and infrequent washing up, I managed to keep it from leaking or, worse still, falling apart till the end of the year.

As I was studying to be a vet, I had a giant animal poster, a gift from Sandra, on the wall of my room. Not a cow but a tiger. Maybe it reminded me of Africa. It didn't mean that I was going to become a zoo vet. Once or twice I invited Sandra to visit for events like midterm barbeques. She most vividly remembers that there was a student whose horse was in the paddock where we parked all the cars. It suddenly took a dislike to its owner's Ute and dealt it several hefty kicks, leaving a slightly dented side. Everyone else was worried in case it should take a dislike to some other vehicle, so the horse was shifted to another paddock.

During our time at the Camden farm, we all got to know the friendly university cows and the farm manager who milked the cows with a couple of milking staff. These cows were our bovine guinea pigs. We had to learn how to examine a cow, find the veins, listen to the heart, or test to see whether they were pregnant. The old farm manager with his farmer ways was always on hand to teach us how to handle cows. We all thought of him as old, but he can't have been much older than us as he was still there and only just retiring forty years later when I met him again. I had come to visit for the forty-year class reunion and, driving past the university farm with Sandra, I decided to drop in and see how it was all going. The same farm manager was still there, and they had just installed a state-of-the-art robotic rotary milking parlour. The cows were still getting used to it, but they seemed to love it, he said. He was an observant farm manager, but he had always thought that the cows were afraid of students who handled them between milkings. Now as his helpers tried to get the cows to load onto the new milking platform, he changed his mind. He realised that it had been the farm staff who had been frightening to the cows when every day they had chased them into the milking shed.

Camden and the university farm were quite a distance from Eastwood, where Sandra lived, so no riding past on my little motor scooter for those two semesters. Instead, I would gather some coins and drive off to the telephone booth in the town. It was during this time at the farm when I first learned that it is a good idea to make friends with the ladies who operate the telephone exchanges. When I wanted to call Sandra from the telephone booth, I would first post in some coins for a long-distance call. The operator would then connect me to the correct number; then, whenever the money was about to run out, she would ask me if I wanted to continue and if I could post some more coins in. Sometimes if I ran out of coins, she would just let us talk a little bit longer for free before she had to cut us off.

All those phone conversations bore fruit, and towards the end of the last semester, I returned to Sydney to propose to Sandra. I took her for a short ride on my scooter to a quiet little spot on the harbour and asked my question. And she said "Yes!" For the next outing, I borrowed my father's VW. It was sort of more appropriate to go and choose a ring in a car.

Graduated and married!

We were married the year that I graduated from vet school and the same year that Sandra graduated from Macquarie University. Brett, true to form, had married Anne, her sister, several months earlier. So it was that at the end of my studies I graduated as a married vet. Ready to take up a job as a vet with large animals and to start my life with Sandra. Many more and longer journeys were still to come.

## CHAPTER 4

# New Vet, New Country (1974)

NOW I WAS newly married and newly graduated from vet school. I was looking for a place to start my vet career. I applied for some jobs in Australia out in the dairy areas of New South Wales near where I had done some of my practical work. They were happy to have me come to work there, but somehow those jobs didn't quite fit me. Then one of my lecturers, knowing my interest in dairy cows, suggested I go to New Zealand, make all my "mistakes," and then come back to Australia as an overseas expert! A good idea, and one thing was true, I definitely knew that I was no expert then, fresh out of university. Nowadays, I tell my farmers that I am still making "mistakes," so that is why I am still in New Zealand! A kinder take on that could be that I am still learning new things and having learning experiences.

I applied for some jobs advertised from New Zealand, and one head vet wrote back to me. In his letter, he offered me a job in Inglewood in a four-man practice dealing mainly with dairy cows – just what I was looking for. But wait – where was Inglewood? I remember he described Inglewood as a small town where there was lots of liquid sunshine, sometimes even horizontal liquid sunshine. So it was to be New Zealand – a land of dairy cows where I was to meet New Zealand dairy farmers like Colin, who were prepared to try new things and who thought about what they tried and were not happy until they had an answer to their questions.

Inglewood under the mountain

Inglewood, we were to find, was a small town in the North Island of New Zealand nestled under the watchful eye of Mount Egmont, as Taranaki Maunga was then called. It was surrounded by relatively small, perpetually green dairy farms. In fact, Sandra had been there about five years earlier with her parents travelling to nearby New Plymouth to meet a florist friend of theirs, little knowing that she had just passed through her future hometown. The town, we learned, had a thriving dairy factory making milk powder from the milk collected from those local dairy farms. The factory, Moa Dairy Coop, was owned by a local farmer cooperative. Most, if not all the dairy factories scattered in the different dairying areas of New Zealand were then owned and run by farmer cooperatives.

All these dairy farms around New Zealand represented thousands of cows whose owners needed a good reliable veterinary service. New Zealand's Massey University had only recently begun offering the full five-year veterinary science degree. Previously, if a New Zealander had wanted to train as a vet, they had had to go overseas, most often to

Australia. Although new vets were now trained in the country, there was still a shortage of trained vets. A group called the Veterinary Council was formed to regulate vet services. Part of the job was to build up rural veterinary services so that if there was an animal health emergency such as an outbreak of foot-and-mouth disease, there would be sufficient vets available to respond. The Veterinary Council saw to it that vets like myself coming to the country would have their travel costs to New Zealand paid provided that they stayed for three years. I was one of many vets who came on this plan, and in this way, New Zealand not only acquired young vets like myself but also managed to import many mature vets who brought with them great veterinary expertise. One such vet from Denmark was soon to be my head vet, the one who had written to me.

We were to move to Inglewood to start work in early March, and here we were in January, just graduated and still on our honeymoon. I had borrowed my father's VW for the honeymoon trip – no hitching this time. We travelled to many of the places that I had visited for vet experience. One of those places was Murray Bridge, where I had met the flying vet. He had told me of a houseboat on the Murray River that I could rent. What fun to stay on board for a few days. We carried on in our trip to Adelaide, where we attended the wedding of another vet friend before returning to Sydney.

For the next few months before leaving Australia, we stayed with the same friends with whom my family had stayed on their arrival in Australia from South Africa some twelve years previously. Déjà vu. We even stayed in the same little cottage. Nearby was a small animal vet practice where there was a need for a short-term locum, so I applied for the job. This was an interesting experience with only pets and no cows, but it did earn me a little spending money to start out with.

One day, when I had been there about a week, the receptionist asked me if I could look at a pet duck. The young girl who had brought it in had said it was lame. I walked it up and down the corridor between the offices and couldn't see any limping, so I diagnosed it as fit and well. Little did I know that although this was my first memorable encounter with lameness in the real world as a graduate vet, lame cows and not lame ducks were to be a huge part of my career. Lame ducks may be easier to treat than lame cows!

On receipt of the invitation to New Zealand, there followed a few months of packing, organising, and saying of goodbyes. This was not a totally new experience for me, having shifted countries twice before and shifted house several times, but for Sandra, this was a big step. It would be just the second move of her life, the first being only a distant memory of a two-year-old moving across Sydney. The amount of stuff that we wanted to take with us wouldn't fit into an airline baggage allowance, but we found that the fare on a cruise ship was the same as an airline ticket and came with a very generous baggage allowance of six cubic metres. So we could pack all our wedding presents and even the now well-used motor scooter, which was destined to eventually become a farm bike in Taranaki.

Then there was the spinning wheel. When Sandra and I were thinking seriously about our future – together or not – we took some time out during one holiday from my studies to consider seriously whether we wanted to stay together. I had found an old spinning wheel under one of the houses where we had lived, and I thought that it would be a good idea to try to make one as a gift for Sandra. So I spent the time in the workshop of a friend up the road who had a wood lathe and was willing to let me try my hand at wood turning. I managed to make a working replica of the old spinning wheel. I gave this to Sandra as a gift, a funny sort of engagement ring! She learned to spin and made, among other things, some sleeveless vests to keep me warm on cold nights on duty. Of course, as you know, I did propose properly and give her a proper engagement ring that she designed sometime later. The spinning wheel and the other belongings we had acquired all ended up in wooden crates painted green and were dispatched to the shipping yard.

We were booked to sail on a cruise ship called the *Ocean Monarch,* which was docked in Sydney just near where the *SS Waterman* had been berthed on my family's arrival from South Africa thirteen years earlier. Unfortunately, there were some engine problems and delays, so most of the passengers had flown ahead of the ship by the time we finally did leave. The remaining passengers boarded one evening when the repairs were complete and said their farewells. Then, instead of the ship departing, all the friends said goodbye and departed for their homes, while we went to our cabins for the night.

Next morning, at first light, the engines started, and we slipped out of Sydney harbour, with no fanfare and no streamers, for our three-day cruise to Auckland. There were no rough seas and no seasickness, so we arrived refreshed and ready to step into our new country. We disembarked and then watched our green-painted crates being unloaded. We organised for the baggage to be sent to New Plymouth, and then were met by some more old friends from South Africa. These were the very same family at whose home we had stayed in Cape Town, 149 steps up Jacob's Ladder, as my family started out on our first ship journey. Another déjà vu. After a short stay in Auckland, Sandra and I boarded a plane to travel to New Plymouth.

It was a freezing cold Sunday afternoon in March 1974 when my new wife and I finally arrived in Taranaki and were met at the airport by a tall, fair-haired man with an accent. This was the head vet, who was to become my boss, mentor, and friend. Gunner was originally from Denmark and had come out some years earlier on the same scheme that had brought us here. And he was wearing clogs of course. The clogs were his most comfortable footwear and easy to remove to swap for gumboots when needed, also very handy for knocking out the old tobacco from his pipe. Gunner was very business-like and ushered us to his car quickly. Just as well as the wind was howling, the rain was coming at us horizontally, and everything was grey and dismal – even the car was blue grey.

One thing that I will always remember about Gunner was his care and attention to detail both with animals and especially where it concerned cars. Not a rattle was permissible. Any strange sound was traced to its source even employing his stethoscope to locate it. We loaded our suitcases into the rattle-free car and set off down the highway for the twenty-kilometre drive to Inglewood, looking interestedly at the small dairy farms we passed. Along this road now there are only six remaining of those original twenty-four dairy farms – all the rest have either amalgamated with neighbours or been divided up and sold on as smaller blocks for lifestylers or market gardeners.

We soon arrived in Inglewood, where we would be serving the thriving community of dairy farmers. Inglewood was to celebrate its first hundred years as a settled town just a year after we arrived. In the early days of Inglewood, the settlers' days were mostly spent clearing roads through the dense bush and forest that had covered the town area, and then clearing fields to grow grass to feed dairy cows. An obvious extra development was a timber industry. However, the main reason for the establishment of Inglewood was as a dairying area, and the first cows were there even as the timber industry began. There was a lot of work involved in clearing the thick native forest in the Inglewood area, and in a novel plan, the council offered plots of land to settlers who could pay them off by working for the council in clearing roads and putting in the railway. This was all celebrated at the jubilee the next year, and a history was published as well.[1]

By 1974, the year we arrived, Inglewood was also sporting several other industries including a pyjama factory and the famous toy factory turning out cast aluminium "Fun Ho!" toys. Central to the town was still, of course, the dairy factory. Moa Dairy Factory was the amalgamation of several small dairy cooperatives which made their own butters and cheeses. But now with modern machinery and transport the central, somewhat larger factory turned all the milk from the surrounding farms into butter and milk powder and a couple of other products. Although most of the factory buildings are still there, they are now idle. These days the milk now goes to Hawera, a town fifty kilometres to the south where there is a huge combined factory complex. After many more amalgamations of bigger cooperatives, the New Zealand dairy industry now has one main giant cooperative with large factories in each of the main dairying areas, and this is one of them. In addition to this, there are also now quite a few big companies owned by people other than farmers.

Inglewood in 1974 was a buzzing old-world town with wooden buildings along a curved main street and a railway line bisecting what might, at a stretch, be called the CBD. Inglewood was a crossroad town where the main highway going south from New Plymouth is met by the side highway which bypasses New Plymouth and follows the railway. The main street runs almost due east–west, so the sun sets in your eyes if you are driving the wrong direction in the evening. Just before the road crosses the railway line, it turns a right-angle bend and heads south towards Wellington. On the corner, there was a brick post office with, upstairs, the telephone exchange. This building has now been replaced with a park honouring the early Polish settlers of the district. Without the settlers there would have been no Inglewood, and many of them had come from Europe and especially Poland. I was to discover this when trying to remember names – which "ski" was that farmer: Dombroski, Dravitzki, or maybe Stachurski?

The town was hunkered down on that freezing day when we arrived with rain blowing across the roads and defying any umbrella to hold together let alone keep the rain off. With many apologies, Gunner explained that the vet that I was to replace had not actually left town yet. This vet was about to move back to Australia to follow his interest in horses. His method of moving to Australia was to sail there as a competitor in a yacht race across the Tasman Sea, but this did not leave New Zealand for another six weeks. In the meantime, until the vet house, where he was staying, would be available to move into, we were to stay at the old Inglewood Hotel, the larger of the two establishments in town. So Gunner invited us for dinner at his house.

He and his wife and two children lived in another house owned by the vet group. As they were Danish, they all spoke Danish at home but English also when they had guests.

After dinner, Gunner took us the short distance to the hotel, and we moved in: through the front door, up a grand staircase and across a landing into a south facing "with mountain view" room. In the gigantic room, the double bed looked kind of insignificant and baby sized. Worn out with all the travel and new sights, we went to bed.

The next morning, we woke early, and all was bright and cheery – we looked out the window, and there was "The Mountain" – covered in fresh snow and against a backdrop of solid blue. What a change and what a welcome! All that was needed was a foreground of cows happily grazing for the perfect rural Taranaki scene. The mountain seems to be an integral part of nearly every scene of Taranaki and Inglewood and not surprising as Taranaki Maunga is truly magnificent and is one of only a few almost perfect pyramid cone volcanic peaks to be found worldwide. Its better known "twin" is Mt Fuji in Japan although we have found, in our more recent travels to visit the dairy industry in Southern Chile, that there is another close lookalike even with dairy country around about it and cows posing in its foreground.

Outside our window in the hotel, the clouds had rolled back, and we felt welcome in our new home town. Since then, I have found that every dull and gloomy day in Taranaki is not so bad because you never know what treasures the next day will bring!

Settling in to Inglewood Hotel was not hard – even meals were provided at the hotel. We were usually the only diners in the dining room and enjoyed the set menu cooked in the huge kitchen. It was as tasty as any restaurant fare – even with the somewhat absentminded cook who often forgot which items she had salted. To compensate, she generally added a bit more salt to something just in case.

In Inglewood, I became part of the vet club or group practice. Each small dairy cooperative had its own vet group or "vet club" which employed vets and provided the clinic buildings and housing for the vets. These "clubs" were actually "not for profits" run by an elected committee of farmers who organised the veterinary service for all the farm animals in the area. As a farmer and milk supplier, you could join the club for a small membership fee and enjoy low-cost veterinary service for your animals.

Soon after we arrived in Inglewood, Sandra and I were invited to dinner at the home of the chairman of the club committee – a nice change from hotel meals with oversalted peas. The Inglewood vet club committee and the farmers who were part of the club were a great group of farmers amongst whom we quickly made many friends – they were great to work with and made sure that young vets like myself were looked after as they started "making their mistakes." My real life learning began with these farmers, who helped me learn and forgave me through those "mistakes" and through all the experiences that they and I shared with their animals.

Very early in my career, even before I knew what to look for, I was writing things down. My lifelong love affair with gathering data really began to blossom. My family calls it an obsession. The best thing about being a country vet is that it is like living in a giant laboratory. Some people have mice or rats in their laboratory; I had cows. Thousands of them. They were all looked after, fed, and milked every day just so that I could study the effects of all sorts of things. As a young vet, I was curious to know what the result of our work was – did we really make a difference? Farmers often were too nice to tell us about our failures – when the cow didn't get better or even died. I wanted to know what the outcome was either way. The answer was to write down what happened or ask the farmer to write it down.

Some jobs that we do as vets are boring, repetitive, and so dirty that you can't go home to your wife without a shower and some liberal application of toothpaste, not to the teeth but to the arm and hands! Some smells can even penetrate plastic gloves, and only by using toothpaste instead of soap can you get rid of it. I often smile (or get embarrassed) thinking of my journey home from a day on farms. There was a little corner shop in a small village in the middle of my group of farms, and I wondered what the lady behind the counter thought of the vet who came in for an afternoon tea ice cream and found out later that his face and hair were generously be-smattered with cow manure!

When jobs were dirty or boring, I found a personal key to making them at least interesting, if not less smelly. That key was to write down what I saw, and then, with all this data collected, I could become an expert on odd things like retained foetal membranes after a calving and extra teats on calves. I found out what sort of treatments worked and what did not. And this way I really did know! I found out that researchers on all sorts of cow health matters often did at least the initial research using very small groups of animals whereas I "had" thousands. So I could collect very powerful data. If one cow gets better and another worse, you could say that they had a 50–50 chance of getting better, but how much better it is to say "Out of my one thousand cases, five hundred got better" – it looks more likely that it really is a 50–50 chance.

For example, nowadays, I often ask farmers if they know that in New Zealand female calves are born with an average of five teats instead of the usual four? An interesting genetic fact that I found when I was disbudding thousands of calves (removing their horn buds), and, whilst they were sleeping under anaesthetic, I also painlessly removed any extra teats. And wrote down the numbers – voila: data.

This data collection that I continued to practise in my "laboratory" was another step in my journey from Colin's paddock to some useful answers and advice for farmers.

# CHAPTER 5

# Settling In (1974–1980)

HAVING POWERFUL DATA was not very useful unless I could pass it on. Early in my career, I started holding seminars for farmers, initially by joining farmer discussion groups where everyone contributed what they knew. I contributed very little but learned a lot. As the years went on, as well as running the seminars for farmers, I also started running courses for vets, usually new-graduate vets. The plan was to help get them up to speed with understanding lameness and safely treating lame cows.

I wanted their early vet experiences with lame cows to be easier than mine. Knowledge that I had had to glean here and there should be more easily available to new graduates. Not to mention that we now know more than we used to know then. I wish that I had known some of this when I was a new graduate just starting out. Not everyone will have someone like Gunner to teach them. I called the seminars "Understanding Lameness" as I had high hopes that this is what we will eventually achieve.

My first years as a vet were both exciting and challenging. For me back in 1974, to begin work in Inglewood was a great place to start, especially with a great mentor like Gunner, with plenty of experience that he was prepared to pass on to me. Little did I know that I would also have the privilege of finishing my veterinary career in Inglewood.

There were still a lot of old family farms around Inglewood when I first arrived. Each farm was relatively small by New Zealand standards with around 180 cows per farm on average. But things were by no means old-fashioned.

In the past, the processing of the milk would start on each individual farm. Each farmer would separate the milk into cream and "the rest" on the farm. Then "the rest" would be fed to pigs and the cans of cream taken by horse wagon to the dairy factory in each little community. Each small factory then converted the milk fat to butter or cheese. By the time I arrived on the scene, there were tanker trucks carting the whole raw milk to the local factories every day, and the only process done on farm was to quickly chill the milk. More logistical changes were to come, of course, as I have mentioned. Taranaki's one huge dairy factory needed a veritable fleet of tankers, most with trailers in tow, to collect all that chilled milk.

The dairy farms themselves have also changed over the years. Many small farms have amalgamated into bigger concerns with modern milking facilities. However, when I first arrived in North Taranaki, most farms were still as they had been in the early days of the developing dairy industry with very little change. That was still to come on my watch. The last walk-through shed in our part of Taranaki closed just at the same time as I was retiring from vet work!

Having arrived fresh from university in the city, I was keen to sort out what equipment I would need. Talking to Gunner, my boss, I discovered that the first thing I would need was a vehicle to drive from farm to farm and a good loud set of air horns for that vehicle. Obviously, I needed the advice of the older vets. Who would have thought that you would need air horns? Gunner gave me an old set of his airhorns until I could find some for myself. Of course, these would come in handy.

I would drive up the tanker track to a dairy shed and sound my air horns to let the farmer know that I had arrived. I had received a list of farms needing a visit in the morning, and I just organised them as I thought fit. We would never know what time we would be able to get to a particular farm and extra, more urgent, calls could come in at any time, changing your route between farms. The air horns made it easier for the farmer as he didn't have to wait around at the yards for the vet but could go home for a cup of tea whilst the vet did other calls on the way.

We now no longer need air horns as some sensible people thought of the idea of booking in appointment times. The old vets didn't like having to keep to a time schedule, but now with better telephone systems if an appointment needs to be changed, we can easily be in contact. The farmers can be more organised and not have to be available the entire morning, and now also the stock doesn't get frightened by a very noisy vet arriving. Progress.

I began looking around for a vehicle to fill my vet visit needs. However, in the meantime, we also needed a vehicle to drive myself and Sandra around outside work hours, something that we could afford as we had very little money having just started out. I spotted a nice-looking 1956 Morris Minor. During my teenage years in Sydney, my family had owned a Morris Minor even older than this, a 1950 side-valve convertible. I had learned to drive in this. Having just a canvas roof, it was really easy to break into, and often, young lads with nothing better to do would take it for a little joyride. Whenever it was missing in the morning us kids would go for a walk, and we would find it not too far away. I guess the main fun was getting the engine started, but the speed was not exciting, and the fun quickly wore off.

This 1956 Morris I had found for sale was relatively modern! Pretty soon we had it set up with seat belts and could travel where we liked all over the province. We christened it Popsie. This car was my first four-wheeled vehicle and stayed with us for many years. In the days before bigger child seats became the law, we could fit four children in the back seat. Popsie was to also be the vehicle in which I taught my children to drive. Some twenty-five years later, we sold it to a friend for $1 whilst we travelled overseas – on our return we got it back again – he had never paid the $1! Popsie transported us faithfully around the local area, at one time transporting a pet sheep and, on another occasion, even a pet calf. Eventually we sold it to someone who wanted a classic Morris to sell in the United States.

When we first acquired Popsie, believing that we were only going to stay in New Zealand (making all my "mistakes") for three years or so, we started out using our free weekends to travel around Taranaki sightseeing. For longer trips, we used the next car we bought.

My first vet car was a shiny maroon Hillman Hunter. This was the first of a series of vet cars – they wore out much more quickly than the faithful Popsie – although they were much better suited to carrying stuff and going a little bit faster. Of course, before going away anywhere further afield on the weekend, the vet vehicle had to be unloaded and deodorised.

As I began working and visiting farms, I started to get to know which road was which. Taranaki is not a flat place with roads laid out in grid pattern. Instead, the back roads to farms wind around the hills and sometimes even bend back on themselves. Most are sealed – a legacy of having to accommodate milk tankers. Our area that we covered as vets was not very large as the small farms were really quite close to each other. We serviced a sort of rough circle with a diameter of approximately forty kilometres around the town of Inglewood, and I was given a slice of this pie, just under a quarter.

This was, of course, before cell phones were around, so another piece of equipment that was needed was a two-way radio. This necessity was duly installed in my Hillman Hunter along with the air horns. The "base" at the office could answer the "real" telephone and call people with messages from the vet on the road. When a farmer called with a sick animal to be seen, Peter at the office would pick up the radio telephone hand piece – "Base to V-one . . .," and the signal would bounce off the aerial on the mountain and end up wherever I was – except if I was behind a big hill. It was at least as good as the modern cell phone. We could all talk to each other whilst driving around the countryside, and everyone could hear all the conversations. In this way, the one who was not too busy or finished early could hear who might need an extra hand.

Before beginning the "real" vet work at my new job, the next task was to set up myself with the smaller equipment that I would need to carry in my car. A builder needs a hammer and nails and drills and screws. I needed surgical instruments but also things you might not usually think of as vet equipment like ropes, and calving chains, and protective gear. Then add the supplies needed like antibiotic injections, bandages, and the list goes on. No wonder the Hillman Hunter was quite full in both the boot and the back seat.

To keep in communication with the farmers the office staff had extra helpers – the ladies who operated the manual exchange located on the second storey of the post office downtown. Making friends with telephone operators as I had already learned was a good idea. Inglewood had the most modern – and the last manual exchange in New Zealand. By turning a handle on the phone, you could buzz the exchange, and "Number Please" was the reply. On occasions if the office staff needed to call a series of farmers, they would give the list of numbers to the operator, and as each call was completed, she would just connect the next one.

As you can imagine, these ladies, despite being so busy that they hardly had time to breathe, still managed to go over and above and even well beyond the regular service. One evening, when I was on after-hours duty and had finished my daytime calls, we were invited out for dinner. Since there was no such thing as a mobile phone, I gave the vet after-hours lady the phone number of our hosts for the night. About an hour after we arrived and in the middle of dinner, there was a ring on the phone. Our host answered and then called me – "There is a call coming through for you from Auckland, and the exchange lady has found you!"

Then there were the "after-hours ladies." These ladies who answered the phones and took calls for us outside the normal hours were great; they were like mothers for us young vets often providing cups of tea when we arrived back in Inglewood and dropped in at their homes. They were also in radio contact with us in the car. One of the ladies had great vicarious pleasure in sending her vets all over the countryside like knights in shining armour while she stayed at home directing operations. She retired from answering the phone, but we still remained friends for many years. As untrained people without even a farming background while they learned a lot from farmers, they often made strange diagnoses over the phone.

Sometimes they needed some other skills. How to decipher odd accents. One day when I was on duty, I received a radio call from Ev, the after-hours lady on duty. I had two or three other calls waiting, so I got out my diary to write the new one down.

"A farmer on Airport Drive has a cow to be seen. He says it has its tongue hanging out, and he was very worried – even panicking. I said that you would be there soon," said Ev. She gave me the address. I thought that this shouldn't be an emergency, so I did a couple of visits on the way. When I did finally arrive, there was a cow with its "tum" hanging out! The midlands English vernacular and accent had confused the after-hours lady. It turned out that the cow had jumped over a low fence and cut its stomach whereupon some of the intestines had started "hanging out." No wonder the farmer was panicking. Fortunately for the cow, I was able to put everything back in place and then stitch up the wound. She recovered and (probably) never attempted to jump over a low fence again.

However, despite the occasional, usually very minor slip-ups, the after-hours ladies were most valuable in keeping everyone calm – staying on the phone and radio at the same time, telling the farmer not to worry, the vet is on the way – even though he might still be getting his overalls on or just finishing another call fifty kilometres away! And telling the vet not to worry even if this is their first caesarean operation.

The first time I did each type of job, it was a bit nerve-wracking, but the farmers were really understanding. I remember being on duty for the first time by myself, and a call came in for a cow with difficulty delivering her calf about twenty kilometres away past Tarata, a small community on the other side of a saddle reached by a really windy stretch of road. In the early days before children came along, Sandra and I would often go out together on the weekend calls. According to the after-hours lady, this one could be a caesarean, so I took Sandra along with a textbook on her knee open at "caesarean on a cow." Along the winding road as I drove the Hillman and Sandra read from the book, bit by bit I revised the procedure whilst Sandra tried to avoid getting carsick on the bends.

Arriving at the farm, we saw a big brown cow standing in the yard looking a little distressed. No need for air horns here.

"Hello, Jim," I introduced myself, "I am the new vet from Inglewood. The after-hours lady said that your cow was having difficulty calving – maybe a caesarean needed?"

A quick examination of the cow proved the farmer and the after-hours lady were both correct – it needed a caesarean to deliver the calf.

"Yes, the lady said she thought it needed a caesarean. Is this your first time?"

"Yes," I admitted.

"Well, let's get on with it – at least it wasn't so long since you learned how to do it."

*Only five minutes or so ago*, I thought. We were in it together. In about half an hour, we had a cow and calf doing well. And the vet and his wife survived the ordeal.

My early vet experiences weren't just with cows. I always tried as a vet to keep in mind the saying that people are as important as their animals, but to some people, their animal is more important. I had only recently arrived in Inglewood when I met Dick, an elderly man who lived a few kilometres out of town. He owned a small car and a dog. Once a week he would drive into town to visit the local corner shop for an ice cream outing. He would drive slowly along the main road in his pale blue Triumph, with his little dog peering through the windscreen beside him, at well below the speed limit, while traffic gathered up behind him. For Dick, his little dog was his best friend, and in fact this was a doggie outing – he would park just outside the dairy, go inside, and buy an ice cream in a cone – for his dog. As a vet, caring for Dick's dog was also caring for Dick and vice versa.

Putting dogs and cows together was sometimes a problem that I would meet. In fact, later on in my career some farmers would tell me that dogs were the main cause of lameness. One dog problem like this that I met was at a farm where there was a dog who loved cows a little too much, playing games with them, that is. The cows were terrified of the dog who would run along behind them and try to nip their heels. I suggested to the farmer that he should get rid of the dog – wrong idea!

"Oh no, I couldn't do that, she is my only friend," he said dejectedly.

It certainly can be lonely on a farm, working long hours with no company – and this farmer was a bachelor. I quickly sent up a prayer for the right answer.

"You don't have a girlfriend?" I asked.

"No," he replied.

"Well, if you had a girlfriend, where would she be right now?"

"Oh, that's easy, she would be sitting on the back of the motor bike with her arms around me."

"Well then," I said, "that is where your little dog should be." Two problems solved. No vet treatment needed, maybe fewer lame cows. And we were still friends.

Another dog I met would have been the least likely to have caused lameness. I had been in Inglewood less than a year when I drove up to a farm dairy shed and sounded my airhorns. I was looking for a farmer whom I had not yet met. I was met instead by a very friendly dog. The farmer was not so happy, however, when he arrived a good ten minutes later.

"Stupid dog," he said, "I will have to get rid of it. She likes people and doesn't like cows. Whenever I send her to get the cows, she just visits people."

There she sat a beautiful Border collie cross, tricoloured like a collie dog, and "smiling" at me. As a vet, I well understood the euphemism that the farmer had used. She was such a nice dog that I immediately said, "I will take her home," without thinking of how this would be received at home.

"Hop in," I said, and she jumped into the car and sat on the front seat. However, "Crunchie," as she was called, was a real people charmer and charmed Sandra at first sight just as she had charmed me. That wasn't her last ride in a car as she accompanied us on many trips. She also learned how to ride in a box on the carrier of my bicycle. She remained in our household for the next fifteen years.

My other girlfriend on the bike

Crunchie also soon was introduced to more people as over the next few years our family grew. First to be born was Gael, while we were living in a house owned by the vet club, right next door to the vet clinic. This had its advantages, only a few short steps to get to work, for example. But also some disadvantages as people could just drop in on a weekend or after hours to "see if you were home and could you look at their possibly sick cat or dog." This happened one night when I was actually on duty. It was our wedding anniversary and we were celebrating – dressed up in our fancy clothes – when a farmer arrived at the door needing some antibiotics for his cow. I don't know what he thought about the new vet and his wife who dressed for dinner.

Our second daughter, Karen, arrived a few days after we moved out of the vet house and into our own house in Inglewood. That house certainly had character and had been the centre of activities quite different to the vet house. Most recently it seems it had been the home of local gang members. All the rooms had bolts screwed onto the doors, and apparently, we heard, the roof had been a great place from which to throw bottles at a rival gang. More about this house later.

Inglewood is not a very large town, and most places were just a short walk from our old house, so Sandra would take Crunchie on the lead. At the same time, she would be pushing a pushchair or pram, and later, there might also be a tricycle in the cavalcade. Crunchie, being an intelligent dog, knew that with two children, Sandra had her hands full, so Crunchie would misbehave and hope to get away with it. One day we had an idea – Sandra carried a small stick – even though she never used it, Crunchie would walk like a well-trained dog. Problem solved.

With each little problem gradually solved and each new experience chalked up, we settled in to vet work in Inglewood. Soon it would be time to begin the lameness lessons.

## CHAPTER 6

# Learning Lameness Part 1 (1974–1980)

IN A COW vet's life, treating lame feet could be called the three "Ds." It's the dirtiest, most difficult, and dangerous job. It is much easier to just give the lame cow some antibiotics and anti-inflammatories (painkillers) and then wait and see – a bit like a doctor telling you to go home, take an aspirin, and, if your leg still looks like it is at a funny angle, come back tomorrow. You can imagine what the person might think of that – and maybe also imagine what a cow might "think" of it.

A doctor who lived and worked in Inglewood in the old days had a reputation for just that – especially if an after-hours visit might be needed. One evening, he was holding a party for his rugby friends when the toilet got blocked. So he rang the plumber. The plumber, not wanting to go out on a cold night, said, "Throw in an aspirin and see how it is in the morning!" Touché to the plumber.

As vets, we also sometimes got to thinking that we were just as good as a doctor. One of our four vets, after a cow had stepped on his foot, was convinced he had a broken bone – so he borrowed the corner of an X-ray plate whilst X-raying a small animal and X-rayed his foot at the same time. Then he rang the doctor and told him he had broken a bone in his foot.

"How do you know?" asked the doctor.

"I X-rayed it," replied the vet.

"You X-ray – you fix," the doctor shot back. Touché to the doctor.

One doctor vet story that we were part of was when our third child was due to be born. Sandra had called me and told me it was time to go to the maternity hospital; the doctor would meet us there. "Is there any rush?" I asked, as I had a vet call to do.

"Well, things are not moving fast yet, but you had better be ready soon," was the reply.

My vet call was not to a sick cow at that time but to a lion with a toothache. The circus was visiting town, and the old lion was groaning in his cage. Another vet was going to deal with the tooth, but they had asked me to anaesthetise it. At the time, I was the only vet with a dart gun for remotely tranquilising or anaesthetising animals. I had made it for wild deer that we needed to treat, now it was needed for this circus lion. The final plan was that we would both go to the lion – as Sandra would not be left stranded in Inglewood whilst I drove off to look at a lion. All was well – the next day, the lion was minus a tooth, and we had a new baby boy. The doctor who was waiting at the hospital still tells the story.

One thing that one of our clients learned was that it was not a good idea to get the doctor and the vet confused. Pandemonium could ensue. Mr E was an elderly gentleman who had retired from dairy farming and now had a small property just outside Inglewood. He and his wife raised dairy cows for their son and kept those old ones who had not got pregnant that year (holdovers), ready to possibly get pregnant the next season. One day, one of those cows became really sick – probably old age. Mr E called the vet who came and gave it some treatment. However, it was not improving, so Mr E rang the vet again and asked him to call in and see what else could be done for the cow. He walked back to the shed where the cow was lying only to discover that she had died. He went back to the phone in a hurry and dialled what he thought was the vet – but was in fact the doctor. "Hello, Mr E here. You don't need to come. The old girl has died."

As a young vet coming to treat a lame foot on a cow, I realised how much I had to learn and not just strictly veterinary things. Starting out working on mostly smaller family-owned farms was a good place to quickly learn how to safely do the "3D" job. I never did solve the D that stood for dirty except with a washing machine and lots of soap and toothpaste as well to get rid of the smell afterwards. But I did find ways to ease the other two Ds, to make the job less difficult and less dangerous . Many methods I used were great tips from Gunner, some were ideas I had myself, and some were time-worn ideas that the farmers passed on to me.

A city boy with very limited cow experience is not a bad position to start from. Anyone might be likely to make one or both of the two biggest mistakes that people make when meeting cows: thinking that a cow is just like a human with four legs or, just as misinformed, thinking that a cow is just a dumb animal. I probably started with a pinch of both wrong ideas, but getting to know cows gradually trained me to get a better perspective.

Before I could do any fancy vet work, I had to learn how to get that intelligent, four-legged animal, the cow, to walk to a suitable place where both the cow and I could feel safe and to ensure that the cow stayed there. A cow doesn't want to stand nice and still and allow you to lift one of her feet, especially if the foot is painful, but for her own good, we needed to restrain her. She likes to feel safe with all four feet on the ground, and if you try to lift one of those feet, she might decide to use it to kick you. Cows don't look all that agile, but they sure can kick and often accurately as well. A calm cow can even lift and lick one of her back feet whilst standing on just the three other feet!

The ideal place to stand the cow to look at and treat her foot should, at the very least, have rails on either side and a gate in the front to let the cow out afterwards. The rails should extend as a sort of lead in. We call this a race. When I was starting my vet journey, most farmers did not have special facilities. Often, as I was frequently going to be working on cows' feet at the farm, I advised the farmer on how to build a safe race with a head bail to catch the cow's head to prevent her backing up. This was a compilation of treatment facilities that I had seen on other farms. No farmers had fancy crushes, or treatment boxes, to hold the cow such as we see nowadays. They were not even invented. In the most fancy, modern foot crush, the cow walks into the box and you just press a button and, presto, the foot is neatly captured, secured, and lifted right in front of your eyes – you can even stand back if the cow lets fly with a well-aimed cow pat! Although not many farmers have the really fancy crushes, most farmers now have much better and safer treatment races or bails in which to hold a cow to look at her foot.

Cow jack

When I was just starting out, most of the time we had to make do with the end of the treatment race or even inside the milking bails. This is where I needed my chain or a rope behind the cow to stop the cow backing up or falling over. If the farmer had a bar, I could use that across the race to keep the cow where it and I were both safe. In some cases, the cow could be really stirred up, especially if it had been kept in a yard by itself for quite a while, or if we had used loud noises or whistles to try and get her to move. Once or twice I have had cows jump over fences like a supercow. Usually, the best idea was to let the cow (and us) calm down and then try again. In some extreme cases, I use my special nonmedical cow tranquiliser. This is a very simple trick with a long piece of rope. Cows feel safe in a close box where they can't escape and nothing else can get to them. I use my rope to tie zigzag over the top of the rails as a sort of a web lid where it will firmly touch the back of the cow. Then when we encourage the cow under the rope she feels safe in a sort of box. In the end, usually we could get the cow to stand in a good position either on the milking platform or at the end of the race ready to tie the foot up to any convenient rail.

Then to lift the foot. Standing on only three feet is tricky for a cow. Imagine a chair which started out with four legs now with only three legs. It is going to fall over without something to lean on or to support the missing leg corner. So we did the best we could whilst often the cow did the best she could to hamper us, being determined to keep all four feet on the ground.

In order to tie up the foot securely when once you had the cow at the front, closed end of the race, farmers and vets would use a piece of rope. These were either too thick or too thin and slipped or cut into the leg. I experimented with all sorts of things. Then I discovered that the ideal "rope" to gently but firmly tie a cow's foot to the rail was not a rope at all but a flat strap. In fact, a seat belt webbing strap such as you find in your car turned out to be the best idea. Safety strap was a good name for it. It is soft, doesn't hurt the leg, and doesn't slip, especially when it is wet and most things in or near a dairy shed are bound to get wet. It is also safer for the vet as the cow feels safer, and it doesn't kick around.

Where to get this seat belting? I tried getting it from cars that had died, but I found that the pieces that I could salvage were usually not quite long enough especially in the days before vehicles had retractable seat belts. When I found a good length, I used it for many years. As soon as anyone saw me using this, they were impressed at how well it worked, so I soon had a reputation for spreading the idea of using seat belt webbing. Many years later when I had started travelling around to advise farmers in other countries and collecting lame stories, I found that this reputation had gone before me even further afield. In about 2016, I was in the United States. In America, seat belts are long enough – everything is big there! I was visiting a farm in Missouri in the

United States with a New Zealand farmer who was working there. The first thing he said was, "I know where to get you a good piece of seat belt webbing to treat my cows." He took me across the farm to a derelict giant "pick-up" RAM that had gone over a bank probably several years before. With the help of a crowbar, we managed to extract the perfect piece of "cow foot rope." I have stopped visiting derelict cars to get my belting – I now source it in one hundred metre rolls from upholsterers who use it as a support for the seats of chairs. I cut it to the right length of three and a half metres.

When tying up the leg of a cow, the first thing you need to do is to get hold of the leg. The easiest way to do this is to throw a rope around it. Most foot ropes had a loop at one end, so all you had to do then was to thread the end through the loop and pull the rope tight like a noose. Then you had hold of the leg, and you could pull it up to the rail to securely tie it up so that the cow didn't kick you, and the foot would be steady so that you could treat it. Although the noose idea was good and generally worked well, it had a problem – how to loosen it afterwards – or in an emergency if the cow slipped and fell over. I had found that when using softer webbing, if your length of webbing is long enough, you can tie a quick-release slip knot as the noose to capture the foot. Then it is really easy to just pull undone and release the foot quickly. At the Stamping Out Lameness course, when I teach young vets about treating lame cows, we have races to see who can tie and release the knot the fastest. This slip knot is the perfect solution if the cow has begun to fall over with her leg still tied up to a bar. If this happens, you need to release the leg quickly by just pulling the end of the strap so she doesn't dislocate a hip. Cows are really heavy, and a cow falling over is a real hazard to people as well. I have a bent finger to prove that it is not wise to allow a cow to squeeze your finger against a rail.

In my early years as a vet, usually the farmer would be available to help, and the two of us would usually be enough to keep the cow and people safe. Times have changed, and health and safety is a sensible consideration now. With the right methods and better facilities, even a new young vet, man or woman, can easily restrain a cow safely. In all cases, cows are big and heavy, and it is always better to insist on good facilities and a helper. Brute strength is not needed – progress.

Early in my time as a vet, I started writing articles for farmer conferences and magazines. One article was titled "Lameness is Physical." But I wasn't only just referring to the physical difficulty of getting the cow ready to have her foot looked at. It was more to do with day-to-day observations with cows and farmers and what I learned at Pete's place.

Pete was a farmer just a few years older than me but who had a lot more farm experience. His was also a smallish farm with about 180 cows like my friend Colin. However, although his farm had streams flowing between the paddocks, it was much flatter than Colin's farm. He, like Colin, also had lots of lame cows.

"Pete has a couple of lame cows," said Lois, the office receptionist over the radio telephone. "I guess I will hear from you in an hour or so."

Can you hear the smile? All our receptionists were great and enjoyed sending their vets out to do the work but couldn't resist a smile when they knew that the work was going to be a bit difficult, tiresome, and time-consuming. A lame cow is not a serious emergency (except for the cow!) and usually not life threatening, but it is a job that can take some time to finish so that the cow is more comfortable and can walk well again. Even today, I can usually only properly treat five or six lame cows in one hour.

As I drove up the tanker track at Pete's farm and blasted my airhorns to tell Pete that I had arrived, I thought, *Back to the "laboratory." I wonder what we will see today.* Waiting in the yard were three cows as usual. Pete didn't lift the feet or treat any of his cows for lameness – he left the three Ds to me – sensible, don't you think? However, he was always on hand to chat and help – both of which were valuable. Working with Pete and others like him was how I learned much of what I pass on today.

I walked over to say hi. "Right, Pete," I said, "what have we got today?"

"Two lame front feet and one back one, I think," he replied.

"Okay, let's check, shall we?" I had found myself in a "hole" on an occasion before this when the cow was waiting in the crush to be treated, and Pete had said he thought that the left back foot was lame. After lifting the foot and poking around, I hadn't been able to find anything wrong. So we let the cow out again and walked her around only to discover that it was the "other left." Then we had a really hard job convincing the cow to go back into the place where someone had just tied her foot up to a rail.

"Let's walk them gently around, and they will tell us which foot is sore," I said to Pete.

The first cow didn't say "ouch," but she lifted her head when the right front foot touched the ground to pull the weight off that foot, in exactly the same way that we would. If you have a sore foot or leg, you will do whatever you can to keep your weight off it. Sometimes we look like we lift our whole body when the sore foot should be on the ground so that it hardly touches the ground.

"Okay, that's the first front foot one," I said. "Remember that!" Pete wrote down number "39." If the cow has a sore back foot, she will drop her head and throw the weight forward off the sore back foot. The second cow was dipping her head like that. The third was another front foot.

"Right, now we have that sorted, let's put the first one up the race, and I will go and get my kit."

I fished out my relatively new lame cow kit from the boot of the Hillman and walked back into the milking shed. I kept my kit in a bucket mostly because it has a handle and will stand up by itself. And, also things can just be thrown in when you are finished. In this bucket were all the things that I needed to do the job as efficiently and as safely as possible. Of course, on top was my length of seat belt webbing usually still damp from the previous farm or because it hadn't dried out because of the damp weather – or both. All three and a half metres of it.

A pair of stainless-steel handles were poking out the top. These belonged to my hoof testers. Under those were my hoof knives keeping themselves safe pushed into old rubber inflations (which are the rubber linings of the milking machine cup). There they are safe from getting their blade nicked or being blunted by something else in the bucket. This also keeps my hand safe when reaching in to get the knives out.

My knives are now very sharp. Once they were out of the bucket and in use, I have found – again, through painful experience – that the knife that cuts the user is usually the blunt one. This is because it often slips when you have to apply more force to try to trim off the hard nail of the cow's foot. And your hand is in the way. And when you forget to wear your protective glove. Another piece of my equipment.

At first, I would buy expensive knives ready sharpened until I learned from Gunner how to sharpen a knife to make it "scary" sharp. Vets could be great chefs when they know how to sharpen a knife like that. However, being a chef wouldn't really suit me because, as you know, I only really cooked baked beans or whatever came out of a tin, and some toast to put it on, burnt. But a vet needs to be a bit versatile – or at least a lateral thinker to work out where to get help.

Sharpening a hoof knife is a matter of knowing a couple of principles and having the correct equipment. A hoof knife is not an ordinary knife – it is a paring knife with a hook at one end. The flat part of the blade is for paring large areas of the hoof, and the hook part at the end is for digging out small shavings from difficult places. Because it is a paring knife, you only sharpen one side – like a chisel. The flat side rests on the surface from which you want to shave a small sliver, and the sharp side directs the slither upwards and away. Knives don't usually come with a nice thin edge on them so I have to spend some time to adjust this. To make a good low bevel, you need a good file and a lot of patience. Or a Dremel with a fine diamond file attachment. The hook part is curved so a flat file will not work here; you need a round one like a chainsaw file, and it needs to be thin enough to fit into the hook. I found it was worth spending some time to sharpen my knives at home and then they only needed a little touch-up at the farm. Often, I would do this touch up whilst I was waiting for the cow to arrive – just like a good chef will touch up his knives before getting to work. Today at Pete's place, the cow was already waiting for me.

I put my bucket down and fished out my safety strap. We managed to lift the front foot and tied it firmly to the rail. Number 39 turned her head to look and see what was happening, and then, as if approving of the knot, turned to face the front again.

## CHAPTER 7

# Learning Lameness Part 2 (1974–1980)

"LET'S HAVE a look at this," I said to Pete. "I am pretty sure we have got the correct foot, it did look like it was in the right foot." So with her foot tied securely to the rail and with Number 39 turning her head again to watch the proceedings, I washed the foot to see what was going on. Nothing visible. Nothing between the claws. No swelling. No heat. Hmmm. I got out my hoof tester pliers. Hoof tester pliers look like a pair of giant pincers similar to what you might find on an insect except that they are made of metal. They open wide enough to "pinch" anywhere on the claw that you might wish. They are the most valuable piece of equipment in my box. It was valuable not only to me but also to the cow as she would have a better diagnosis and therefore a better outcome.

I gently squeezed here and there. As I squeezed lightly over a small speck on the bottom of the foot, the cow twitched with the pain – and so did I as I thought of the dentist checking to see which tooth was needing attention! I guess I would have complained if he had drilled the wrong tooth – just as the cow might have complained if I started digging with my knife in the wrong place.

Before I started to use hoof testers, I had definitely been making real mistakes. On one occasion, I had seen just with my eyes what I thought was the problem, treated that very nicely, I thought, then let the cow go out. She was still limping badly.

"Hmm," the farmer had said, "looks like she is still lame." I had missed what I was about to find on Pete's cow.

By now I had begun to get a bit more confidence with treating lame cows, and I had a better protocol. I said that treating lame cows was the three D job, it also should be the most "S" job, satisfying. I always love to see a cow that was limping and obviously in severe pain walk away with less of a limp after I have treated it. I think that the cow was probably happier too.

"Ah ha, here it is," I said as Number 39 twitched with the pain again. "Looks like something has gone in under the sole here, at the toe."

"That's microscopic," was Pete's comment.

"Sure is," I said, "but the pain is anything but microscopic." I fished out my sharp hoof knife from my kit bucket and started to gently pare off a bit of the sole to relieve the pain and pressure of the little abscess. Pop, splat, pus in the face. A painful abscess burst all over my face – did I say this job was dirty?

"We got it," I said, wiping my face on my overall sleeve, and set about making sure there was no more pus under the sole and that gravel wouldn't be able to get stuck in the hole that the pus had been filling.

"Are you going to put a block on this one?" asked Pete, grinning, as he remembered that the last block that I had glued on had fallen off as the cow walked away. The quick-setting glue mix had obviously not cured properly – or I had put it on too early or too late. How to make the block stay on was something that I had had to learn quickly!

"Let's give it a go," I said.

These are the last part of my kit – the blocks, and I am not talking about the sort of blocks that children play with. Indeed, the block can be made of wood, but these days you can also choose rubber or plastic or even hard foam plastic. But for "block" substitute "orthopaedic device" or "sole support." Blocks are the best invention for helping the lame cow get back on her feet literally. God made the cow with two claws or toes for each foot, giving them two flat surfaces side by side on which to stand and walk. In the past, when dairy farmers in the Northern Hemisphere had a lame cow, they had the fantastic idea of raising the one claw that was injured above the ground. They added a block underneath the good claw so that the good one would support all the weight whilst the sore sole was lifted up above the hard surface. They initially used wooden blocks and nailed them on just like a horseshoe. This needed really thick soles on the foot of the cow, not to mention the added problem that the cow might stand on a nail if it fell out. Then this would be a worse problem.

So the next idea was to glue them on. How to find a good glue? An Irishman named Ernie Logan was working with horse shoes and had invented a plastic shoe for horses that was able to be tied on. He thought that glue could be a better solution. He experimented with two-part glues and eventually found the best formula for a glue that worked for the stuff that cows' and horses ' feet are made of. He made his blocks not from wood but from hardwearing plastic. The original old wooden blocks looked like an extra sole, but this new plastic cow shoe was shaped to fit on the foot just like a slip-on shoe. This gave more surface area for the glue to stick, as the glue was on the front of the hoof as well as underneath. It also made a handy mixing place for the two-part glue – inside the shoe. So now with the glue well mixed and spread on the front of the hoof as well, the block stayed on so much better.

He also came up with a great name for his new block – "Cowslip" – slipper for a cow! This block that now stayed on better was a revolution in treating cows' feet. When I was visiting Ireland years later, I had the opportunity to call on Ernie, the inventor of the Cowslip and glue which for many years was the one and only glue.

There was only one problem with the blocks initially. Although the problem was with the vets not the blocks. You had to learn how to prepare the hoof by scraping it clean and making sure that it was dry. Then you could glue the block on properly so that it didn't get lost in the paddock or, worse, drop off before the cow had walked out of sight. Now there are many different types of glues and many types of blocks, but it still applies that you need to prepare the hoof and use the glue correctly. You can no longer blame the glue as I did when the block had fallen off Pete's cow as it walked away from us.

I set about cleaning up the claw that was to receive the block, making sure it was quite dry, by using a gas burner. Then I mixed the glue and fitted the block. In this case, the cow did manage to walk away with the block still attached. I was learning all the time.

With a block glued on and the sore claw elevated above the ground, it was much less painful. So after any painkillers that might be needed to cover the pain of treatment wore off, there was still less pain as the block stayed there as a physical painkiller. It might even stay on for three or four weeks, and so the cow's foot had a great chance to heal completely before she had to use it again full-time. It also meant that the cow could soon walk well enough on her orthopaedic device to be able to get to the good grass with the rest of the cows, and she didn't have to stay in "hospital" and away from her herd mates – all good outcomes. "Hospital" was usually a separate herd of cows called the "lame cow mob." These cows were kept in a different paddock closer to the milking shed, where the grass was not as good.

Another great outcome of using blocks, as I learned, is that a treatment like a block indirectly reduces use of antibiotics. There is no need to try antibiotics as a first response. The block is the first response. First do your paring and let out any infection, then apply the block to the good claw and usually it works so well that no antibiotics are needed – the cow is already on the road to recovery. Just a bit of painkiller is needed.

"No antibiotic needed, Pete," I said, wiping the remaining pus off my glasses and watching as the cow walked away and feeling my usual satisfaction. "We've already let out the pus, and the air will kill anything else." He knew we were right as Pete was one of my "laboratory" farms. I had done a survey on his farm. When I treated an injured foot with pus under the wall or sole, I wrote down the case. I gave half the lame cow cases antibiotics, and half of them had none. I found no difference at all. They recovered at the same rate. In fact, it was the block that was more important – as long as it stayed on. So no antibiotic was even in my bucket kit. If I decided that it was needed, as it is in most foot rot cases where the infection is inside the foot, then I could fetch it from my car.

Most farmers don't write down what happens to their cows unless the vet gives the cow an antibiotic injection. Then they know it is really important to write it down and mark the cow with a big red splash of stock marker paint. No farmer wants to accidently get milk contaminated with antibiotics into his milk vat. If antibiotic is in the milk, it will kill off the bugs that make cheese or may cause some pasteurised milk contamination. For this reason, the factory collecting the milk would collect samples from the bulk milk vat and test them for antibiotics. If even a tiny bit was found, the milk was regarded as contaminated, and the farmer was heavily fined. Whenever a cow that I treated needed antibiotics, I would write its details in my pink-page book and tear out the top copy to give to the farmer to remind them not to milk that cow into the main collecting vat.

"What is the tag number of that cow again?" I asked Pete, picking up my pen and pink-slip notebook. This was a sort of docket book with carbon copy pages. This book was not only our reminder for the farmer; we also used it as our record for making up accounts. But I felt it could be a reminder for myself, too, and it was fast becoming a place to record even more data for later. "I will write it down whilst you get the next one for us." I wrote "39 lame RF M SA," which meant cow number 39 was a lame cow, and I found that her right front foot was lame and had an abscess in the sole of the middle or medial claw.

Finally, having finished with the last cow, I packed up my kit back into its bucket – a good morning's work. In those early days, I was often learning from the farmer, but sometimes we both learned something new. I got a call from another farmer; this time it was Mac.

"Can you come and look at three lame cows?" On the road again, I went to visit Mac.

"The white antibiotic isn't working – I need the brown one," he told me when I arrived. There were three cows all limping on one or another front foot. "They each had a swollen foot with foot rot four days ago, so I gave them a jab, of the white one," said Mac. "The swelling went down a bit, but they are all still limping."

Back in those days, there were two brands of antibiotic; one was white and one was coloured brown but in fact there was very little other difference.

I looked around for a crush to put the cows into so that I could safely get to a front foot to examine it. Nothing really suitable available. So we brought them into the milking bails and managed by some fancy rope work to lift the lame front foot of each cow. All three cows had a small stone stuck in the cleft between the claws of a front foot. I jokingly said to Mac, "When I find an antibiotic that dissolves stones, I will give you that, but in the meantime, pull out the stones by hand and just use the white antibiotic. It will kill the infection."

It wasn't the pulling out of the stones that was the problem; the real problem was the lack of a good place to safely check the foot and then remove those stones. I checked out the stones – they were all around the same size approximately one centimetre in diameter and quite smooth. A snug fit in the groove between the toes of the cow. The stone was quite happy to stay there, but the cow wasn't happy, as the stone kept rubbing and damaging the skin. I knew from my lectures at vet school that sheep get foot rot when the paddocks are damp. They get damp patches between the claws where the foot rot infection gets in. But now I was seeing that cows' feet are much stronger and damp doesn't damage them. However, a small stone continually rubbing will do damage in the end, and that damage will let infection inside the foot.

It seemed like I was getting lots of different experiences in different situations.

Another day, I received a call from a farmer on New Year's Day – normally a holiday, but I was on duty that day. He said that his cow had probably dislocated her hip.

"What happened?" I asked the farmer when I arrived, expecting to hear of an accident or that the cow had slipped over.

"I don't know. She looked a little bit lame yesterday, but today she is a three-legged cow!"

I thought to myself – *a gradually dislocating hip – not likely?* But out loud I said, "Well, we had better look at the foot first." It turned out to be an abscess in the sole just like the one at Pete's farm when I had got pus in the face. The foot was so painful that the only relief for the cow was to stand on three legs. In fact, since then, whenever I see a cow standing on three legs, I find it is often this type of problem. It was through experiences like this that I learned that usually, in fact, in ninety percent of cases of lameness, the problem is in the foot. My pink-slip notes confirmed this.

As I travelled from farm to farm writing my notes, I was starting to see a bit more of a picture of what types of lameness were out there. How much of a problem generally lameness was, I didn't know. Farmers like Pete used to call me to all their lame cows, so I got to know that out of every one hundred cows he usually had about twenty become lame during the milking season (in New Zealand, this is usually from July to May). And he wanted to know: is this twenty percent normal – or too much? Or maybe everyone else had many more? We didn't know; we only knew that some farmers seemed to get a lot more of what they called "foot rot" than others. No one in New Zealand really knew how much lameness there was – did one in a hundred cows get lame or twenty of them? And what sorts of lameness were we dealing with? What had happened that ended up with a limping cow? Initially, I was mostly just dealing with these limping cows.

"What do you think happened?" asked one farmer. "Here is another one the same."

"Can you come and fix my lame cow?" asked another.

"What is the best antibiotic for lameness?" said yet another.

"How long will it take to get better?"

These were all questions that I was faced with on a daily basis during the milking season, still working towards the biggest question that Colin had posed: "What do I do to stop this happening in the first place?"

Gradually as I wrote down each case on my pink slips, I began to see that there were distinctive types of lameness injuries. We were not usually dealing with an infection (like foot rot). In fact, over forty percent of the cases were an injury to what we call the white line. The first category: White Line.

A cow's foot has two claws or toes and each claw is alike. Each has two visible parts, the sole and the wall. The wall is a bit like your fingernail, it protects the front of the foot. Around the edge and underneath the foot of a cow, there is a line which marks where the nail that wraps around the front half of the claw joins to the sole or hard surface underneath. It is called the white line because it is white, and when the hard nail is black, it is clearly noticeable. This was the place where many injuries that I was seeing would occur. Obviously they were called white line.

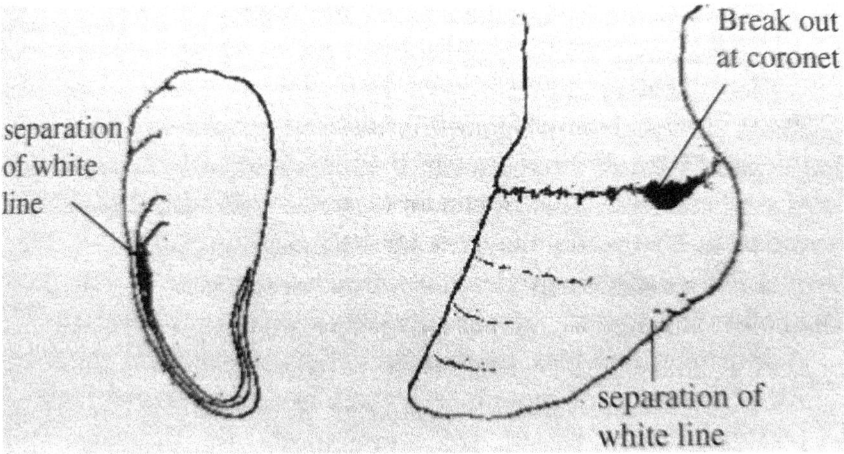


Diagram so you know what I am talking about

The second most common lameness I saw was caused by an injury in the sole itself. Category two: Sole Injury. This injury was underneath the foot, like the case of the three-legged cow.

There were a few other injuries caused by stones or something sharp between the claws breaking the skin as in the case of Mac's three cows where the stones were not "dissolved by the antibiotic." Then infection could get in. This foot rot was the third most common problem, but usually this happened much less frequently than the two most common injuries. I put this as category three: Footrot.

Interestingly, although all three cows with the stones between the claws seemed fully recovered shortly after we removed the stones, one of them had to be treated again three months later when what looked like the original injury had grown down the nail between the claws, just like a bruise on your fingernail will grow out. Hidden between the two claws, a crack had formed on one side where the stone may have rubbed. This sort of injury I find is very painful, and it occurs as the fourth most common lesion. Category four: Axial Crack.

The more I wrote down, the more I saw that what we had in New Zealand walking cows was something physical, to start with, an injury, and not initially due to a bug or infection. Maybe my title "Lameness is Physical" was near the truth?

So would antibiotics fix this? Would these injuries heal themselves? Farmers said yes to the first question and yes to the second. Often, I heard farmers say, "I just give lame cows a shot of penicillin and leave them close by, in the paddock with the mastitis herd for a week or two, and they usually come right."

I was enjoying treating the cows and the beautiful Taranaki landscape as I drove around. Treating lame cows was something that I could now passably manage, and it was satisfying. But maybe this was a bit like being an ambulance at the bottom of the cliff. Going to university and having a degree so far hadn't given me many answers to the big questions although I was collecting quite a lot of information. This lameness wasn't turning out to be simple, and, when you think of it, lameness or limping in people isn't simple either. "What did you do?" could be "Oh I twisted my ankle," "I stepped on a nail," "I've got an ingrown toenail," "I have always had a gammy leg," or "I need a new hip." Most of us would not think of asking the doctor to tell us what medicine we should take for "sickness." We would tell the doctor a bit more about it and maybe some of the symptoms.

I was now beginning to sort the information and ideas to answer my first question of where to start. And here was the first lightbulb right there in front of me. The problem: What was the problem anyway? Farmers were telling me that they had lame cows, so I would say I will come and treat them, but I hadn't thought to ask the bigger question: What sort of lame cows do you have? Are they all the same "sickness"?

These experiences and stories with farmers along with the data from the pink slips was helping me find out what the symptoms were and what treatments worked better than others. What was less clear was what was causing it and how to stop it happening in the first place.

I wasn't the only one getting desperate. My friend Colin also needed help. It was time to do some more serious investigations.

# CHAPTER 8

# Real Live Data (1980s)

IF I HAD not written anything down, I wouldn't have known where to start. I was the sort of person who was interested in how many and how much and how often. Early in my life I was already counting things, like the 149 steps to our friend's house in Cape Town. I still have a desire to count steps!

Fortunately, right from my early years of being a vet, I had started collecting data. By the truckload. I sometimes wonder if I had an overdose of curiosity and not just about lame cows – about everything that I was treating. What happened in my laboratory? It could be significant so I wrote it down.

There are two types of data – and I collected both. The first one is raw data from the field, and it comes in the form of numbers or yes/no, such as: Did the cow die? Or the number of days before it recovered. So early in my life as a vet, I began to give the farmers like Mac and Pete in my "laboratory" a record sheet that I would fill in on the farm with the cow's tag number and what it was that was the problem that I had seen. Then I would write what treatment I had administered. I would ask the farmer to fill in later what happened or what was the outcome. On my copy of the records or my "pink sheets," I had even included such detail as which claw on which foot was affected if it was a lame cow that I had seen. Front foot or back, left or right, inside claw or outside.

And not just on Pete's farm, on every farm that I visited over the first years of my vet career. Such a wealth of information on treatments. This all sat in drawers for years waiting until I found a way to turn it into useful information.

There is another type of data that is found in observations, stories or anecdotes, and casual comments from my "laboratory staff" – aka farmers. I call this "anecdata," and there is often only one way to obtain this data – over a cup of tea when the job is done. So I always accepted a cup of tea – even if I was in a hurry – and many were the cups of tea that I put on credit and drank later after everyone had had time to think. Ideas brew just like the tea. Soon farmers got to know that I was interested, and they collected ideas maybe remembered from their old boss, or their father or grandfather. Sometimes the chats were a bit longer than planned – when I wanted to get home in time for dinner!

Late one afternoon I was called to see a lame cow at a farmer named Sam's place, and I knew that it might be a long chat afterwards. I had already talked at length with him earlier that week. This was the last call of the day and time to get back to the office to catch up on the day, so I organised with Lois, the receptionist, to give me a call on the radio telephone to ask if I was available for another call on the way home. I finished the lame cow at Sam's place and called up on the radio to see if there were any more calls and Lois, as we had organised, told me of another call waiting at the opposite end of my area. "Sorry," I said, turning to Sam, who was waiting at my elbow listening in to the radio conversation. "I can't stop today. I have got another call waiting. Let's chat another day." And off I went back to the office where I went to the tea room to find the other vets sitting with cups of coffee in their hands. At that moment Lois came in, saw me and exclaimed, "What are you doing here – you should be at Fred's place – the cow is waiting." Sometimes my subterfuge goes astray.

At the end of the day and when all is said and done, the "anecdata" and the data must complement each other. The one is needed to frame the question; the other is needed to scientifically examine the question and then to convince the scientists. After this, the "anecdata" comes again to confirm and to convince the farmers. Take amputation, for instance.

If a cow has a white-line injury in a claw where the abscess goes up the side under the wall or nail of the foot, it usually bursts out at the top of the claw at the hairline or coronet. In some of my cases, even when treated well, the foot didn't seem to get better and in fact got worse. The cow would end up with one toe turned up and still limping. This was despite treatment and often antibiotics. What had happened was that the infection had gone into the joint instead of draining out the top. This is called septic pedal arthritis, and anyone who has arthritis will tell you it doesn't get better – ever.

Well, the usual solution for this was to amputate the claw that was affected, and then the cow would have no pain and could walk on the one remaining claw on that foot. We could demonstrate that this could work because when we put a block on the good claw of a lame foot, lifting the sore claw off the ground, the cow could walk with a block on one claw, not even using the other painful one. Some vets were already doing this amputation operation, and my head vet, Gunner, was one of them. It seemed to be a great success, so I learned how to do it. Over the years, along with other vets, I worked out easier ways to do it. However, the farmers and many vets remained unconvinced that it could work.

Being lame is really painful for the cow. This is an animal welfare issue, and we need to do the best we can to minimise discomfort and pain. When a cow has a claw that is really painful, the very best we can do to take away the pain is to amputate the claw. When you amputate that affected claw, as I keep telling other vets, it is like throwing the pain away. One vet student who had come for a week of practical experience happened to be with me when I was doing an amputation, and so she was able to add amputation to her experience. After we had finished, she asked could she have the claw that we had just cut off for a photograph? So I gave it to her – "Can you photograph me as I throw it away?" She smiled, taking aim for the middle of the nearby paddock.

The big question that needed to be answered was how did this affect the cow. "Anecdata" was not going to be convincing enough. Did the cow remain in the milking herd and continue to milk or maybe they just never recovered and no one knew? Many wouldn't believe that we could do this with a cow that still had to walk a long way to get grass in the paddocks, going back and forth every day to be milked. So I started recording amputations on my pink-sheet records. This would to be a long-term investigation – how long does a cow continue in the herd, producing milk and being happy after losing a claw to amputation? Well, some cows actually ended up not lasting the whole season out as they were either culled because they became lame in another foot or because they didn't get pregnant – an apparent failure – but at least they could walk around and enjoy the part of the season that they had left. However, many of my amputation cases carried on being the greatest producers, and one even lasted nine milking seasons after the amputation. I know because I collected the data.

I had convinced myself with the data records, but how do I convince – first, other vets, and then the farmers – that this was indeed successful as well as the kindest solution for the cow? For the vets, I began teaching the method of amputation and showing how quickly and easily we could do the procedure. On one occasion, I was visiting a large corporate group of farms in South America and discovered there were a lot of cows that needed amputation of one claw – hundreds of cows, in fact. I was working with another vet, and often we had two crushes to work in, so we had a competition to see who could finish the operation in the fastest time – the other vet won with only thirteen minutes from local anaesthetic to bandaging.

To make teaching about amputation more visual, I planned to make a video to illustrate my seminars. I was looking for a good practical example to film. It needed to be in a shed with good lighting, and the cow needed to have a white foot that would show up well. One day, I was at one of my friendly farmer's milking shed to treat some lame cows. This was an as-yet-unconvinced farmer. Three of the cows that were waiting had turned up toes and needed amputation as the kindest thing to do. I turned from the badly infected foot and said to the farmer, "Ned, we need to amputate these claws."

"No way," he shot back in a most emphatic tone, a frown appearing on his normally jovial face. "They won't be able to walk."

"Yes, they will," I replied in my best professional manner and quickly added, "I have done hundreds of others who are still walking around." I asked Ned if I could borrow his new cell phone to call my wife. Taking a few steps away, I spoke clearly enough to be heard.

"Hello, Sandra," I said when she replied to my call and then carried on without a break, "I have an amputation case here that looks like it will be a good one. Bring the video camera out to Ned's place. See you soon." And then I gave the address.

I turned back to Ned, excited – "I will do this cow for half price if I can video it. My wife is on the way."

He reluctantly agreed. Even though we filmed the amputation procedure and the cow walked out without a limp Ned was still not convinced and didn't want the other two cows to have the same operation that day. I thought that I had failed

Two days later, he rang me at the office. He got straight to the point and I could hear the smile when he spoke. "Can you come and do the other two cows? Will it be half price?"

Nowadays, the "anecdata" convinces the farmers and the data convinces the vets that this is the best treatment once the lameness has gone into the joint. I teach young vets how to administer a good local anaesthetic and amputate a claw quickly and easily. One farmer had been watching from a distance and heard about the success of amputation from another farmer. I was at his farm to do some pregnancy checking and noticed that there were quite a few cows with amputated claws – ten or twelve of them. I couldn't remember ever doing one on his farm, so I asked him who had done them for him.

"I will tell you the story if you don't tell anyone else," he said conspiratorially. "I go to the clearing sales to get a few extra cows every now and again, and if I find one or two that have had a toe amputated, I talk privately to the agent and say, 'Look at that – you will never sell that cow, it only has one toe on that foot.' 'Oh my, you are right,' the agent agrees – we quickly settle on a much lower price and I relieve him of the 'burden.' When I bring them home, I find that they are often the best producing cows in my herd – no one would have kept a cow like that unless it was a good one."

However, although treating cows that had become so lame that amputation of a claw was the only, rather drastic, solution, I was sure that it would be a much better thing if we prevented the cows from becoming lame in the first place. Amputation was simply that ambulance at the bottom of the cliff again.

The problem of lameness wasn't on every farm Taranaki-wide. In fact, there were some farmers who had very few lame cows. This was the first thing that my data was telling me. Somehow, they had solved or avoided the problem. The trouble was it seemed that, if they had solved their lameness issues, they had done it without knowing it and without knowing what they had done right. Visiting Colin on his farm, I had been looking for some source of the problem to jump out at me, but maybe the farmers who were doing well could have answers. How could I find out what it was that they had done differently? What question should I ask? A general one about other farmers should work, whilst talking over politics after the cow had been sent back to the paddock. Every farmer had different opinions. Often, I would chat to a farmer and stories wouldn't add up and raised more questions than answers. But there were also many farmers who had really useful knowledge to pass on.

So I kept asking farmers, "What do you think is the cause of lameness on farms?" I was beginning to compile quite a list. "It's the rain." This was near the top of the list. The obvious answer in Taranaki. And maybe they really had something there.

Having our iconic mountain, Taranaki Maunga, creates beautiful scenery. The mountain also sees to it that we get lots of lovely liquid sunshine as Gunner had informed me when he offered me the job in Inglewood – the closer to the mountain, the more metres of rainfall. Since the sea is nearby, clouds coming in from the sea rise when they meet the mountain, cool down, and drop the rain fairly evenly throughout the year. Lots of little streams gather the water and take it down the mountain, across the farm land, among the hills, and off to the sea. And a good deal of the water travels underground so there are springs in many places. All the beautiful Taranaki green scenery is a product of the rain. This also results in grass growing by the ton because of the rain adding to the great volcanic soils. The good old volcanic soils served us vets well – you could easily drive an ordinary car, which is what we drove in those days, right up to the cow that was unable to stand, even only hours after the rain stopped. The downside of this is that even only a few weeks without rain spells a drought.

And there were other good benefits with downsides. Those beautiful little streams everywhere have to be crossed and kept clean. It also means that it is hard work to keep walkways walkable for cows and passable for farm vehicles. Boggy paddocks and maybe lame cows could also be a product. Could this be a source for lameness? But why on some farms and not on others?

What is a great advantage for the grass is also a challenge to manage in spring when there sometimes seem to be only rainy days and mud everywhere! The year that I arrived in Inglewood from sunny Sydney, there was hardly a day it didn't rain for three solid months – it rained cats and dogs, horizontally, lightly, heavily. Although that year was, in fact, a record-breaking year, I was soon to find out that this is a fairly normal "spring" calving season. Farmers and cows get literally bogged down, and there always seemed to be more lame cows – so a reasonable answer to my question of what causes lame cows. Rain. Nice to know but impossible to control. Would we need to somehow learn to work around it? Well, I thought, some farmers didn't get many lame cows whatever the weather, so there must be something else going on as well.

More questions came up. All farmers knew that when there was wet weather, there were nearly always more lame cows – was this because the rain caused lameness or because the rain came at the same time of the year as we would normally get lame cows anyway – a coincidence? – or did the rain just make other things that did "cause" lameness become worse? And what sort of lameness was more common in the rain? By now we knew that muddy, wet feet on cows don't get foot rot like sheep. Now I had lots of anecdata and lots of questions, and my collection of real data was getting large and unwieldy. And I still didn't have many answers. No wonder it felt like I was not much use to my farmers and to Colin in particular.

Time to do something more scientific.

## CHAPTER 9

# Right Place, Right Time, Right Friends (1985)

OUR VET PRACTICE in Inglewood was very much a family affair. A retired farmer, Peter Austin, and his wife, Margaret, did the office work and answered the phones. They had two daughters, who also worked in the office. They were fanatic about two things: their vets and their rugby. Peter, although he was now too old to play rugby himself, supported the local team with great enthusiasm. If you went to a rugby match with him and his family, there was no need to cheer or to tell the referee how to call, Peter would do it all for you. Peter and Margaret also looked after us vets, and Sandra and I were treated as family. Margaret was the one who "chose" our house for us. We had not long been in Inglewood when one day Margaret had said, "I have found just the house for you to buy." We were not even thinking of buying a house – after all we had come to stay for just three years and then return to Australia, and we were now in our second year. We certainly weren't about to buy a house and certainly not one that we had heard had been the centre of the local gang activity.

To keep Margaret happy, we went to look at the house. It was a cute bungalow built nearly eighty years ago. It was looking old and now very rundown. It was definitely in need of a great deal of work. But it had a veranda around two sides just like old Australian houses. And it had a big yard with large trees. There was a cherry tree in full bloom and two kowhai trees both also in flower the day we first looked at it. For some reason we really liked it – the trees and the yard, that is, and the potential indoors. Also, it was very cheap – about one-third the price of other houses on the market. The idea of buying a house took root, so we looked at a few other houses, but none of them really suited us. So we scraped together our small savings, took out a loan, and thus we ended up the proud owners of a nearly derelict house to renovate. Our five children grew up in that wonderful old house. It was the ongoing project for the thirty-five-or-so years that we owned it.

Our old house as my father-in-law saw it

Immediately after we purchased it, there began a steep learning curve. A new hat for the vet to wear. New concrete piles underneath, new veranda, new roof, new driveway, and so it went on. Some of our friends had already renovated houses, so we had lots of advice and ideas as well as helping hands. The first three months of owning the house were spent in replacing the piles that supported the house. They were made of wood, and everything below the ground had rotted away. They no longer supported the house very well, so some of the rooms had a definite slope on the floor. A marble would roll from one side of the room to the other with no help at all. Then the kitchen was replaced with a second-hand one as Sandra had said she was not going to move in until there was at least a decent kitchen. Four months later we moved in, and two weeks after that our second little girl was born. Sounds like a good time to take on a new project!

When we first arrived in Inglewood, we had joined a local church and soon had many friends there. We were just a little older than the various youth in the church – so we were the leaders. They were often at our house, and we sort of grew up with this younger-than-us youth group, some of whom are still in Inglewood and still our good friends. As time went on, we welcomed another baby into the family, this time a son, so now there were five of us. Shortly after this, one of the youth group had a friend in trouble, and we became stand-in parents for him as well. Six.

This young man staying with us for a short while had had difficulties at his home, and he had serious problems with reading, so Sandra decided to help him with this reading so that he could get a driver's licence. He only stayed with us for about six months, but by then Sandra had found something that she really enjoyed – teaching reading. After the first young man moved on, several other younger children came visiting to learn how to read or get better at numbers.

So when our third child was nearing five years old and about to go off to school, Sandra decided to do some study. The obvious choice of topic was teaching reading, and she added numeracy and parent education to make up a graduate diploma in education. For the next few years, there was always some study going on at our house, either hers or mine. Sandra graduated the same year as the first of our two younger boys was born.

Towards the end of the three years completing this *diploma in education* by correspondence whilst raising the children, Sandra had come across a book on homeschooling. She discovered that in New Zealand, it was legal to teach your children at home – it just required permission from the Department of Education. I was sceptical at first, but the community of homeschoolers from all over New Zealand won me over. So permission was obtained, and we began a period of nearly twenty years of school at home, wherever home happened to be in the world.

While all this activity was going on, I was still collecting data. And asking questions. By now, I had lots of answers from farmers to my first question: What do you think "causes" lameness? There were a lot more answers than I expected – all reasonable – in fact fifty-eight of them! So many different ideas came up as to what was the root cause. Now all fifty-eight answers can't be right, can they? Were fifty-seven people wrong? Or were most of them partly correct? Solving this was to occupy me and clever statisticians for many years – and we are still getting new ideas and information. We needed to find out how much of each answer was right – how important was each factor in the resulting lameness? We were discovering that this problem of lameness in cows is not the result of a single factor but a combination of lots of things happening at once – being a walking cow in Taranaki is a risky business. That sounded like a good title for a seminar: "Lameness Is a Risky Business." How easy was it to get lame on this farm and not on that one? Standing and watching in a paddock at Colin's farm was a good start, but there I might have spotted just one or two of the many factors. The picture needed to get bigger.

Time to do some science and then to call in reinforcements. These fifty-eight ideas of what might be a risk factors for lameness became the basis for my first investigation into the "causes of lameness." As you might have guessed by now, I am not very "scientific." I love collecting data – and "anecdata," but what to do with it? How could I address my data and ask it questions and get some answers that would help my farmer friends? This would be easy if you had a simple problem and only one or two things that could affect it, but fifty-eight factors – all changing from farm to farm . . . my head was a bit full. Of course, I had my own ideas as did the farmers. It was worse than doing a jigsaw puzzle without being able to see the picture and not knowing if all the pieces were there. A grandson of ours did a jigsaw puzzle with Sandra some years ago. It had no straight edges, no picture to go by, and some extra pieces – they did it in the end, but it was really challenging.

My first plan was to go to farms and write down everything

that might affect lameness. So I went back to Colin's farm as he had first requested and wrote down all my observations in the fifty-eight categories that had been suggested. Then I found four more farms with lameness problems and did the same list of observations, looking to see whether there were any common factors.

How to work out which was right or what was the most important factor was the next question. Time to call in the experts. I went to visit Massey University in Palmerston North, New Zealand, where there was a veterinary school.

What sort of person could help me? I found out that I needed an epidemiologist. I didn't really understand epidemiology – it was too big a word for me – all I knew was that lameness was an epidemic, not of infection like a flu epidemic but of injury or damage to the feet of cows – a sore feet epidemic. What were the "bugs" or mixture of "bugs" in a sore feet epidemic? What circumstances did you need for an epidemic to break out? These "bugs" were really circumstances or possible circumstances that might result in the accident or "disease" of a lame foot. At Massey University, I met Roger Morris and his team in the veterinary epidemiology department. He was keen to guide me through the labyrinth of the valleys of science to get some light on the subject.

I presented him with the data so far collected from my five farms. To get answers to my big lameness questions would take a lot of investigation and a lot more data collection, he told me, his eyes gleaming at the prospect of having lots of data. Not only would I need to find out what was "wrong" on farms with lots of lame cows, but I would also need to find out what was "right" on farms that only had a few lame cows. Roger called it a "case control" study. I would then be looking at differences between farms and farming practices, and differences between farms with lame cows and farms where there were very few of them. I already had the data from my five farms but, said Roger, I would need data from more than ten times that number of farms. Not just truckloads of data, mountains of it!

Talking with Roger, I realised that this was going to be a mammoth undertaking, but he really encouraged me and was so enthusiastic to get his hands on real live data that I went home much inspired. When

I got home and thought about what Roger had said, I realised that this project would take lots of time and money. I had neither. I could either give up the idea or press on, and of course I chose the latter. So I had to find someone or some group interested in finding out about and preventing the sore feet epidemic and who had money to spend on it. This I found in Taranaki – the McKenzie Trust – set up to research and support work in the area of welfare for animals in Taranaki – perfect.

I now found myself carried along by the flow into the river to solve the puzzle. It seemed that this was almost too good to be true – you could say the "stars lined up," but I say it was a "God coincidence," being in the right place at the right time when this needed to be done for the welfare of farmers and cows. Some research is just waiting there to be done, and the results are just waiting to be discovered.

We wrote a proposal (another new word for me), with all the proper information, submitted it to the McKenzie Trust, and got the go ahead. Full of enthusiasm, I then employed a locum vet to do my usual day to day vet work, and I was free to proceed to do my part of the study. I sat down with Roger and a few others from his department and from my list of observations devised a sort of survey. Using this survey, I planned to visit some Taranaki farms and see how much of each possible "bug" or circumstance was present operating on each particular farm.

Then I began by phoning the other vet practices in Taranaki to get a list of farmers who might be interested in taking part in this study. I asked each practice to recommend the three farmers who had the worst lameness problem and the three with the least lameness over the last three years. Next, I called up each farmer for a chat. There were to be sixty-two farms in the end, thirty with lame cows and thirty-two with very few.

Then came the fun part – to go out and collect the data. For some people this might look like a lot of donkey work, but I really enjoyed being out on the farms asking more questions but now with a purpose – and with a good survey tool in hand.

I had based the survey on the answers that I had gleaned from farmers over the years. All the farmers of whom I had asked my original question, without exception, had told me that poor tracks or walkways with rough surfaces were guaranteed to cause lameness – so that had to be measured. How long, how wide, how many bends, how muddy, how steep, and what the surface was like, all these might have an effect.

What if cows were more likely to become lame if they were milked in a herringbone shed rather than a rotary? Another thing to take note of.

So on each farm I measured all sorts of other likely and seemingly unlikely factors that could affect the cows and end up with some becoming lame.

During the months of October to December for the next three years, I visited those farms and watched cows. And by default, the people with them. I filled out sixty-two survey forms and made friends with farmers all around Taranaki. Now I had a big collection of information or data about all the things that farmers said might result in lame cows – yes, all fifty-eight of them. For each I wrote the degree in which it could be "bad." Was it a steep piece of track, or very steep, or maybe excessively steep? I had my ideas about what was causing lameness, but now, was the data confirming this or telling me something different that I hadn't thought of at all?

This was all on paper – miles of it. Now I had to sort it and get some sort of analysis of it. Here technology stepped in for the first time.

This was completely out of my area. We had only recently acquired a home computer for homeschooling – not many of them were around in those days. Sandra had a better idea of it than I did, so she entered the data and organised it into a database – I didn't even know what one of those was! Fortunately, she had studied computing at university, along with biometry – or the basic statistics that you need in biology. At her university, they had had a computer which filled several rooms. It read data from punch cards. Hardware had progressed exponentially since then, but the principles were much the same and much more user-friendly.

I brought all the survey forms home and handed them to Sandra. Then the digital version of the data was loaded onto floppy discs to be sent to Massey. There the statistics and analysis people went to work on that mountain of data to find out the answers to my questions – or in layman's terms, see which ones of my farmers were right. The result was a combined effort that set the whole direction for study of the prevention of lameness on a new pathway.

By this time my own ideas were being refined by all the things I had seen on the farms that I visited. I could see that the cows were being affected by the people with them, and the people were affected by the cows. Some people were very friendly with their cows, others not so. For some people, the cows would walk really well, and the trip to the shed to be milked took only a short time; for others, the cows just would not walk at all. What was going on? How to get your cows to walk and do what you wanted them to was a question that different farmers answered in different ways. Some farmers were simply more patient than others.

However, things were not as simple as that, as I could see we had another problem – what if the cows didn't like the track or the shed to which they were going in order to be milked? Or what if the track was rough or slippery, so that the speed that the cows walked was too slow even for patient people.

We had measured a big conglomeration of factors that could affect whether cows were likely to get lame – or not. To make sense of it all, we found that all the data could be grouped into just three categories: things about the cow itself, things about how the people and the cows worked together, and the design of the facilities, tracks, and sheds.

We looked at what there was about the cow that might be a lameness tendency – just like we say of some people that they are an accident waiting to happen – maybe some characteristic of the cow herself might make it more likely to get lame. Things like the breed, the colour of the foot, or even the shape of the claws.

Then we also looked at the way the cows were handled by the people on the farm; maybe what they did could affect the chances of getting lame for the cow. Were the people very patient? Did they use dogs or backing gates? We called these people factors. And finally what sort of facilities were there. Were they comfortable for the cow? Were the surfaces rough or slippery, or maybe there were sharp corners? These were the environmental factors.

In the end, the main result of all those years of investigation and my gut feeling was that the two biggest risk factors for lameness were impatient farmers and poor tracks. Both of which my farmers had been telling me along with the dozens of other suggestions they had given. Of course, there were other things acting in the mix, like biting dogs and electric gates, but the things with the most effect were the patience of the people and the maintenance of the track.

With the help of Roger and the others at Massey, we published the results as a paper in the *New Zealand Vet Journal* – the first major study on what might be some of the risks for lameness in pasture-fed cows.[1] One of our group took the paper to a conference in Europe, and we were on the world stage. In 1989 as a nice little outcome for all my data gathering, my old university in Sydney awarded me the medal of the Australasian College of Veterinary Surgeons for this work.

Back at the coalface, it felt good to have this confirmed, and now I could tell farmers that they were right when they said, "It's the tracks." I also now had a few ideas on how to help them avoid getting lame cows. Much simplified it was "Fix your tracks and be patient." I could fine-tune this advice depending on how each farm operated. I could go back to Colin and other farmers, work out which of the two factors was their main problem, and give useful advice. On Colin's farm, it was mostly the very steep tracks that were the problem and the biggest risk for his cows.

But now what I really wanted to know was how this all worked together. What was the mechanism? We could probably guess at what the poor track did to the foot of a cow, and we are still guessing because we can't see inside the foot! But what exactly was happening to the foot of a cow when a farmer got impatient – even just a little?

A new piece of technology now more available to me might help: the video camera.

## CHAPTER 10

# Cow CCTV (1986–)

WHEN I WAS growing up, a well-off person might have a movie camera and be able to show movies at home. Each film had to be shot, developed, maybe edited, and then you needed a projector to show it. My parents had a friend with a movie camera who took a movie of their wedding, but they rarely ever got to see it as they didn't have a movie projector. When we moved from South Africa to Rhodesia and then to Australia, the movie of the wedding came along, but it wasn't until the advent of video technology that we got to see it whenever we wanted. Since then, of course, video technology has come a long way. Today, if I want a video of something, I whip my phone out from my pocket. It can do slow motion, time lapse, and almost anything I want with a few little taps.

In the late 1970s and early 1980s, when I was just starting out as a vet, the latest toy to own was a video camera – as big as a suitcase! This would be a great tool for observing cows, I thought. I didn't own one myself, so I borrowed a camera from a farmer friend. This was the early type that took a full-size video cassette. And it also made a whirring noise. Now the cows could really see me! A really good zoom mostly fixed that, as long as there was a handy fence on which to rest the camera.

I really caught the filming bug and videoed everything, from cows coming in to milking, to walking-along cows, and standing-still cows, plus all the scenery around them. I considered a video of cows second rate if there was no mountain in the background. Since we lived in New Zealand and our family all lived in Australia, whenever I could borrow the camera, it also become a tool to use to send moving pictures and birthday greetings. However, cows were the main stars of my videos.

Cows were not very good movie stars. They would stare at the camera instead of doing their normal stuff. Or they would run away or, worse, come up really close and try to sniff the camera. I have some interesting pictures close-up of a cow about to lick the camera just before I rescued it. At first, I tried to get sequences on video that were abnormal – or of what not to do, but that was a matter of very good fortune to find one scene that worked in fifty minutes of otherwise boring tape. Usually all the people and the cows became self-conscious, and what they did was not typical of anything. I tried taking really long videos and then searching for the best bits. As in the early days of photography, we were limited by cost as to how many videos we could take. As I wanted to keep each one that I took, I would squeeze as many as possible onto a long tape.

One day I visited a farm where I noticed that a big Friesian heifer was being beaten up and afraid of the little Jersey cows around her. Could there be something interesting going on here? There was also a big dog. I decided to video this scene to see what I could spot in it, so I got the farmer's permission and set up the camera. It was after some heavy rain, nothing unusual in Taranaki, and the cows were coming in to get milked. This farmer let the dog do all the work, and I think that the dog had a bit of an idea that he wanted to show off to the camera and get those cows in as fast as humanly, or "dogly," possible. What a scene, no mountain, but the cows made up for that. The cows and the farmer were all busy with what they were doing, so I caught on camera a scene of real life for those cows. This video was to become an eye-opener on how cows might get lame. However, this had to wait for a few years for some better technology combined with a bit more insight. Then I would know what I was looking for, and I would be able to see what was really happening.

I kept on borrowing video cameras until finally I bought my first video camera. This one took mini cassettes. With our own camera, our older children were now into the game making family videos to send to grandparents overseas, especially as there were babies to show off. Then they made home documentaries as part of their school work. No wonder that sometimes I had to line up to get a turn with the camera.

We then purchased a video player which took two cassettes so that we could copy from one to another. My cow videos would be really great as teaching aids, I thought. I soon had quite a collection of videos of cows. Some should have been on YouTube if we had had it then, but some these days really should be rated R-18 – although we didn't realise it at the time. I wince when I watch the way cows behaved and how some were treated before we knew better.

Not only had I been asking farmers about lameness, but farmers were also asking me questions about what to do about lameness. Lots of farmers wanted to know about lameness. This made me realise that talking to more than one of them at a time would be a good idea. I could get them together, and I could pass on what I was learning, and they could also discuss it. I had amassed quite a bit of "anecdata" and observations from all over New Zealand, as well as my research data and findings. This really needed to be passed on to those who could use the information. So I began giving seminars and talks for farmers on how to design a good shed, how to fix your track, and how not to handle cows. I called my seminars catchy names like "Lameness is Physical" and "Stamping Out Lameness."

Making these seminars interesting and fun was a challenge, but I had plenty of stories and enthusiasm. I love telling stories, and so I would illustrate my talks with stories of farmers who had struck a problem or solved a problem – names and places changed, of course. The dairy farmer's world is very small, so I had to be careful. "Was that my cousin in that story that you were talking about?" "My brother had exactly the same thing happen here in the North Island!"

Stacey, one of the other vets in the practice, had an amazing talent drawing cartoons, and he drew me some lame-cow cartoons which were funny but true and where the people and cows couldn't be identified!

I didn't give handouts at my seminars, and this was before the Internet, so I organised my seminars and talks into a little booklet of ideas and observations called *The Lame Dairy Cow* and later *Lameness in Dairy Cattle.* I used Stacey's cartoons as illustrations.

It was much better, however, to come to a live seminar where I showed the cartoons and photos on acetate sheets using an overhead projector. You had to be really careful with those overhead projectors. They had a very powerful lightbulb which, as the presentation went on, progressively got hotter. When it was time to turn it off, you had to make sure that the fan was still running for a while to cool everything down. If someone accidently turned the power off before the lamp was cool and then someone bumped the projector, the lamp could very easily burst. This happened a few times so I always carried a spare bulb. Cleaning up an exploded bulb was also quite an exercise.

By now I had a good collection of videotapes to supplement my photos and overhead projector acetates. There was no PowerPoint in those days. I added a video player and television screen to my seminar equipment. The next problem occurred when I wanted to show one segment of video. How to find it and how to go back to the right spot to repeat? Solution: use the short demo tapes that companies sent out to vets as advertising, and, using my two-cassette video player/recorder, tape over the advertisement. Each videotape contained just one short sequence and was cued at the beginning. To show a video, I would grab the one needed and post it into the video player and press play. When I needed another segment, I took the used one out and found the next tape and played that one. I had videos of poor handling in sheds, on tracks, and in yards along with sections of poor tracks and poorly designed sheds. I could now demonstrate why it wasn't a good idea to have the entrance to the yard close to the entrance to the milking parlour – the video showed the cows just going around and around in circles trying to get into the parlour whilst others were coming in at the gate and getting in the way. I was also becoming better at taking video footage now that I knew what was needed.

I discovered that it is better by far to show people what good handling looks like, and they can quickly see whether or not their cows look like that. I was working on the banks' theory. When banks train their new tellers, they practice with real money, and when they see a counterfeit, it really stands out. So the idea was to show a cow or a herd of cows behaving normally, and then farmers would know what to look out for. So what is normal for a cow? We had a good idea of what was normal, but when it came to catching it on camera, it was really hard. Then which of the things I was seeing cows do were actually normal? Did cows ever behave normally, or at least when I was there with a camera?

I started to ask more questions, such as: how does a cow walk, where is her head, and what happens when there is a stone on the concrete, and so on. Now with a video camera, I had another source of answers for these questions. Often, I would be talking to a farmer and asking a question, and we couldn't work out an answer but watch a video, and there it was. For example, do cows turn to the left or to the right when backing off a rotary platform? Answer: both ways and almost half and half. That is normal. Then I visited a farm where I saw nearly every cow turn the same way, to the right, not normal. We discovered a problem with the flooring. The cows knew about it and could avoid it by always turning to the right and only turning to the left when they were forced to. Normal behaviour interrupted seemed to indicate a problem.

I had begun thinking about lameness and cows even in my sleep. My poor wife would have to put up with random midnight questions like "Do cows get lame in the paddock?" and various other unconnected exclamations at two o'clock in the morning. Who is watching when the cow gets lame? Where is the cow? What is she doing? Are there any people there to see anyway? Some stories gave me ideas.

"I saw her stumble on her foot on that stone in the race, and now she is lame," said the farmer. "Actually, she stumbled and limped for just a day or so. I rang the vet office and asked for you to come – but then she got better – so I cancelled the call. Then blow me down, if today she is limping so badly that I had to get you out."

I lifted the foot, and there was a stone stuck in the sole and an abscess spreading under the sole – did the farmer "see" the cow get lame? If so, this is very rare. To video-record it would be even less likely, but one day I did happen to catch a cow stumbling on a stone on my video of cows walking past, which goes to show how much video footage I took.

It seemed that usually beef cows which just graze in paddocks don't get much lameness except for foot rot infections – or if they do, nobody notices. So probably it would be true that a dairy cow seldom would get lame in the paddock either. It must get lame during the time of walking to the milking shed, getting milked, or walking back to the paddock. That was what my study project had shown. The most important factors in lameness were track maintenance and farmer behaviour, both during that time. So that will be the time to be watching, I thought, when every self-respecting vet is either still in bed or in the afternoon, back at the office having a cup of tea.

But how to observe without being observed? The cow is an animal of prey and always on the lookout for anything unusual like a vet in green overalls with a notebook and a camera. I was reminded of this once when I was in Germany. We went to see a herd of wild beef cows and tried to sneak up on them – we couldn't get closer than five hundred metres away without them running off in the opposite direction. Domesticated dairy cows are a little bit tamer than that, but they still got scared of me when I went to watch them, probably because they smelled a vet or because I was a stranger. I would stand "unobtrusively" in a paddock waiting for the cows, and they would come around the corner and spot me. Usually, they would just freeze until they decided that I was not a threat. One day, however, some of them got such a fright – maybe I had a scary look that day – that they all turned around and charged back to the paddock. Needless to say, the farmer wasn't exactly happy. But that is science for you; things don't always go as expected.

How to hide and still be able to observe the cows was my question. Would it matter if they did notice me? Shall I try behind a hedge? That was a disaster – I went to watch some cows that the farmer said usually walked very slowly along the track to the shed. He was having real trouble getting them to walk to the milking parlour.

"I will watch them walking and see what is going on," I suggested. I arrived at the farm in the dark and lay down behind a hedge peeping through a small hole. What I hadn't taken into account was that cows walk with their heads low to the ground looking for where to step next. The first thing that I spotted was a pair of cow's eyes looking at me. In fact, they all spotted me – and panicked and ran as fast as they could up to the milking shed. When all the cows were in the yard, the farmer told me that it was the fastest the cows had ever come home.

"Best cow flow yet," he said with a grin. "Can you come every day?"

The lesson – don't get in their line of sight near the ground; climb a tree or find somewhere high up like a shed roof or a water tank or silo. Pretty soon, I began to get a reputation for climbing trees or getting on roofs! Just like my little friend with appendicitis from my student days. None of the cows appeared to notice him on the roof, or else they figured that he was not dangerous as he was out of the way.

I found that the best trick is to use camouflage – sit up on something that is usually there and that they are used to, such as a tractor or motorbike. So now I could usually trick the cows, but sometimes I had to hide from the farmer as well. His cheery "Hi there" pointed me out to the cows.

I was also observing and sometimes filming normal farmer behaviour – or sometimes poor behaviour. With permission of course. Often, if the workers knew I was watching, they might do things differently, which would lose the point of seeing what usually happens. If I wanted to see what happened when there was no observer watching, I tried some subterfuges, such as "accidentally" leaving a hoof knife at the farm and calling in quietly at milking time to collect my "forgotten" piece of equipment. At other times, I had to resort to asking the farmer if I could come at a random time when I passed by – sometime in the next week or so. Then I would come to the farm and put myself somewhere I couldn't be seen. On one occasion, I was hiding up a tree, and the farm worker, upon arriving at a stream crossing, looked all around to see whether I might be watching. He couldn't see me, which was lucky, as I probably looked funny sitting up in the tree. He got out a piece of plastic pipe with which he drove the cows across the stream. Normal for him but not the best for the cows. This wouldn't happen now as farmers have to have bridges over all farm streams – better for the cows and better for the waterways.

However, there was another trap that I found out the hard way – you need to make sure that everyone has been told that you are coming. One day, I was watching cows getting milked whilst lying down under a milk vat with my feet sticking out. The farmer's father, who had come to get his billy of milk, thought I was a robber or some intruder and shouted, "What the h— is going on here?" I got such a fright that I sat up and banged my head on the vat – painful lesson. Fortunately, I was able to explain myself and also to tell him that what I had observed was all very good.

In the end, I learned that it is better to be obvious as a part of the normal scene and to be observing whilst doing something else that was needed as part of the investigation. So I could be checking on the size of the yard whilst also checking on how the staff were handling the cows. The cows seem to just glance at me and give me the okay without batting an eyelid. I guess they know that a farmer wouldn't let just anyone sit on their bike or tractor or walk around their yard.

Now I had literally hours of cow CCTV footage, and I thought, *Observing cows – got it sorted!* Time to take a different tack for a few years.

# CHAPTER 11

# Lame Vet (1990–1993)

## Part 1

"CAN YOU TEACH me to pregnancy-diagnose?" asked the vet.

"Don't you know already? I just saw you check that cow for the owner and write the diagnosis in the record book."

I was talking with an Afghan vet in Peshawar, Pakistan, at a free training clinic where we were training "paravets." This was 1990, and the Russians had just left Afghanistan, and the three million Afghan refugees who had fled the war at home were planning to return from Pakistan to their own country and rebuild. I was there in Pakistan as part of the rebuilding effort. This was a real change from my life in New Zealand. The lameness I had been concentrating on for the last sixteen years was not a problem here except in horses, donkeys, and people.

Four years earlier, in 1986, I had travelled in Pakistan with a friend for a few weeks. He had asked me to come along as a travelling companion as he had lived and worked there in a school for expats fifteen years earlier. He was visiting old friends and looking to see whether there were opportunities for him to return with his family to work there again. He was enjoying the trip, but I was discovering that I was not cut out for being in a country where they ate green chillies for afternoon tea! We were sitting in a tea shop eating a Pakistani speciality – pakora. Pakora are little deep-fried fritters made with vegetables in batter made from chickpea flour. However, this one had not cauliflower or green onion but green chilli. One bite and my eyes watered so much that I went blind and clutched my mouth in agony.

When travelling with my friend, we had visited Peshawar, near the border with Afghanistan. The road from Peshawar heading to the west rises into the hills and then over the Khyber Pass and into Afghanistan. While in Peshawar, I had met a band of dedicated people, most of whom were working with nongovernment organisations (NGOs) helping Afghan refugees. There were literally millions of these displaced people in Pakistan who were now living in modified tent cities in semi-friendly Pakistan. They couldn't return to their homes in Afghanistan because of a war going on, where the Russians were backing a communist group to take over.

Three years later, when the Russian forces left, I was contacted by one of the people who was working in Peshawar who happened to be from New Zealand. A small NGO which was breeding karakul sheep to send to Afghanistan to rebuild the flocks needed a vet in their team. They had thought that a kiwi vet would be great and asked if I could find one. I contacted young vets that I knew in New Zealand, and none were available. Then we realised that maybe our own family would be a good fit for the job. We were now a family of seven as we had added two more boys to the family since we started homeschooling. I had reached the end of one chapter of studies on lame cows – and now could be a good opportunity for a useful interlude. One day, we were at a training session with a person speaking on advice from God. Without knowing any of the backstory, he gave a flippant example, saying to me, "I could say something like, 'Neil, go to Afghanistan'!" A sort of word from God just like I had given my parents years ago in Zimbabwe saying we should go to Australia. We decided with the backing of our church that as a family we would volunteer to go and do what we could whilst avoiding the chillies. This was to be a real education, and I don't mean for the locals.

My family about to leave for Pakistan

So we packed up our house in Inglewood, loaded our suitcases – one each – and prepared to live in my fifth country, Pakistan, for a few years. We figured that we would just take basic things, and the rest we could buy in Pakistan. For the children, that included school books and just a few favourite toys. Some of those toys even made it back to New Zealand and are still around as well-travelled toys. Armed with our three-year single-entry visa and with my wife and five children in tow, we arrived in Karachi Airport one late afternoon in September 1990, the day before our youngest turned two years old. There was a huge crowd milling around with families, children, and older people with porters trying to wrest your bags from your hand to carry them for a small fee and other semi-official looking people. The real official people were looking down on us from high desks. Have you ever noticed that officials at airports are often at higher desks – maybe so that they can look down on us lower individuals? Sandra and the two girls were waved away to a separate desk which was behind screens in this majority Muslim country. I went to the regular men and boys' desk with the paperwork. At that time, we were still holding Australian passports which I handed up to the immigration official at his elevated desk. He frowned down at me and then, picking up the bundle of passports, threw them on the desk. "Fake, all fake," he said.

Not realising that what he actually wanted was some money folded into the passports, I picked them up and proceeded to explain. I thought maybe he was confused by the address in New Zealand whereas the passports were Australian.

"Oh, sorry – it says we come from Australia, but actually we have come from New Zealand," I began.

The frown suddenly evaporated and was replaced with a wide grin and friendliness.

"Richard Hadley," he exclaimed. "You know Hadley (a well-known New Zealand cricketer)? He is playing in Peshawar next Sunday. Oh, I would love to see that. Give me your passports." (stamp stamp) "Welcome to Pakistan – would you like some tea?"

So we "uneventfully" moved to our new home in Peshawar and joined a large expatriate community of aid workers and their families where we began to learn that "uneventful" was normal in Pakistan – or "T.I.P." (This is Pakistan), as the expats would say. We had had our first taste of how different life is in Pakistan and maybe in any other culture where you have not grown up.

Fortunately for us, there was a large community of expats, and they had people who knew how to live in this foreign culture. We moved into a duplex next door to an American couple, an older doctor and his wife, without whom I don't think we would have survived the adventure. Our half of the house was actually the rented home of another family who were away for four months, so we didn't need to rush out and buy household goods yet. In the big expat family, there was always someone either going home for several months – in which case you could borrow stuff – or going home permanently as they had finished their job – and in that case, there would be a big garage sale. It was at those garage sales that our children obtained much of the Lego that still resides in our toy cupboard in Inglewood.

Right from the start, we began to learn the Afghan trade language, a version of Persian called Dari after the ancient Persian king Darius. Sandra built it into our homeschool curriculum. I was not a good language learner, and anyway, most of the vets I was to work with spoke English well enough for me to understand. However, the two girls and Sandra did much better as the ladies that they spoke with often spoke no English, so it was a case of sink or swim.

We acquired local-style clothing, which consisted of very baggy pants and long shirts for the men and boys – called a shalwar camise suit. For the girls, it was similar but in a feminine style and with a large headscarf. We all visited a tailor who took our measurements using a length of cotton thread in which he tied knots at the various lengths he needed to remember such as shoulder width, sleeve length, etc. Then we went to the cloth bazaar to find our choice of fabrics.

As in most Asian cities, the bazaar is divided into areas depending on the merchandise. There was a cloth bazaar, a copper bazaar, one for kitchenware, and one for gold. The most exciting one for the girls was the bangle bazaar where you could buy glass bangles made in such a small size it was an art to get them onto your wrist. Our daughters bought dozens of them. In the cloth bazaar, we bought lengths of cloth, delivered it to the tailor, and were told when the suits would be ready.

In the bazaar

The house that we were borrowing for a time came complete with a chowkidar, or doorman, guard, cleaner, and even cook. Yusef was our helper in everything local. He would do the gardening and answered the gate for us. Every house had a high wall around it so that the family living inside had complete privacy. There was a wall-sized gate where anyone wanting to come in would ring a bell, and Yusef would go and check them out. Yusef himself was a refugee from Afghanistan, so another thing he did was to help us with our language practice.

Then another event occurred that gave us a new perspective – a Yusef view of life – how to be a refugee.

Before our programme could really get going, the Gulf War erupted. In the Persian Gulf, Iraq had annexed Kuwait, and now the combined U.S. and Saudi armies were endeavouring to right the situation. Central Asian Muslim peoples can be very volatile – especially where the West is involved, so there was a lot of anti-Western feeling in Peshawar, so much so that it became dangerous to stay there. So many of the expat families went overseas for a while. We ourselves became temporary refugees in Islamabad, the capital of Pakistan. One way to find out what it feels like to suddenly become displaced people.

Our small NGO had a vehicle for the project, an older Isuzu four-wheel drive. It had a bench seat in the back as well as a seat along each side in the back luggage area. It also had no power steering. When Sandra had to drive it occasionally, it was hard work for her. We loaded up the vehicle with what we thought that we would need to survive for up to a month. Fortunately, not too difficult as we had not long ago unpacked our baggage from New Zealand. By that time, we had all obtained local clothes, and I had grown a beard so we looked somewhat like locals – until we spoke! We ended up camping in the basement flat of a friendly church in Islamabad for several weeks until the rioting had died down when we returned to continue on with the project.

Soon after our arrival, the leaders of the NGOs which were involved with veterinary work had been gathered together by the United Nations Development Program (UNDP). The meeting was to discuss how to rebuild the livestock of Afghanistan. Sending new livestock wasn't going to be feasible, so we needed a better plan. The new and much better plan was to set up local vet clinics with vets or "paravets" in every Afghan province. For "paravet," think of paramedics for animals. In this way, the animals that were surviving in Afghanistan could be kept healthy, and the flocks and herds could increase. The UNDP was to fund this, and I was asked to write the proposal. The writer had to be a vet, and the proposal had to be written in English, so I qualified, just. English – check (provided that I could check the spelling), vet – check, but experience in writing proposals – virtually nil, unless you counted my very brief research proposal a few years earlier.

This was a step above what I had thought that I was to be involved in. I had never had anything to do with vet work in any developing countries, let alone one that had been decimated by war. Before I started writing a proposal, I thought that I had better get some background and see how vet programmes work in poorer countries. The first thing that I did was to travel to the poorer high-altitude valleys of Pakistan to see how they set up vet programmes in an area very similar to northern Afghanistan. The Afghanistan we were talking about then was made up of impoverished people who had been at war for upwards of ten years. Northern Pakistan was similar in that there was very little infrastructure and very few vets. In Gilgit, up near the Himalayas in the northern mountains of Pakistan, I visited a Pakistani NGO which was doing veterinary work for subsistence farmers. They had a very sensible plan designed for this sort of scenario to avoid creating an aid-dependent community. It was working well. In their plan, the local people, although they had very little money, had to pay for their vet services – just a little – and that way, the vets, when they came, would get paid and have their own small business. The people didn't have to pay for the vaccines – these were provided by the government – and the vets themselves found ways to get medicines. Each farmer or animal owner with just a few animals spread the cost of vet services over many. Everyone was happy; they got the services they needed and supported the vet to be there for other jobs as well. That was where I learned that it always pays to check out what the locals do before coming in with a ready-made solution from another culture.

Back in Peshawar, I had to convince the other agencies to join me in the same proposal, including the idea of user pays – a little bit. We were twelve different NGOs, and each one was in charge of one province of Afghanistan. I was the only native English speaker, and there was only one other European agency. All the rest were local, homegrown, Afghan-run agencies. My job was to convince them all to combine and write one proposal (at least I would write it), and they would agree. Anyone could see that if we differed on the basic user pays idea, we would have a problem. If the vet services were free in one province and you had to pay in the neighbouring one, we would have an outcry from the places where they had to pay. No one would use their own vet where they had to pay; they would just cross the border to get services for free. I guess it was a bit unfair as I was the only English speaker and experienced vet in the group, so I kind of had them over a barrel. We eventually agreed on the proposal.

I then had to sell it to the UNDP, which had the fixed idea that all aid should be free to poor people. If the aid was free and the salaries of the vets were paid by the UNDP, then what would happen in a few years when the project finished and there was no money for salaries? Or if there were no longer free vaccines and medicines from the United Nations? The whole project would finish, and the vets would stop work. End of story. But if the user pays system worked, it would be the beginning of a story. Fortunately, I found an ally among the Afghan staff of the UNDP who had worked in Africa with a similar programme. Together, we talked to all the others who finally agreed, mostly because of my friend. After all, who would believe a Westerner who was just out to "rip off the poor"?

Having gotten the project approved, we got to work. The first thing was to train "paravets" and upskill vets to run vet clinics in their own villages. Because of the ongoing civil war in Afghanistan, none of the university-educated vets who were refugees in Pakistan had had any practical experience. Organising the practical experience was my job. So here I was in Peshawar at a vet training clinic, run very much along the same lines as the university training clinic where I had done my own training. Local Pakistani people would bring their animals to the clinic, and the vets in training would practise their examination and diagnosis under supervision.

This was the scene when I was asked, "Can you teach me to pregnancy-diagnose?" by the vet working at the clinic who was supposed to be training others how to pregnancy-diagnose. Then, in answer to my surprised question, he said, "Actually, I have no idea what I am doing, but they all ask me to tell them whether their cow is pregnant or not – so I pretend that I am doing something and then make up an answer: "Yes, she is 'in-calf' (pregnant), or, 'No, sorry not in-calf'." But I don't know if I am right or not, so to protect myself, I write the diagnosis in my record book – except that instead of writing what I said to the owner, I write the opposite."

"Why do you do that?" I asked, totally in the dark.

"So if the cow owner comes back six months later and says, 'You were wrong – you said my cow was in-calf and there is no calf,' I just say, 'Oh, is that right – let me just check my records – what day was it that you came? Yes, here it is in my book – see it says that she was not pregnant. You must have forgotten what I said!'"

Our clinic in Peshawar, Pakistan, was mostly for the poorer local farmers and families who often only had one cow or a horse or a donkey for their livelihood, so it was pretty important to them that whatever treatment we gave was effective. If a cow came in with a little package tied to her horn, then you were in all likelihood the last resort – the local religious leader had already prayed for the cow to get better, and it hadn't worked straightaway. If, now, the Western medicine worked, you still didn't win, as the religious leader would then say, "Why did you go there? You should have just waited."

Sometimes the most effective treatment was to rest the animal. "Rest" was not an easy treatment to suggest to a tonga (horse-drawn buggy) driver. If we asked him to rest his horse for a few days – how was the family to eat? One tonga owner came to work in our office as a respite whilst his horse recovered from a fall on the tar-sealed road that had grazed both its knees to the bone. Rahim Khan soon became great friends with our two youngest boys. Every week after his horse recovered, he would drive to our gate and take Sandra and the boys shopping in the little "corner shop" bazaar where you could buy fruit and vegetables and some other groceries. In the part of Peshawar where we were living, there were many other aid workers and their families from all over the world, so these shops often stocked things that we might like such as canned cheese, and English Marmite. Rahim Khan would drive them there and stop the tonga outside the shop. While Sandra went inside to find what we needed, David and Peter would sit on the driving seat with Rahim Khan and pretend to drive the tonga. Inside the shop, Sandra would tell the shopkeeper what she wanted, and it would appear on the counter. There was no need to haggle as this was a fixed-price bazaar.

Every day was an eye-opener. One day, I saw a flock of goats and sheep coming down the road following the young boy goatherd, as they grazed from one dumpster with tree prunings and other garbage to another. At the same time, another flock was coming from the opposite direction. They met at the dumpster, ate for a while, and then the two boys called their animals, and both herds continued on again in the opposite directions. I guessed that the sheep knew whom to follow – sounds biblical, doesn't it?

Learning to live well in such a different culture was vital, and I think we did well as we were a family just like the local families. Every house had a front room where you could have guests. No furniture but just a carpet on the polished concrete floor. Around the edges were thin kapok-filled mattresses called toshaks. Each one was about the size of a narrow single-bed mattress. We and our guests would sit on these at floor level, and the tea tray would be on the floor in the middle. If we were having a meal, we would spread a tablecloth to cover the entire exposed carpet on the floor. Then it could be covered with dishes. No need for knives and forks though, as most Asian and Central Asian people eat with their fingers. Much to the delight of our younger boys. We had a basin and jug of water that was passed around to wash hands before eating, so our hands were possibly cleaner than the knives and forks. One of our friends said to us the reason he ate with his fingers was that he knew where his hands had been, but, as for the knives and forks, who knew where they had been?

We filled our guest room many times. Sometimes the family was the family of a person who was working for the NGO. Other times it might be a friend who was helping us practise our language skills. Sandra needed to learn how to make proper tea to serve. She also learned to cook rice and meatballs Afghan style – very delicious.

We also had other expats with whom we worked side by side who had families with children and teenagers the same ages as our family. We would go on picnics to remote places as a large group, where the younger ones could swim in a river or play volleyball. There was a local university – this was why our part of town was called University Town. Part of the university consisted of a large experimental forest where different varieties of trees were grown. It was the perfect private playground.

However, we couldn't play all the time. I had a clinic to run and projects to organise. But before that could happen – it wasn't the animals needing a doctor – it was myself.

## Part 2

Adjusting to a new country with different diseases, we had to learn how to sanitise everything, wash fruit and vegetables in water to which some iodine or Condy's crystals had been added, filter or boil all the water we drank, and never, never eat salads prepared by someone else. We had a bit of sickness here and there in the first few months as we sorted out the system, but somewhere along the line I had slipped up, as six months into our stay, I came down with hepatitis A. I blamed it on a fruit and water drink that the locals traditionally drink to celebrate the Afghan New Year, Nao Roz. It is called haft mewa or five fruits and consists of a mixture of dried fruits soaked for several days in cold water. At the time I wasn't feeling all that well and was really ill the next day. Our doctor friend and neighbour looked after me and gave the rest of the family booster vaccinations so no one else got sick. However, for the next several months, I was rather useless. Then one day the tide turned, and I began to recover, thanks to the prayers of our friends and family at home in New Zealand.

Miraculously fully recovered, I got back to work. At the clinic I taught the practical skills, and the local vets taught the academic stuff – all the things that I had forgotten over the almost twenty years since my university studies. Each NGO was in charge of a different province. Our NGO, ComDev, was to set up clinics in the far northeastern province of Badakhshan, bordering Tajikistan, China, and the far north of Pakistan. The trainees came from villages all over Afghanistan, each small group representing their own province. Our group of paravets graduated, and they were now ready to return to their country to rebuild veterinary services.

This was to be a major undertaking. Inside Afghanistan there was no shop selling vaccine or medicines or veterinary equipment, so we had to buy this in Pakistan and package it all up to survive the journey. For a short while, our office yard was full of packages, sacks, rope to tie them up, and tin trunks in which to put items that should not get wet or squashed.

A few weeks later, I accompanied them to the north. Our convoy set off from Peshawar with the load of medicines and vaccines to do their best for the animals in that province. The trip started on a bus in Peshawar with the bus full of their equipment. When we arrived in the far north of Pakistan, all this had to be transferred to donkeys and mules to cross over the high-altitude mountain pass that was the doorway to Badakhshan. I accompanied them to the border post where they loaded the donkeys, and then, having waved them off, I returned to Peshawar to keep organising supplies. As a Westerner, I was not allowed to cross the border at that time.

There was work to do in Peshawar keeping the office open and supervising alterations to our little building. I sent an Afghan who was a qualified vet to visit the clinics in Afghanistan to collect reports and see how they were doing.

While we were in Pakistan, we did have a couple of opportunities to see the countryside. We visited the fabled old city section of Peshawar with its beautiful buildings. The old bazaars were really crowded, so when we went as a family, we had to work on sticking together. I would go in front, followed by Sandra and the girls each holding hands with a small boy, then in the rear guard was our older son.

Since we had the use of a vehicle, we were also able to travel further afield. Driving on the roads was also an experience. Travelling on a main road was a bit like joining a fast-flowing river. You just jumped in and hoped for the best. People would blast their horn at you just so that you knew they were there.

One winter, we followed the Swat River valley up to Mingora with a group to have some snow fun. On the way, we were amazed by the canal system that the British had built. This system transports water all over the fertile valleys to grow crops to feed this populous nation. There were amazing siphons under the roads or even under another canal going in a different direction. There were also canals in our part of the city of Peshawar where the water buffalo would cool off in the hot summers.

Another legacy of the British was the railway system. We went by train right across Pakistan from Peshawar to Lahore to take the youth to a holiday camp nearby. The mountainous areas north of the capital Islamabad were my favourite. Pakistan's lower areas are very hot and humid, so anyone who can afford it tries to escape to the mountains for a while in the summer. There are many guesthouses – another legacy of the British. We stayed in one that was situated on top of a mountain where there was an almost 360-degree view of the Himalayas and the Hindu Kush mountains – all still snow-capped.

Another legacy of the British, however, that we were continually meeting, was the bureaucracy and paperwork that was part of everyday life. To visit the bank, you had to fill in what you wanted in triplicate – at least. Every step needed a different person in a different office. Getting visas renewed was the biggest problem – you had to wait for what seemed like years to get a piece of paper signed by the right person, who was sitting behind a huge desk drinking cups of tea. In the end, I managed to secure the relevant papers to go and visit the clinics that were our responsibility in Badakhshan. I would visit over two weeks to see how they were faring.

Travelling into the far north of Afghanistan to visit and check on clinics was quite difficult and even dangerous as there was a civil war in progress now that the Russians had left, and various parties were vying for control of the capital, Kabul. There was no air service, and the roads were very basic. To cross from one province to another might be dangerous as you would have to keep all the warlords happy, not to mention the danger of unexploded antipersonnel mines which were everywhere. Fortunately, our province was bordering Pakistan – supposedly eliminating some of those problems but creating different ones. In order to travel into Afghanistan to reach the northern province of Badakhshan, where our clinics were, we had to travel to the far north of Pakistan – almost to the Himalayas, then cross over the Shai Saleem pass, a high-altitude mountain pass. Our vets and "paravets" had travelled by horse, and the medicines (as all other supplies) were sent in carried by donkeys or mules. We were reliably informed that they had just opened a new road across this pass, so travelling there became a possibility for me. We combined forces with another NGO and prepared an expedition.

There were no banks in Badakhshan, and the only way of getting money to our projects was to carry it in as bank notes. This was a little problematic as, due to inflation, the afghani (the local currency) was worth very little, so we had to carry literally trunk loads of these bank notes to our workers. This was to pay for such things as renting buildings. I was going to visit our clinics and the other NGO with whom I was to travel, had medical clinics to visit, so the timing seemed good. It was spring, and so the snow had only melted a bit, and the road should be passable. Also, the other NGO directors wanted to deliver a vehicle to their people and I could drive. The vehicle was a small 4WD Suzuki, box on wheels. We loaded up, Asian style. Five large people, trunks of money and supplies, including petrol in tanks tied to the roof, and all the relevant permits to cross borders.

I had travelled a few times up the valleys to the north and had found that even in the far north of Pakistan I didn't escape the cricket mania, and my five countries came in handy. I also found that I was starting to try out their cultural styles before we crossed the border into Afghanistan. I was in a little guesthouse with my travelling companions who were about to watch the TV broadcast of a cricket five-nations event. Then came the loaded question, "Who do you want to win?" "Well," I said, "I was born in South Africa so that would be good. I studied in Australia, so that would be good. I worked in New Zealand, so that would be good, and now I am living in Pakistan, so that would be *great.*" There was a burst of supportive laughter. In those tribal villages, it turns out that everyone is on the side of the locals or those who are next to you – real pragmatism or maybe self-preservation.

Travelling up the valleys to the north of Pakistan was uneventful, apart from the tight squeeze to fit us all into the vehicle. As the driver, since no one else knew how to drive, I had the best seat. We crossed the border and set off to the mountain pass. At the top we were told that the road was no longer passable because of the early spring snow melt, so we would have to leave the vehicle there and hire horses to take us and the baggage the rest of the way to Faizabad, the capital of Badakhshan. Fortunately, I was travelling with local people who knew how to bargain and get us the horses we needed. There were not enough good horses for everyone, so the good riders (Afghans) got the best horses, and I got the last choice – the dregs – slightly lame in the left front foot. Did anyone mention lameness?

A day or two of beautiful scenery passed by – fields with pink flowering poppies and with red poppies growing in the cracks of the little mudbrick walls we passed by. All the fields were irrigated by little channels bringing water from higher up the rivers – an amazing system that has been there since antiquity. There is very little real rain, and so the fields need to be irrigated, and certainly the Afghans are expert water engineers. We were crossing fields the next day and stepping over little canals (or at least the horses were) when my horse with the limp stumbled and fell over onto its side, landing on my left knee. Crack! Ouch! They managed to pick me up and dusted me off, gave me a more dependable horse, said I will be okay, and we set off again. However, if the pain was any indication, I was not okay. A few days later, still not feeling any better, I managed to have a carpenter make me a pair of wooden crutches to help me get around when I wasn't on a horse or donkey and in order to continue on to my clinics. Going back by myself was not an option. We were out of contact with Pakistan, so we just carried on travelling.

I travelled around mostly by donkey, and with the help of my crutches, I visited each of the three clinics. It amazed me how the staff were managing to vaccinate and treat minor problems such as worms and wounds so that the animals could do better. They had already found a cheaper source of medicines and were setting up their own businesses. It looked like we were seeing the beginning of a good story. I wondered how long this would last and determined to come back sometime to see.

On the one opportunity that I had to phone back to Sandra via radio, all the local people forbade me to tell her that I had injured my leg – and they stayed around while I talked to make sure that I didn't make any slips. If I had told her that I had had an accident, it would look bad for them. So eventually, two weeks later, when I arrived home on my trusty crutches to finally get an X-ray, I was not popular with Sandra or the family. An Iranian doctor whom I visited in Peshawar told me that I had broken the top of the bone below my knee. "Don't have surgery here. That is too dangerous. We will just plaster it for six weeks, and it will heal itself. Then in eighteen months you will be back to normal."

That is how I became known as the lame vet on crutches in Badakhshan. I didn't see any lame cows in Afghanistan. And after our project concluded, we went back to New Zealand and, still slightly lame, I got back to work again on the lame-cow problem.

# CHAPTER 12

# Videoing Myself and Cows (1993–1999)

THE IRANIAN DOCTOR was correct, in eighteen months after the injury to my leg, I was no longer a lame vet. But now I was focused on a different question. I knew exactly how I had become lame, but how does a cow become lame? What happens? The cow certainly doesn't fall off a horse or even usually fall over – what really happens?

I was now back in New Zealand and able to concentrate on my local vet work including a few new ventures. Before we had left Pakistan, I had received a letter from one of the other vets in the Inglewood practice. He reminded me that the head vet, Gunner, was due to retire shortly, and he thought that this would be a good opportunity to change the structure of the vet practice a bit. Ray, always a go-ahead person, had the idea of turning the practice into a contract practice – a semi-private vet business. What he proposed was that he and I would be partners in a contract with the vet club to do all their dairy work. We would lease the vet club premises and operate in the same area. The dairy members of the club would still get service, but Ray would also develop the business to include more pets and horses. I liked the idea – it would be a nice new start for me back into vet work in New Zealand although I did make the proviso that I would like to travel overseas again especially to Afghanistan to check up on my vets in Badakhshan. Ray would have to provide most of the money to set up and purchase stock and equipment from the club, whilst I would contribute my small amount and work with him. So I arrived back in New Zealand to attend a retirement celebration for Gunner and to help open a new business.

This wasn't the only business that Ray and I were to start. As my lameness investigations had progressed, and before my short interlude in Pakistan and Afghanistan, I had been travelling around in New Zealand doing seminars as well as writing short articles and compiling a little booklet. I now had the idea that, instead of travelling everywhere to give seminars, I could make a teaching video to sell to farmers or vets with all the ideas that I had collected to reduce lameness. Many of these ideas were specific to New Zealand dairy systems and not in other books that were designed for the Northern Hemisphere. This was not going to be another home video, the plan was that the video would be professionally made. This would cost a lot of money. So Ray and I thought, why not make another little company just for teaching materials? With that purpose, we created Vet Education Transfer Services Limited (VETSL).

The next job was to find a person to make the video for us. We found the ideal person in New Plymouth who was already making short teaching videos and also taught video tech at the polytechnic. Keith was really interested in the project and came on board – boots and all – literally. There were learning curves for both of us. He had to learn how to video cows and how to get me to remember my lines. We had to learn how to script the videos, I had to learn to present to a camera what I had memorised and then edit what we filmed. Sometimes it seemed that most of the editing was to take out the bloopers where I forgot my lines. I definitely was not a natural film star; the cows were more natural than me.

I didn't realise how much work was involved in creating a teaching video, but Keith patiently led us through it all. The first job was to write the script. This was mostly compiled from my teaching seminars. Then the next thing was to suggest what picture should be showing whilst each segment of words in the script were being spoken. If I was talking about a cow with a sore foot, I would have to find a cow like that to stand next to and point out that particular foot problem. Keith was amazing, often dropping his other projects to come and film the perfect case to show a particular problem. Many of my laboratory farms were the backdrop for my video, and their cows were the film stars, and occasionally the farmer or worker appeared.

Next step was to edit and do the voiceover. This was almost as difficult as talking straight to a camera. Luckily, Keith was very patient.

This project was to take several years and many dollars to finish, but the result was a set of three videos with most of my knowledge on lameness treatment, lameness prevention, and cow management. We advertised it around New Zealand through vets, and after three years, we broke even on the costs. Over the next few years, we used the income to upgrade some of the sections, put it on four DVDs instead of tape, and make a vet supplement. By this time, Keith, the cameraman, had taught Sandra how to take and edit video as well as he could, so she could now make more segments to illustrate my seminars. This skill was also to come in handy later when we made a second set of DVDs with information on cow flow.

We were getting into the modern world now. Sandra's brother came over from Sydney for a holiday and suggested that we needed a website to sell videos, and it would also serve as a good base to share information. His workday job was at a university in their computing department, so he was certainly the right person to do this. He asked for some suggestions on a website name – and then he proceeded to make www.lamecow.co.nz.

The idea of the video and website was that information about how to prevent lameness could travel worldwide. In theory, I wouldn't even have to travel around New Zealand myself to give seminars. This was true to a certain extent, but just as in the case of a music band, everyone might enjoy the recording, but the live performance is much better.

My travelling didn't only just occur for work. We also really enjoyed travelling for family holidays. Almost every second year, we would visit Sydney as a family, often for weddings or Christmas.

One year, the family went to Sydney for Christmas, and I had to stay in New Zealand on after-hours duty until the day after Christmas, when I would fly over to join them. The day after the children left with Sandra, I received a phone call from Immigration New Zealand.

"Did you know your wife has just left the country with your children?"

"Yes, of course" I replied.

"Well, then, can you tell me their names and birthdates?"

"Names I can do, but birthdays . . ."

The lady laughed and said, "Well, give it a try, and see how you go." I didn't manage to get them all correct, but apparently, I was close enough, and maybe I was just like many other fathers who forget dates of things like wedding anniversaries as well.

Another time we went to a wedding where my two daughters were to be flower girls – wearing dresses that had been worn by Sandra and her sister some twenty-three years earlier. Just before we left New Zealand, our eldest daughter had recovered from chicken pox – so of course when we arrived, the second one came down with it – recovered in time for the wedding – but left the bugs in Sydney for their uncle and aunt!

With all these minor ups and downs, an upside was combining business with pleasure. In 1998, there was an international conference in Sydney, and I had a paper to present. It had grown out of my mountains of data and questions that farmers suggested. Then an added lightbulb was a video with cows as the star performers just doing what they normally would do.

Treating lame cows on an almost daily basis, I had noticed that most frequently when the problem was a white-line injury, it would occur on the outside claw of the back foot. Farmers that I asked said that they noticed the same but also added that it was often different for the two-year-old heifer. I had been keeping records of all my lame-cow cases for quite a few years now, and I thought that it would be a good idea if I looked closely to see whether the records or data could confirm these anecdotes that my farmers told me.

My collection of lame-cow cases was getting quite large – every year brought in over five hundred cases. When a cow had become lame, many of my farmers had called me in, and I had personally treated the lame foot. I would write on my pink sheets anything of note about each case. After I had used the records to make up my accounts to charge the farmers, these pieces of pink paper were stacked away in piles in a cupboard – not much use and very difficult to sort information from. Then enter the computer with spreadsheets. By now the software had progressed significantly, but it was still beyond me. Fortunately for me, another vet in the practice could set up spreadsheets, and my wife and our teenagers could enter data – for extra pocket money for the teenagers, of course. Then came the fun bit – asking the spreadsheet questions.

We had records from ten years of lame cows, and when we checked the data, now nicely organised, to see if the "back foot outside claw theory" stood up to the scientific test, we found it did. The farmers were correct. A cow three years old or more and in at least its second milking season, when it had a white-line injury, it nearly always occurred in a back foot and on the outside claw. In fact, seventy-seven percent of the injuries were in that exact same spot. *Why?* I wondered.

Even more interesting was the other observation to be confirmed by the data. Farmers had also told me that when they treated a heifer or two-year-old, it would often have its white-line injury on the inside claw of a front foot. Now we had numbers – front foot inside claw in heifer: fifty percent, back foot outside claw in cows: seventy-seven percent. Confirmation twice over.

How could this be? Why was it not random? What was happening must be something physical – it must be something to do with too much pressure on the foot, I thought. But why did the pressure occur on the outside claw in the back foot and on the inside claw in the front foot? By this time, after quite a few years of watching cows, I had a theory that a cow and heifer reacted differently to herding pressure. It seemed to me that the bossy, more confident cows in the herd, when they were pushed or were trying to escape from something like a dog, would just shove forward against other cows. The less confident cows (and this usually meant the heifers, or two-year-olds) would back up and then turn to hide in a good-looking safe space far away from any bossy cow. But my question was: just what exactly was the cow doing with her feet when that happened, and what was different for the cow compared to the heifer?

Cows' feet are complicated but in actual fact simpler than our human feet and hands. They are not feet as we think of feet; they actually walk on their (overgrown) toenails. Instead of having five fingers or toes to walk on, cows only have two on each foot. The flexing ankle or wrist is above the claw and then further up come the leg bones or "arm" bones if you are looking at the front feet. The Spanish language that I tried to learn in South America is much more helpful in this, as it calls the front feet of a cow "manos" or hands. Looking at our finger, it would be like walking on your fingerprints, which are specially hardened to make a solid sole, and the fingernail. In the cow, the "nail" is wrapped around much further like a wall around the bones inside the foot, making what we call a capsule. And in fact, that is the reason that the nail is called the wall. It joins to the sole at the white line. When you scratch hard using your fingernail, it is not very hard to pull the nail away from the skin – and also it is really painful. A cow's claw is much tougher at that white-line junction than your finger, but then a cow is much heavier, and twisting and turning might possibly pull the wall and sole apart ever so slightly.

A white-line injury on a cow's foot is where the side of the wall has become separated from the bottom of the foot or sole just like this. Sometimes there is enough space for a small stone or some sand to get stuck there, and this results in a problem, usually an abscess, which moves up the side of the hoof underneath the wall until, if nothing stops it, the infection gets to the top where the abscess bursts out. My question was – what was causing the separation to happen in such specific places? One obvious answer could be that this is the weakest point, which might explain the site in cows, but why in a different place in heifers? I thought that it might be something to do with how they behaved.

So now was the time for me to look more closely at my collection of videos and see what was going on with the "toenails" of the cows and the "fingernails" of the heifers. Something interesting was happening here.

By now, we knew that one of the risks for lameness, including white-line injury, was having a herd of cows bunched up under pressure or being forced to go somewhere in a hurry or into a yard where they didn't want to move as fast as the farmer wanted or trying to escape from something scary like an electric fence wire or another bigger cow. Thinking about this I remembered an old video that I had taken years ago of a farmer whose dog was pushing cows onto a concrete yard area that was covered in mud, and the cows had not wanted to go in. I had labelled it "Poor handling." Inappropriate behaviour by the dog, but probably the cows would be doing what they always do in that nasty pressure situation, and this was what I wanted to see.

I went back to my collection of videos. Soon I was watching the old (R-18) video of some cows coming in to be milked, where there was a Friesian heifer afraid of the Jersey cows. Jersey cows, even though they are smaller, can be quite feisty. However, the Jersey cows at the front were afraid of the rocks on the concrete in the yard. They knew it might be painful to step on one of those stones. The ones in the middle were afraid of an electric wire along the edge of the track and of the other feisty cows getting too close. And the ones at the back were afraid of the barking dog. A good place to see what happens when cows are scared and under pressure. Sounds like a soap about cows. I am happy to say that this rarely, if ever, happens these days as farmers are much more aware of what the cow is feeling.

Now that I had the digital technology, I started to watch that sequence in slow motion. Older cows in the video were indeed pushing forward to escape danger as they saw it. They went in among the other cows, and when I looked at the feet in slow motion – goodness me – I could see that the older cow, in order to push forward and sideways to make a space, would actually cross a back foot over under her body to give an anchor and to push harder. And the weight all landed on the outside of that hind claw! Definitely a possibility of damage here. There was one cow who was in the middle of the mob and who was accidently being pushed by other cows towards the electric fence – in slow motion I could clearly see that she crossed her back foot over underneath and pushed off from the ground near the fence whilst leaning against the other cows more firmly. This used the outside claw of her back foot to take the main pressure. Repeat this many times on hard surfaces, and there would be a high risk of white-line separation in that specific place. Now to look and see if I could find a heifer.

Another bit of technology came in handy – the digital zoom. The heifers in the same video, when I zoomed in and watched the film in slow motion, were doing something different. They wanted to get away from the bigger bossy cows in front and on each side because those big cows were likely to swing their head around and wallop little heifers like them. One small Jersey animal, which I assumed was a heifer, was being shoved towards the stone covered yard, and she didn't want to go in. Besides there were other big cows in there who might deliver a well-aimed head butt. So rather than challenge the big cows, she backed up. She anchored her one front foot and pushed backwards with her other front foot – using the inside claw. Here was an indication of behaviours that could account for the injury being in two different places. Now I began more determinedly watching cows in the yards at the farms I was visiting, looking out for this sort of thing – and sure enough, I could see it everywhere. Bigger bossy cows were strong enough to push sideways and push their way forwards past another cow, while littler younger cows, less bossy and afraid of the heads of the bigger cows, backed up and tried to find a place in between the rumps of the other cows for protection.

I even tried pretending to be a cow and performed both these actions, first for the cow and then the heifer. Definitely the pressure could be felt in the places I thought it would.

This certainly seemed like a plausible mechanism, and a possible explanation for the pattern of the positions of the injury that we all saw. Also, as these behaviours occurred in high-pressure situations, it was a good connection between poor handling and pressure on the herd from facilities. This mechanism then could account for a more frequent lame-foot outcome in those circumstances. So I wrote this as a conference paper along with the "movie" or slice of life of the cows on my video and presented it at the Buiatrics Conference in Sydney, whilst the family visited with the grandparents.

Having now found a possible answer to one of my questions, this caused me to start thinking of a lot more of my questions: Are the cows at the back of the herd always under more pressure than those at the front? Are the same ones always first, or are they different cows each day? I suspected we were going to need more research, more data collection, and more of what I enjoyed most – getting out on farms where the cows were. I might have to (temporarily) pack away the video camera and do some real science.

## CHAPTER 13

# A Scientist in the Field (1997–2003)

IT WAS REALLY cold and rather dull, but I could still see the large orange numbers on the sides of the cows as they walked by me coming up to be milked. I needed to be quite a distance away; otherwise the cows would get spooked and not follow their normal behaviour. I whispered the numbers into my little Dictaphone as they passed by. I was out in the field again, literally, and watching cows.

It seemed that every idea or result of my studies and research turned up more questions, and every conversation with farmers turned up more "anecdata" to confirm. Now I had heaps of questions that I wanted to answer before I could back up my advice to farmers who were trying to avoid getting too many lame cows. I had come up with an idea that worked in theory to explain why cows got white-line lameness in back feet and heifers in front feet. This idea was connecting the way the cows reacted to herding pressure compared to the way heifers reacted. So now the thread seemed to be going along the lines of cow behaviour, something that could be observed.

If you have a herd of three hundred cows, which cow do you think is more likely to become lame – old ones, small ones, big ones or ones that are low in the pecking order, or the ones at the back of the herd?

If we knew the answer to that question, we could know which cows to target with our prevention strategies. More questions that needed answers. Farmers told me that the cows that got lame were at the back of the herd, easy to spot. Were these cows always at the back of the herd, or did they get lame somewhere else and end up walking or limping slowly at the back of the herd where they were noticed?

I have always found that farmers have favourite cows even if their herd is quite large or cows that they just notice because of something that a particular cow does.

I was visiting a farm in UK, and I noticed one very large white cow standing in a corner of the waiting yard. Being white, she stood out amongst the other black-and-white cows. I had earlier noticed that when the farmer brought them all into the yard for milking that this cow was the first to arrive, well ahead of all the others. Milking began, and the staff were busy with the cows that came into the milking area. Gradually the cows moved in and then out the other end and back to the barn – except the white cow. She was still there quite a while later, so I pointed it out to the farmer, who said, "Oh yes, she is always there – that is her favourite spot in the yard, and she gets here early to claim it. She also likes to be milked last at the very end – you wait and see." He was right. Other farmers confirmed this, telling me about cows that liked to be milked at the front of a row or maybe in the last round of the rotary – with a space between them and the second to last cow. Or, even more curiously, cows that liked to be milked in the second row and not the first. More interesting "anecdata" to confirm. If you ask a farmer which cows are the dominant ones, they will be almost certain to be able to tell you the one or two cows' numbers who are really bossy. Maybe something was going on here with the cows that we were unaware of.

Cows have a secret weapon always at hand, I mean at head, as it is their head. I suppose this is because some cows have horns to defend themselves not only from predators but from other cows. With their head, they can knock another cow right off its feet. We know that bulls fight each other and tackle each other head-to-head, but we often don't realise that the sweet cow called "Daisy" could be "Danger Woman" to the rest of the herd. She is the "Godmother" who rules the rest with her head. If that cow were a hen, we would say she is at the top of the pecking order. I supposed that every other cow has a rank as well, and they all seem to keep in order. If they are low in the order, does that mean that they will be more likely to get lame? I thought that it would be a good question to find an answer to, so back to the observations.

So here I was out there in the cold getting more data to address these sorts of questions. The first question that I was wanting to find the answer to was – when the farmer always said to me that the lame cows were at the back of the herd, were they there because they couldn't keep up with the faster ones, or did they get lame because they were at the back and got pushed around more, even, maybe, by the farmer, or his dog? Were the same cows always at the back anyway? Maybe the herding was random, although farmers told me that they thought that cows were always in nearly the same order when they came in to get milked. . My questions were all about what the cows were doing – cow behaviour.

So, I got to dreaming about how to do this and woke up with lots of ideas. I had the idea that I would find out which of the cows got lame in the herd over the period of nine months while they were coming every day to get milked. Then I would find out where they were in the walking order of the herd when the farmer brought them into the yard. Were they at the front of the herd, in the middle, or part of the back group? Then maybe we could get some clues as to why those particular cows got lame. Was it something that the farmer was doing, or was it something that the cows were doing? Then, we could take the right actions to prevent it.

Then I had another bright idea. Why record the numbers of the cows that were walking along when it would be easier to read them after milking? I thought that if the cows arrive at the collecting yard in the same order as that in which they walk forward into the bails and are milked, I would only have to check the order of the cows coming out past me as I stood on the other side of a bar where I could easily read their numbers – or even where a machine could read the numbers. Then we could compare the records of which cows got lame and find out where they were in the order of the herd. In the back of my mind were some stories I had heard from farmers similar to that about the white UK cow. So I thought that first, I had better check whether simply reading their numbers after milking was a good idea.

I enlisted some farmers, ten of them, to help and began my second major study. This time I was looking at the habits of cows. Which other cows did they usually walk with? What order do they keep, if any? Where were the bossy, dominant cows – if I could find out which ones they were? Stories that farmers had told me and that I had observed for myself told me that I might be able to confirm my "anecdata" with some real facts.

Cows in New Zealand herds all have a herd number from one to several hundred depending on how many cows there are in the herd. This number is displayed on a brightly coloured tag in their ear like an earring, which you can easily read – if you are close enough, and if the cow is looking in your direction, or if you are behind and they are looking ahead. But virtually impossible to read at any distance. So we came up with the idea of writing their numbers giant size on both sides of their back with spray stock marker paint so that at a hundred metres away, they could still be identified. I don't know what the cows thought about having their numbers written largely on their backs but it certainly made it easier to identify them. I read out and recorded the giant orange numbers from the backs of the cows, first as they walked into the collecting yard and then later when they left the milking parlour.

Next, we took a random group of twenty-one of those cows and put them in a small separate paddock to eat, away from the rest of the herd. I climbed up a ladder to be able to see them all at the same time – and watched which cows won the little "face-off" battles. One cow would approach another as if to say "That is my patch of grass!" and the cow that "won" the grass I recorded as the winner. I watched about 150 battles or face-offs and then took my notes home. At the dining room table, we all shuffled twenty cow numbers into a rank from top cow to bottom of the pile.

That was at the beginning of the milking season when every cow in the herd had calved. I went to each farm five times. We repeated the whole procedure about three months later, and, would you believe it, we waited until the end of the season and did it all again. The result of this was another mountainous pile of data to be analysed. Various ones in the family transferred it from tape to spreadsheet. The family had done the sorting out of who were some of the dominant cows in each herd and that joined the rest of the data. Then I enlisted the help of my university friends again, who found a lovely lady called Carola from Germany, who was working on her PhD at Massey University in New Zealand whilst her new husband was left behind in Germany. She relished the idea of real data from the field, so I handed it all over to her to see what the mass of numbers really meant.

Then I flew off to Afghanistan again with my two younger boys and Sandra for a time to watch mostly people and only a few cows.

When I visited the vet clinics that we had started in Afghanistan in 1992, I said to myself that sometime I would like to come back and meet up with those people again. In fact, I had said to my New Zealand partner in the Inglewood vet practice when I came back at the end of our three years in Pakistan that someday I would like to go back for an extended visit, but this time I wanted to be near the clinics.

So here I was in 2020 back in Afghanistan to check on how the vets and clinics that I had worked with were faring. This time I was able to live with my two younger sons and Sandra in the town where the clinics were based. I looked down a valley from the cottage that we had rented, at the view of huge mountains passed by a raging torrent of a river. This was Faizabad, on two sides of a river with irrigated ground beside and steep rocky hills behind.

Cottage in Faizabad

I had actually been to Faizabad eight years earlier on my "lame vet" expedition. I was now able to introduce the town to some of my family and my family to the town. Where our cottage was situated was called "New City" about thirty minutes' walk from "Old City." Faizabad was not just old though; it was ancient. It is situated on a sort of tributary of the old Silk Road where it runs up the river to the ancient lapis lazuli mines. There was one rough road that was just passable by vehicles from New City to Old City, and it passed through the narrow bazaar. Almost all the houses, including the one we rented were flat-roofed and built from handmade, sun-dried mudbrick. The roof was also made of mud spread over a sort of thatching made of twigs supported by logs. Excellent habitat for scorpions! Most gardens had a few trees and usually a mulberry tree which would have provided leaves for the silk worm but also mulberries for people to eat either fresh or dried. Needless to say, we were more interested in the berries, which were delicious. In the garden of our little house were literally dozens of fruit trees, so we ate fruit nearly all the year round, harvesting and drying apricots and pomegranates and eating peaches and cherries as soon as they became ripe.

When we had first arrived, we found the pace of life was probably much as it had been for the previous thousand years. There were a few modern amenities such as a sort of electricity which lit up just a few lights in a dull sort of way. There was no running water or sewage; it was a case of make our own arrangements, which, just like all the local people, we did. An outdoors long drop was built in our backyard, and we built a sand filter to filter the water from the nearby canal. Whilst we were there the World Health Organization (WHO) installed piping from a nearby spring to taps in each block. Before they did this, we would give gallon containers of water each day to our neighbours. The children would gather in the afternoon outside our gate each holding a bright-yellow plastic container.

Our little cottage had a stunning view of the river and valley. We bought some fabric, and Sandra sewed curtains and mattress covers. Soon we had a little home. There were just three rooms and a bathroom and hallway. The hallway was quite wide, so we made it into a sort of kitchen. Our local friends had a kitchen outside with a fireplace for cooking, but Sandra preferred to cook on a little kerosene stove which we placed by the door at the end of the hall in a box with a vent to the outside. I found a carpenter who built us a kitchen dresser. The last thing that we needed was a pressure cooker, and we could cook meals. Sandra tried some local recipes but also even managed pizza and steamed puddings. We invited people to our house and got to know our neighbours.

Faizabad was quite a conservative society, and usually the men would meet men in a guestroom beside the gate, while the ladies met each other in the garden or inside the main house. Just down the road from us was a girls' school, and the wife of the owner of our little cottage was the headmistress. Sandra soon became great friends with Hasiba, and Hasiba would bring other schoolteachers to visit. They asked her to help them with their conversational English, and Sandra was happy to oblige. Most of them read English well but hadn't had the opportunity to practise talking.

Our two boys were befriended by one of the local young men who watched over them as if they were his brothers. The boys arranged for someone to send us a rugby ball, and then they tried to teach the boys to play rugby. Rugby was incomprehensible to the local boys, and usually they ended up laughing too much to run. However, playing football was universal, so they tried more of that. We became part of the local scene. And sound as the boys experimented with the local musical instruments – a drum made from pottery and a sort of stringed instrument made from a used milk powder tin with metal strings and a horsehair bow like a violin.

There were a few vehicles in town, mostly belonging to NGOs that were there giving aid and helping to guide the province into the twentieth century. To get around town, everyone simply walked – it was often quicker as the roads were really rough and clogged with donkeys, donkeys pulling carts, the occasional large truck, sometimes camels and lots of people. Whenever we wanted to go to the bazaar or visit friends, we also would walk.

I was volunteering this time for a different NGO and they had a vehicle in which we could drive between our house and my office and go further afield.

I quickly found the vets and local people I had met on my earlier visit. Most of the work that the vets did at the clinics I had started nine years ago consisted of vaccinating cattle, sheep, and goats, and treating lame donkeys or mules. I went with them into the high summer pastures to vaccinate sheep and goats. For a bit of excitement, there were sometimes injured horses after a buzkashi game. Buzkashi is the national sport and a sort of cross between polo and maybe rugby. It involves a team of riders whose aim is to transport a headless goat carcass from one end of the field and back again whilst the other team is trying everything in the book and not in the book to prevent them and steal the carcass. The horses visit the vet afterwards, and the riders visit the hospital.

Checking on vet clinics was not my full-time job, and I was only working part time with another NGO, so I could fit in other stuff like checking the cow behaviour paper and Faizabad-style "emailing" it to Carola, who had by this time moved back from New Zealand to Germany. This entailed working on the text on my laptop – battery powered and charged by a solar panel – transferring to floppy disc, sending the disc by United Nations mailbag on the weekly flight to my office in Peshawar, Pakistan, and then they would email it for me to Carola in Germany. The return answers had to go the same route in reverse. From email to reply was at the quickest one week and sometimes up to two weeks. For urgent communication we had a satellite phone, but cow papers don't rank as urgent or merit spending USD$5 per minute.

We had some fun with that phone as it was the only way the local Afghan people could talk to friends and family who were not living in Faizabad. Within Faizabad, there was a manual telephone exchange that was virtually the same as the one which had been operating in Inglewood when we had first arrived in 1974. Many of our local friends and acquaintances had relatives overseas and would often come and request to call them up on our phone – at $5 per minute – the only problem was that culturally to say "hello" in less than about two minutes was impolite and unthinkable – so by the time they had said "Hello" and "How are you and your family?" etc., their dollars were finished, and no messages had been passed. We hit upon the idea of me doing the first minute of the call and passing the messages on to people whom I didn't know and therefore didn't need to do the whole "hello" thing, and then I could pass the phone to the relative standing there, and he could do the proper hellos until the time ran out. Everyone was happy.

My other part-time job in Afghanistan, apart from phone operator, was for a German NGO as assistant administrator of a drug rehabilitation programme amongst the poorest people I had ever come across. The main administrator, Yaqoobi, was well-known in the area and was much better at doing the day-to-day work, and he could speak the local languages better than I could.

Much opium poppy was grown in that poorest-of-the-poor corner of the world as it fetched the best return for any crop that you could get. Unfortunately, the local people discovered that opium smoking was a great way to relieve pain from ordinary ailments, such as arthritis, when there were no medical services anywhere near and unaffordable anyway. It was also a good relief for starvation and you could spend your days drugged and not notice the pain of an empty stomach. Worse still, opium blown into the face of a crying infant quieted the baby as well – the result: an impossible situation of drug-addicted people when almost all the able-bodied people in the village were using opium. Our organisation employed local doctors and social workers to set up cold-turkey detox and rehab centres in villages. There they delivered good food and vitamins and, later, medical care for these people. I was able to just be the Western person there who reported to the donors where the monies were spent. Several times I drove with Yaqoobi up the river valleys to visit these villages – well, Yaqoobi drove, and I accompanied him.

In the meantime, Sandra and my two younger boys were living in the town of Faizabad with me continuing their school work and working out how to live Afghan style. Watching life in front of us, we would often wish we had a video camera to record great ways of doing things with very little resources as well as lots of interesting animal behaviour. These days you can see lots of great and curious cow behaviour on videos on the Internet – is it real? Yes, usually, and probably they didn't even have to train the cows. Very often we would see amazing things when cows were left to themselves to be themselves.

I would hear early in the morning the young boys collecting the one or two cows and a heifer from each household, calling them to follow up the steep hillsides to graze on what they could find amongst the rocks or what leaves they could reach on the trees. These were not your typical three- or four-hundred-kilo New Zealand milking cow – they looked about the size of a yearling – and neither did they give a lot of milk. However, when your daily requirements for milk consist of enough for a cup of tea and maybe a little yogurt, then one "chinnie" or about three hundred millilitres is enough. And on the sort of feed that these cows were getting you wouldn't expect any more.

Later in the evening as the sun was going down, the boys would return to the town with the cows behind them. At the edge of the town, the boys would say goodbye to the cows, and the cows would wander off towards their own home compound. At the gate, they would lift the latch or bang on the door to enter, cross the yard, and find their sleeping place. Clever cows. At least they were clever enough to learn where to go home. Just the same as the cows In New Zealand, that I had painted with orange numbers for my research, it seemed had easily learned which cows were their group and which cows were the bosses, and which order they liked to come to be milked.

I wondered how the data analysis was progressing.

I was sitting in our little cottage in the village in Afghanistan, reading the newly arrived "email." The final draft of the paper Carola had written using the data we had collected had arrived. Her analysis actually showed that some cow behaviours that everyone thought were obvious really did exist on paper, scientifically. It also showed some things that were not so obvious. One such observation being that cows maintained a sort of marching order in the herd which was not the same as the order in which they preferred to be milked. It was also evident that the dominant cows knew each other and were spread throughout the herd where they could run things as they liked. They were not, in fact, as we had thought, at the front of the herd, but they each had a place in the herd where they ruled, some at the front, some in the middle, and even some at the rear. What I was seeing in the village was a small picture of how cows can learn where to go and can organise themselves without too much fuss. I never saw any lame cows in Faizabad although I did treat a few donkeys, so maybe the fuss driving cows to the milking sheds in New Zealand was part of the problem.

Unfortunately, our stay in Afghanistan was cut short on 11 September 2001 by the terrorist attack on the World Trade Centre towers. Many people around the globe can remember where they were when the news broke of the aircraft flying into those buildings, and we are the same. We were sitting in our garden enjoying the last of an autumn evening when some guests who were staying with us suddenly ran across the yard holding a short-wave radio: "Listen to this," they said – and we did. It was many weeks later that we got to see the whole event on television, but by then life had changed abruptly for all the Afghan people. And sad to say it has not improved much since.

Several days before this happened, there had been an assassination attack on the main leader of the resistance to the Taliban forces. The Taliban wanted to take over the entire country and impose their version of strict Islamic Law. The only things standing in their way were Masood and his Northern Alliance forces, and the city of Faizabad where we were living. Now with the U.S. news, there was an immediate reaction – everyone knew that the USA would attack the Taliban in Afghanistan as they were hiding the leader of Al Qaeda, who was the possible mastermind of the 11 September attacks. Mixed with mourning for Masood was the knowledge that the Taliban would surely increase their attempts to gain the stronghold of Faizabad. All United States citizens had to immediately leave the country, and we also thought that we may have to leave. In Faizabad, where there had been upwards of a dozen expats, there were now just us and one other person. I had the dilemma of safety for my family and looking after the local internally displaced people who had next to nothing with the winter fast approaching. The weekly UN flights for NGOs like ours, and who would carry families, stopped, and the Red Cross flights also stopped flying. Winter would soon close the mountain passes, so we decided that we would travel overland to Pakistan by horse and then travel by minibus back to Peshawar the same route that I had travelled earlier before there was any air service. I would return to work in Faizabad, whilst the family would stay in Pakistan. I completed my work, the U.S. forces did their work, and life in Afghanistan continued on in much the same manner as before.

We returned to New Zealand in April of the next year in time to see the publication of our paper on walking order and milking order in cows, which did seem a little of an anticlimax.[1] Since then, we have managed to revisit Faizabad a couple of times and are still in contact with friends from there, who now use cell phones and apps instead of our satellite phone.

Back in New Zealand, I was now able to say that the farmers are right – I have the data – cows walk into the yard to be milked in one order and then shuffle themselves to another slightly different order to enter the actual parlour and then walk back to the paddock. But further than that, I can now tell farmers that this order, although not perfectly exact, should not be tampered with by, for example, not giving the cows enough space to move around in the collecting yard or by trying to force Number 48 to get milked before the right place in her timetable.

Cows will literally dig their toes in, and the result is that life for the foot becomes a bit more risky. Cows, although they are not humans, are not dumb animals, and they have their own routines which keep every cow under control and safe – that is, as long as we let the cows be cows and provide them with enough space.

A farmer in my own area had real problems getting his cows to come into his herringbone bails to be milked. He would move them from the feed pad where the extra feed was in big troughs to the round yard which led into his milking shed, and then he would shut the yard gate. The cows would then just stand there all close together and refuse to come any further; several would get pushed into the herringbone entrance but didn't come any further. I had been several times to try to think of ideas to solve the problem. One day he rang me.

"I have solved it!" he said and added, "My worker just broke his arm."

"Whaaaat?"

"Well, I was just getting the cows in when my worker came off his bike. Someone took him to the hospital to get him checked out – his arm was broken – so that left me to milk all the cows by myself." I was racking my brains trying to see how this was going to be a good solution.

"So I thought, I will just open the gate from the feed pad and hope they come by themselves, and they did. I didn't even have to come out, or push them, or even close the gate." He said all in one breath.

"Don't change anything. I am coming with my video camera to the next milking."

I duly came with my camera and tripod and caught perfect cow flow on video. The gates were open, and some cows were in the yard just standing around the edges whilst the others were walking right between them and into the milking bails. With plenty of space in the yard, the cows had room to overtake and change their order. Usually, the farmer had pushed them all into the yard where they were so tightly packed that the ones in the front, who usually tried to get milked later in the day, were in the way of the ones wanting to go first. Result – traffic jam.

A bit of a pity that someone had to suffer a broken arm to discover a solution. Surely it would have been better to have the right information at hand, the very information that I had just printed in my paper. I now use that video to teach about getting good cow flow – without any more broken bones.

There were other solutions that I now was able to pass on, which required some experts in fields other than veterinary.

# CHAPTER 14

# Lameness Solutions: Making Tracks (–2008)

AS OUR FIVE children grew up and started thinking about careers, there was not one of them who wanted to be a vet. Maybe I had shown them the worst side of it, or maybe they didn't like after-hours work, or maybe they were just interested in other things. Maybe the seeds for the various careers that they chose were sown around the dinner table.

We had a large dining room table where everyone was welcome. When Sandra and I got married, one of the things that we decided was that we would have lots of guests and lots of talk around the table. She said, if I did the inviting, she would do the cooking. She had learned this while growing up. Whenever I had visited Sandra's home, which, as you might remember, was quite conveniently on my way home from university on my motor scooter, there was always food and talk around the table – never much quiet with six children in her family ranging in age from five to twenty or so. Sandra had told me that her university biology professor had said to the class one day that he was educating mothers to be so that they could talk to their children about all sorts of things – as well as be good scientists. The around-the-table discussion covered a wide range of subjects – practising ideas on the rest of the family – who could rubbish them or hone them. Everyone got to say their thing, opinions flowed back and forth, and one particular person was usually declared right, more often than not, in order to finish the discussion! One of my sisters suggested to Sandra that she should write a book about what went on around the rosewood table. In our New Zealand home, the table was no longer rosewood – it was now sturdy oak – but the talking tradition was something that we certainly carried on. Any topic could be discussed and everyone usually got to say their piece. This proved an oddity to visitors who were raised in smaller families. My son's girlfriend was rather overwhelmed but survived the new experience. Now they are happily married and have gotten used to around-the-table discussion.

Our homeschooled children tested their thinking and debating skills around the table and then launched out into the big wide world either to further study or the workplace. Whether the table discussion had anything to do with it or not, we found our eldest son studying, not to be a vet but rather to be a civil engineer. His course was at a nearby polytechnic to begin with and then extramurally via a polytechnic in Wellington. During his second year, he needed to get a job to get experience – and to get some cash, of course – so he started work with a roading firm nearby. They had a contract to reroute a section of road between Inglewood and New Plymouth, which included a bridge over a river, a long section of road, and a culvert to allow a stream – and the fish in it – to go under the road. Lots of experience and more talk around the table. We call that section of the road "John's Road" as he did all sorts of jobs whilst practicing on that road, from surveying to driving a roller on the final surface. Now people can drive in comfort and at a good speed on a well-drained straighter road. And so began the roading, drainage, etc. discussions with my civil engineer son, who went on to university and now is much more able than me to advise on cow tracks and drainage. Just as well he didn't decide to be a vet, or I would have been no wiser concerning roading and cow tracks. The first thing that I learned was that it is always good to ask the experts. When you want to build a road, ask an engineer, not a vet. Or maybe we should also ask the user of the roads or the tracks – the cow.

I for one, as a driver, knew what sort of roads I liked – or didn't like. There was one local section of road that always annoyed me – something wrong with the camber possibly – and I thought that the engineer who designed that or made it must not have been thinking of drivers that day. Some roads are nice to drive on, others so-so, and others, well, not good at all to drive on. In my travels around Afghanistan, I have driven on some of the worst roads in the world. So bad were the boulders that were strewn on what was called a road that on our return from every road trip all the springs on the Toyota HiAce had to be replaced and sometimes the body welded back together. So now I began to think about cow tracks from the point of view of the user. What is a nice track for a cow to walk on, what do they like and not like? These are the sorts of questions that I was asking myself as farmers kept telling me that it was obvious that the cause of lameness was the tracks that cows walk on. This piece of observation by farmers had turned out to be true – bad tracks were part of the problem. I had confirmed by my studies that the maintenance of the tracks definitely was one of the big factors in lameness.

So if you were a cow, would you like a steep track, a bumpy track, a long track, a bendy track or "scenic" one, or a what? I think that cows, like humans, seem to like straight, level, soft surface tracks, not muddy and as short as possible. They will "tell" you if they like it or not by how well they walk. If the track is really well made, they will walk at a good speed, and you won't be getting impatient waiting for them to get a move on.

Our son, John, having completed his university studies, started work with a large engineering firm. He was part of a team working on the drainage of a new section of motorway north of Auckland, and listening to him talk about it, I discovered the astronomical cost of roading – he didn't just talk in hundreds or even thousands of dollars; it was into the millions. How does a farmer budget for this sort of expense? One thing that I learned was that if you do a good job the first time around, it makes economic sense. One of my farmers near Inglewood found out that one of the best materials to use to build a long-lasting walkway for cows and vehicles is concrete. But it is expensive, so he embarked on a project to concrete all his tracks, ten or twenty metres at a time, and by hand as he could afford it! Patience paid off, and now, forty years later, the tracks are still there and still in great condition.

Of course, that is the ideal in order to avoid constant maintenance. So how to design and make tracks like this from the outset? Or alternatively, how to upgrade or fix what you are stuck with? Of course, when you are starting out to build a new walkway or road, you need to consider what sort of traffic will be on it, most of which will be cows but also more often these days heavy tractors and machinery. Then, you ask yourself: what sort of weather will it need to survive through? And if you are in Taranaki, that means rain, and lots of it.

My civil engineer son is now a water expert and teaches me about the damage water can do and how to avoid that with good initial construction and drainage. Just as we had three Ds for treating lame feet, we also have three Ds for looking after tracks. Drainage, Drainage and Drainage. That means that in the wetter places like Taranaki, you really have to work on getting the water off the surface of the track. As much as it is fun to walk through puddles, they need to be gone quickly before they do damage by soaking into the surface and destroying the structure of the road. But perversely, if you make the track really steep and crowned so that the water runs off too fast, it will cut channels into the surface and scour out sections, not to mention that the cows don't like to walk on steeply sideways sloped surfaces. This building of walking tracks begins to get rather complicated!

Back in my early career, before I had all that civil engineering knowledge, the best thing was to go out and see how people had done it and what worked. Most of the farms around where I was working were old, established, and small family farms. As the years went by, most of them were adding more cows (traffic) and adding more land by joining with the neighbour but keeping the old walkways. Mostly they just extended them. Is that going to be good enough?

Here is a question – how heavy is a cow? The answer is not as heavy as a truck. So does it need a highway to walk on? In fact, a walking cow puts more weight per square centimetre of surface than a truck or tractor. And a cow is not rolling along like a tyre when it is not braking or doing wheelies. The cow's foot, when it is walking, is pushing its weight forward. And there are dozens of cows all with four feet and all walking together – this spells damage to a track. No wonder they need constant maintenance.

Walking also might spell damage to the cow's feet. Just like tyres wear out with driving, cornering, and braking, so do cow's feet – at least where the sole hits the road. However, fortunately for the cow and unlike tyres, the cow's foot is continually growing, just like your fingernail. Mostly our walking cows manage to balance wear and growth quite nicely. But if the cow is not walking along, if it is housed in a barn and only has to walk a few hundred metres or less in any day, the nail of the foot can easily get too long and needs to be trimmed off. If the nail is not trimmed, the toe gets longer and longer, and the cow ends up standing on her heels with her toes pointing upwards a bit like Persian slippers – we even call this "slipper foot" – very uncomfortable and resulting in lameness. Where cows are housed, the feet need to be trimmed sometimes as often as two or three times each year. The walking cow is different – it self-trims. But it can also have the opposite problem where the sole gets too thin. This could be because the track surface is too abrasive or simply because the cow is walking too far.

I received a call from a farmer who had a lameness problem.

"Over half my herd is lame," he said.

This was going to need some detective skills. He had really good records of which cows were lame. We sat down with his records and a map of his farm. It turned out that most of the cows getting lame were from one of his two herds. Typically farmers with a large number of cows will divide them into groups or separate herds. This farmer also had a long farm. The only difference between the two herds was that one of them walked twice as far as the other. So now my question was how far is too far? Well, that depends on what the surface of the track is made of. Usually, I found, the tipping point at which there began to be a problem was when the main track was more than one and a half kilometres long. That's not far – except when you consider that the cow has to walk both directions twice a day in order to get milked and to return to the grass. That adds up to six kilometres. A good solution is to let the cows feed in a nearby paddock, and then the next feed can be in a further paddock. And of course, the further the cows have to walk, the better the track needs to be.

So where this farmer had one herd always walking a long way, it spelt disaster for them. Another solution which can be tried is to only milk those cows once in a day – it cuts the walking distance in half and often reduces the lameness.

It was hard to make the leap from a small track to what amounted to an almost highway-grade road. Many would upgrade them by simply adding a new top surface, but if the camber was incorrect or if the drainage was poor or if the base was poorly constructed, the new surface didn't last long.

I was visiting a farm and saw a beautifully drained track, no puddles along the side and all in good condition. I asked the farmer where he found out how to get a track as good as this – "Well, I used to be a drainage contractor before I took up farming," he explained. "So, close to the milking shed, I cut these drains every five metres on each side of the track."

I had often found that many people who took up farming as a new career had experience in their previous jobs that helped them in farming and helped me with advice to pass on to other farmers who didn't have the benefit of that background. My main drainage tip came from this drainage contractor–turned–farmer. It was to cut small drains like he had and then use the cut-out section for a sort of dam to direct the water into the opening.

Farmers are very inventive and come up with all sorts of solutions for difficult sections of track. When I think I have seen everything, there is always some new creative idea. I have seen tracks made from one metre wide concrete where cows have to walk single file; tracks that are as wide as a paddock; tracks made from old concrete railway sleepers made from cast-off astroturf, second-hand fishing nets, shredded rubber, carpet, even small sections of track reinforced with plastic sacking fabric over sand. Finding the right material is sometimes a lucky dip.

Often when traveling in parts of the country with which I was unfamiliar, I would go to visit the local quarries. I was visiting a farm in another country and watching the cows come in for milking. The cows were walking very reluctantly along what looked from a distance like a nice enough track. On closer examination, however, I found that the track surface was made of really sharp stones – I would not like to walk on these even with boots on. No wonder the cows were slow. What to do about this – the track was well constructed but just lacking a softer walking surface on the top. According to my experience, the top layer should be a nice soft crushed rock that binds together to make a smooth comfortable walking surface. The best material that I know of is a certain type of crushed limestone. So we got into a vehicle and set off to visit some local quarries. At one quarry, I spotted a pile of what looked like the perfect material. I picked some up in my hand. It did indeed appear to be the right stuff. "Maybe we could give this a try," I said. One week later I was back at the same farm again and was standing on the newly resurfaced track when the cows appeared around a bend. They were running, actually bounding along, not running away but enjoying the new surface – what a difference! We had found what the cows liked to walk on. One problem solved.

Another problem I often see is steep and slippery surfaces. One day in my rounds, I went to pregnancy-check some beef cows on a small farm that used to be a dairy farm. After the job was done, I had a bit of spare time. So I had a look around the old dairy parlour built in the 1930s. At the exit where the cows went out to go to the paddocks after being milked, there was a door to a steep slope, but instead of a slope, there was a flight of stairs with a narrow strip of sloping concrete down one side. I asked the farmer about it – "O, the strip is for me to ride the motorbike down. The cows like to use the steps." Sometimes steps could be a solution to that steep-track problem.

In Wales (*on the same farm that my mother-in-law and a cow had a slight mishap)*, there was a big problem with a long slippery slope down a hill then through an underpass underneath a road and up the other side, a quite complicated and treacherous piece of walkway for the cows to negotiate. The farmer said it was always slippery and muddy. I suggested steps. These steps would have to be not too high for the cows to go either direction – up or down. On the way up, as we learned from the old step-up milking sheds, cows could manage to step up quite a high rise, even up to forty or forty-five centimetres. But going down is a different story. With her head out in front as the heaviest part, the centre of gravity is quite far forward. To go down a steep step is very scary and dangerous. But cows don't seem to mind going down a height of just ten centimetres, as long as the landing surface is flat and solid. So, looking at my Welsh farmer's problem, whatever fall they had from the top of the slope down to the underpass, we had to divide this into ten-centimetre-high steps. We came up with fifty steps – that is a lot. How long should each step be? Well, whatever the ideal might be, we had to fit them in the space that there was. In order to fit them in, they could only be seventy-five centimetres long or half the length of a small cow. This turned out to be pretty much ideal. In Wales, as indeed in many parts of the U.K. in houses and guesthouses, we had been faced with many staircases that were quite steep – a major difficulty with Alice, my mother-in-law, who was travelling with us, aged almost eighty and a little bit tottery. Often the problem was uneven steps or sloping steps. So for the cows, as long as we kept within the guidelines – even short steps should work. In fact, the farmer built the steps, and the cows loved it – it felt much safer than the slippery slope. I show the picture of those steps to farmers who are planning to build a track up or down a steep slope, and I suggest instead that they try steps. One farmer in New Zealand in a neighbouring province to Taranaki had a similar problem to the farmer in Wales. I persuaded him to try steps down to his underpass. He first just made steps down the exitway from the milking shed right down to the underpass at the bottom of the hill, all fifty of them. Then, because the cows liked them so much, he built a second stairway going up for the entry pathway. I often hear comments from farmers about that cow staircase as it is easily visible from the main road and an impressive sight.

Cow stairway

All the time I was learning about building and maintaining walkways, I would write down what I learned and soon had a section in my little booklet from which I could teach farmers. Not everyone has a civil engineer in the family.

I wrote about the main problems, what needs to done to fix them, cheap quick fixes, and also how to build the best sort of track that will outlast the farm. It was a sort of layman's guide to track building and upgrading.

In many cases when the farm tracks were improved, the lameness reduced, but sometimes, the lameness didn't get better. And I still saw terrible walking surfaces with very few lame cows. This was going to be a balancing act between the two main contributing risk factors for cow foot injury: track maintenance or facilities and cow flow or cow handling.

## CHAPTER 15

# Ballroom Dancing (2002–2004)

"ONE TWO THREE, one two three."

"Not that foot, the other one."

"Now the men turn around." And so it went on. I thought that I would never learn to dance – not sure that I wanted to anyway. We were in a local hall and practising, brushing up, or just plain faking our ballroom dancing skills. Some of my farmer friends were experts, and some were just like me with two left feet. Sometimes we laughed, and sometimes we just gritted our teeth and tried our best not to step on other people's toes or run into them as we twirled around. Well, twirled is a euphemism. Just as well there was supper at the end of the practice/lesson.

After returning to New Zealand from Afghanistan in 2002, having published my second paper – the one on cow walking order as compared with their milking order and dominance position, I was back at work at the coalface. I was still talking to farmers and university people. *How to connect the world of research and theory with the real world,* I wondered. I was giving seminars to farmers on how to be patient with your cows because, I could now confidently tell them, their cows all know their place in the herd, and we shouldn't try to change that – or cows will react maybe in ways that are unpredictable and damaging. The whole life of the cows is sort of choreographed – a bit like ballroom dancing.

When we arrived home from Afghanistan to return to the business,

I found that Ray, my vet partner, along with the staff of the vet business, had come up with a brilliant idea to get to know clients and, at the same time, celebrate the end of the milking season. This idea was to hold an old-fashioned black-tie ball. Inglewood Vet Services had run their first ball in 2001 in the grand town hall in Inglewood before we arrived home. Now, back in Inglewood, I was roped in to the next one to be held that July. Sandra was asked to help with decorating the hall which she loved and ended up taking over for the next eleven years with each successive ball getting better and better. Our garage is still full of various boxes of drapes and props that were part of these decorations and reused year after year.

I was now faced with learning to do the various set dances! Luckily, not many of the others knew how to do them either. So a farmer and his wife who were part of a dance club had been enlisted to give lessons in a six week lead up to the next ball. These became great social nights – and I did learn a bit of dancing. First it was the waltz, one two, three, one two three, and so on. This was easy enough as it was slow. I was supposed to lead Sandra, and so we sort of had four legs. Then came the foxtrot and other fast dances. Luckily, Sandra had a better idea of what to do, and I usually just followed. Rather like the cows. Following the cow in front was on my list of twelve cow characteristics as number six.

By now I had a bit more of a grasp of what normal cow behaviour was, so I had listed twelve things that I thought all farmers should know about cows. Sounds like quite a formidable list. Number one was that cows have a particular style of walking, where they very cleverly put their rear foot in almost exactly the same place that the front foot occupied. Definitely smarter than I was, who didn't know where my feet were whilst trying to dance the can-can polka. Cows know how to stand to balance and see where to put their feet because they keep their heads down – that was number two. The next three characteristics (three, four, and five) were what had been the subject of the study and paper just recently published – cow walking order and dominance. They have a walking order and a milking order, this is maintained by the dominant cows who are spread throughout the herd and who thus set the walking speed of the whole herd. Number seven was about cows bumping into each other side to side – which they try to avoid, just as I tried to avoid the other couples on the dance floor. Eight to eleven were related to the cow as an animal of prey. Number twelve reminded us that cows love routine – they are creatures of habit, and just like me with the ballroom dancing, once I knew what to do, I could just follow along.

All this was a compilation of what various farmers had told me and which I had verified by watching cows for myself and now also by good research. However, research is no good unless you can get the new information out to where it is needed. This was the beginning of a new direction for me not just in learning a new skill, ballroom dancing, but also moving from the coalface of vet work to teaching and training of farmers and vets.

I decided to try this out full time for a short period. We would go overseas again – this time just across a little bit of sea – Cook Strait – to the South Island of New Zealand. I organised a tour of the South Island. It was to be a seminar roadshow – travelling from north to south down the east coast and then back up again following the west coast. If I could teach farmers about cows, I surmised, they could understand why their cows acted the way they did and what normal behaviour was. It was no use teaching them to let a cow be a cow when they didn't really understand what a cow normally did.

In order to transport the whole staff of the vet clinic to the vet ball and other functions, the vet practice had acquired a large green van. This would be our transport. We packed all my lameness gear, seminars, videos, and data projector along with our baggage for a three month stay in the South Island. Taking our two younger boys with us, along with their school books, Sandra and I set off across the Cook Strait by ferry. Then dairy vet practice by dairy practice, we worked our way down south. I booked us into camping ground cabins so that Sandra and the boys had somewhere to do their homeschooling during the day while I went off to run a seminar for farmers or vets. And on the weekends or when there were no seminars, we were tourists. I was enjoying the bonus, combining business with pleasure. Not sure which was which, as teaching was such fun. The South Island tours were to become a regular event every two or three years, but this was the only trip when I took some of my family.

New Zealand is such a scenic place that much of the trip was near to tourist sites, but we soon learned to be more like locals than tourists as it was much cheaper. At one tourist-serving corner shop, we thought that we would like to get an ice cream cone before going to see the attraction. We were amazed at the price for a single ice cream, so we went to the local supermarket and purchased two litres of ice cream and four spoons for less than the price of one cone. This was not very long after our return from Afghanistan, so we could often compare the sights of the two countries and noted many similarities. One area where there was no similarity was the roadway. We remembered driving along roads in Afghanistan cut into the side of a mountain with no safety rails. Or along the edge of a flooding river. Once on a trip up the valleys we were passing another vehicle coming the other direction, and there was only room for one car between the side of the cliff and the step drop down into the river. As we drove slowly past the other vehicle, ours started to drift sideways off the road. "Get out, quick!" said Yaqoobi. We did. And he drove through without any further slipping. We never had an accident, but I am sure there was a whole crowd of guardian angels keeping the vehicle on the road.

We arrived home from the South Island, and I went back to normal clinical work but with a new dimension and desire to reach a wider audience with what I had learned.

My second paper, on cow behaviour including milking order and walking order, was presented at a conference in Europe by one of the other collaborators. The connection with lameness was part of the discussion, so the people at Massey University suggested that I should check out another conference that was specifically about lameness; maybe I could go along and learn and share my pennyworth with the world experts on lameness. "They are held every two years in different countries around the world. How about you go to the next one in Slovenia and talk about your ideas?" I have to admit, I had to look in an atlas on a map to find Slovenia, snuggling between Austria and Croatia, with borders also with Italy and Hungry, and a tiny slice on the Mediterranean Sea.

New Zealand has a name for innovation in dairying, and often people had come from other countries to see how dairying was done in New Zealand. A group of farmers from Ireland with a similar system of dairying with outdoor cows had visited several times and seen what I was doing in the area of lameness and cow behaviour. They hit on the idea of inviting me to Ireland to teach on lameness. Much as they loved coming to New Zealand, it was a long way from home and cheaper anyway to bring just the one of me to Ireland than to bring a dozen farmers to me. So the idea arose to combine a trip to the lameness conference in Slovenia with a visit to Ireland. Of course, my wife jumped at the idea of joining me, and at least I knew where Ireland was to be found. Business with pleasure again.

By now, our two younger boys were in their late teenage years, so we were free to go by ourselves. So we simply booked tickets to travel, no visas needed – such an easy place to get to compared with Faizabad in Afghanistan. Just fly to Frankfurt, change planes, and go on to Dublin. Other progress had occurred to make life so much easier with the technology which now we all take for granted.

When we had travelled to Pakistan fourteen years earlier, we had needed a whole crate to take our computer, printer, and monitor. We had fax machines and only the beginnings of Internet. Eight years later, when we travelled into Faizabad in Afghanistan, we had taken a laptop, which was much easier to travel with. The laptop in Faizabad ran by battery power, charged by a solar panel and a couple of truck batteries. We charged our camera batteries the same way. Camera digital technologies weren't quite as advanced or as portable as cameras that used film. We took lots of photographs, and our exposed camera film went on the same weekly UN flight as our emails on their floppy disc. The film was developed in Peshawar and returned with printed photographs as well. Travelling off to Ireland, we had a digital camera in our bag – several steps eliminated.

Since then, Faizabad has caught up with technology too. We had the opportunity to return a couple of times to see what was happening and to attend meetings to support the ongoing work. On a visit the same year that we went to Ireland and Slovenia, we saw people driving cars instead of four-wheel-drive vehicles in Faizabad, whilst a man rode down the road on a donkey while talking on his cell phone. On another visit, we were to fly by small plane to the Faizabad airfield, which is just a few kilometres out of town. The pilot, wanting to know if the weather was fine, called up our friend on his cell phone and got the local weather report and the all-clear to fly in.

In our suitcases to fly to Ireland, we had fitted all our technology – laptop, cell phone, navigator, and digital camera – as well as clothes for winter. Just as well. We landed in Frankfurt in a snowstorm and flew on to Dublin over snowy fields in the south of England. We had left twenty-five-degree temperatures in New Plymouth to arrive in Dublin at four degrees. Luckily, the cold snap was short lived, and we were able to enjoy Ireland, complete with a visit to the makers of Cowslips in Belfast. What we saw there were many Irish farmers who were doing dairy farming in ways that were very similar to the farmers whom I knew in New Zealand and having the same difficulties with working out what was the root cause of their lameness. Even the cows that produced the milk for Baileys (Irish whiskey and cream) got lame from time to time. Farmers all over the world come up with brilliant ideas using just what is handy. I was really impressed to see a great idea to take back to New Zealand using a tractor steering wheel to turn a hoist for lifting a back foot of a cow – in just the perfect position.

In between visiting farms, we got to do a little bit of touristing. Ireland was about the eighth country I had been to, and my world was getting broader but also more connected. One day in Dublin, we stopped off to see the Book of Kells in the Trinity College Library in Dublin. The Book of Kells is an ancient manuscript of the New Testament of the Bible copied out in around the ninth century. There in front of our eyes was blue paint made from finely ground lapis lazuli that had come all the way from just near Faizabad in Afghanistan – right near where we had been living – to Dublin in Ireland!

The scenery in Ireland is magnificent, being old-world green instead of new-world green. And we could now take a few more photos – although the storage disk in the camera was limited to mere megabytes. But which castle should we photograph?

On our way around the farms in Ireland, we visited several that were part of old estates complete with castles. One that we visited also had a museum of science from the nineteenth century and a well-kept walled garden. Sandra was delighted by this and enjoyed looking around – we now have crocus growing in our garden in Inglewood. It was great being able to travel around on good roads, albeit torturously narrow, to speak (mostly) the same language as the people we met, and to enjoy great Irish hospitality. This trip also coincided with our thirtieth wedding anniversary, celebrated in Galway. Our keepsakes from Galway were a cladagh ring and a tweed hat. We have since returned several times to Ireland doing training for farmers and teaching farm staff about cows as well as enjoying catching up with old acquaintances and those who visited us in New Zealand. And all the time sharing and hearing stories about cows and hearing what works with Irish cows and might work with cows in other places.

After our time in Ireland, we flew on to Austria and then bussed to Maribor, a ski resort in northern Slovenia, where the lameness conference was to be held. "The International Symposium on Lameness in Ruminants" was an impressive title, and an impressive conference it was. Maybe small in numbers but vibrant in innovation, ideas and a driving curiosity to work out how to solve lameness in dairy cows as well as sheep and goats and other ruminant animals. Here I met the authors of the textbooks on lameness that I had studied at university and referred to in my work in New Zealand. These were excellent books for the housed cows in the northern hemisphere, but they had not given me the answers that my farmers needed to manage lameness for the outdoor walking cows in New Zealand. Then there I was about to tell the authors that although they may be right about Northern Hemisphere lameness in housed cows – our cows in New Zealand and maybe in Ireland were in a different situation. I was definitely the new boy on the block, but despite this, they were all interested in what people from "down under," like myself, had to say.

Here also, I met the second Roger, Roger Blowey, who was to encourage me in my research and questioning. His book was one that I had referred to in New Zealand about the different conditions of lameness and how to treat them. He became another great role model. He was also a questioner and one who asked the farmers for their opinions and what did they think about how cows had gotten lame.

We had another thing in common – looking at the bones of the feet of cows. Whenever I amputated a claw in order to relieve the pain for a cow, I would take the claw home and bury it in my compost or leave it in a bucket with holes just big enough to let in the flies. Months later, I would be able to collect the meatless bones and horn to examine. Roger and I were to confer on these bones over the years. My family knew not to go near any old bucket at the bottom of the garden. I did make progress in that area – I began to boil the feet to retrieve the bones, which was much quicker. Roger and his wife, Norma, kindly took us under their wing, as I discovered they had done for many others before us. He encouraged me to keep questioning, and he became my go-to when I needed answers for tricky problems later. Meanwhile Norma also looked after Sandra and introduced her to the other ladies. We shared many great times together.

After collecting data for years, from every cow that I had treated for lameness, I had been able to compile records from nearly two and a half thousand lame cows with white-line injuries. This was the data that had proved the farmer's observation that white-line injury seems to most often occur on back feet of older cows and fairly often on front feet of young cows. I had written already about this and connected the position of this injury to cow behaviour. I had presented a paper about this at a conference in Sydney a few years previously. This time, instead of talking to cattle vets and researchers about lameness, I was talking to lameness vets and researchers about cow behaviour. I had found that the behaviour of cows when they are afraid or pressured by being too close together, although it wasn't their usual behaviour, was still distinctive and could result in injured feet.

My paper at the lameness conference along with other research at the time was heading in a new direction, away from the traditional idea that all lameness was the result of poor diet in indoor cows, to the idea that there were many risk factors all operating at the same time and resulting in a really complicated situation. And lots of interesting – and still ongoing discussion. So there was I to add a few more risks to the list – and risks that were rather hard to measure. Impatient people, for example. Or poor cow flow caused by something maybe in the facilities or the people. My earlier research in the 1980s had established that poor walking surfaces would contribute to more lameness and that is fairly obvious, but impatience – how did that work?

With my ideas of what could be risk factors for lameness I had listed cow flow or movement of the cows along tracks and into the milking bails, as something that could indicate whether the cows were doing their "ballroom dancing" well or not. And if not, maybe a reason why there was more lameness. Maybe a measure of how patiently a farmer behaved might be tied to cow flow. If cows were pushed to go faster than they wanted to go it certainly didn't look like ballroom dancing. Even if no one was stepping on anyone's toes, there certainly was a lot of shoving and slipping.

More like rugby! One farmer I was talking to over a lame cow pointed to his neighbour who was an ex–All Black rugby player.

"You should see him bring in the cows," he said. "I leave for my cows after a cup of tea in the afternoon, and I am about halfway home with the cows when my neighbour leaves to get his cows – and he still beats me home. I think he learned his cow-handling skills at the back of the scrum on the rugby field because that is what it looks like from here," he concluded.

The simple solution, it seemed to me, was to let the cows do what they wanted to do at the speed they liked, and all would be well. That depended on knowing what speed a cow was likely to go and what was normal for the cow. But what if that speed was not fast enough for the young workers who wanted to get home to dinner? Would better design of facilities work – or better management of cows? Or both? This raised a bunch of questions or areas to address.

Maybe I should concentrate on patience. How do you define patience – or better still, how do you encourage patience? Patience when playing rugby is called biding your time and quite different from the sort of patience you might need to herd cows – or passengers onto a plane.

## CHAPTER 16

# From Vet on the Ground to Flying Vet (2004–2006)

"THAT IS TWO and a half kilometres to this end here," I noted. I was with a farmer on a farm track riding in an old ute that he used as a farm vehicle to get a measure of the length of his track. "That seems a long way," I added. "What sort of lameness are you seeing the most?"

"A bit of this and a bit of that, mostly foot rot, I think," answered the farmer from behind the wheel as we bumped and slipped around a corner on the track. This made writing a bit difficult, and later deciphering what I had written would be a problem.

In my early years of working with farmers, being a vet on the ground, I was always trying to work out how to solve the lame-cow problem, or at least get a clearer idea of what was going on. I had hit upon the idea of a check list to try and quantify the various contributions of each factor to the likelihood of some cows becoming lame. This check list arose out of my first research paper with the fifty-eight factors. The list then morphed into a sort of audit form where I scored everything that I could think of, giving each factor a score from 1 to 5. Now that I was back in New Zealand and still having a reputation for my interest in lameness, I would often be asked to come and look at some farm or other somewhere in New Zealand, to audit it in order to see why there were too many lame cows on the farm. I called this an "investigation," and I was a bit like a lameness detective. I didn't have a Sherlock Holmes hat or a magnifying glass; I just had my checklist. This audit form was my equipment, and these investigations became another part of my job along with seminars and training.

"Let's just stop here and measure how wide this track is," I said, fishing out from my pocket another tool – my measuring tape.

"Oh, this track is the widest," said the farmer, "but the cows only use part of it, so maybe it doesn't need to be this wide." I made a mental note of this observation.

Life always seems to become more complicated before we can get it simple. The question was what to write down and what to just ignore. My audit form by now had become fourteen pages long! There was a section to fill in about the tracks or walkways – including some questions on how the cows walked on the tracks and whether it caused people to get impatient. There was a section on the design of the milking shed. Did the cows like it and move through it well, and what did the people do about encouraging the cows to move? Did they use gates, shouting or maybe even dogs? If a track was five metres wide, I gave it a score of 1 – very little risk; if it had right-angle bends, it scored 3 – a bit more of a potential problem; if it had too steep a camber, measured with my spirit level, it could score up to 5 – high risk.

"What time do you bring the cows for milking?" I asked. In my lameness investigation, visiting the farm and filling out my form, I was trying to find out what was the normal life for a cow on that farm. This could sometimes be difficult and often involved detective-like skills as you have heard earlier!

Walking across the yard, I felt almost dizzy. It felt like the ground was on a slope. "Do the cows like this bit of the yard?" I asked.

"Well, no, they all try to avoid it. Sometimes they even fall over here." Another note was written on my form.

Filling out my form helped me remember what to ask, and helped me get more than the farmer's perspective on life on the farm. I could soon tell by the behaviour of the cows whether they liked the farmer or milker and whether they liked the milking shed. In fact, sometimes I found that the cows were acting as though they were afraid of something, and then the detective had to find out what it was. Very often the culprit was slippery concrete or stones on the concrete that the cows didn't want to accidently step on, or, as on this farm, a section of sideways sloping concrete in the yard

I wrote down everything that I saw on the farm and took my form home. Then I wrote a list of recommendations, my report. In this case, the farmer was right, there was a lot of foot rot – and I thought that the piece of track that the cows were avoiding where they walked in single file was probably where the cows were picking up small stones between the claws – a risk for foot rot. I suggested that he upgrade that particular piece. I also suggested that he roughen the slippery, sloped part of the yard with a scabbler. He managed to do this, and his lameness certainly did reduce.

Roughening slippery surfaces so that the cows could get a good grip was a common solution we tried. But this was not a one-solution game.

I once visited a farm where the cows didn't want to come into the milking bails. On occasions I had found that there could be electricity shorting into the pipework of the milking shed, meaning that the cows would sometimes get a little shock from touching the pipes. Many farmers were convinced that this was their problem. Just like us, cows don't like little electric shocks. In New Zealand, farmers routinely divide up paddocks with an electric fence,[1] which can be easily moved, instead of a permanent fence. By visiting many farms, I had found that often the stray electricity was coming from an electric fence, especially if the main unit where the fences were "plugged in" was near the dairy shed. There were lots of other possibilities though, and I had found a technician who could find even the tiniest bit of electricity that the cows might be feeling.

"I am sure there must be electricity in the shed," complained Bill, "but your technician can't seem to find it." I had watched Bill trying to get cows to come into his herringbone area to be milked, and all they did was turn around in circles at the entrance, terrible cow flow and most likely damaging their feet.

"No, I don't think so," I said. "I am sure there is no electricity here."

But Bill was convinced and wouldn't think of anything else. Lameness detectives sometimes have to take extreme measures to prove a point. One rainy day, I visited his farm in bare feet and walked where the cows walked and leaned where the cows leaned. No electricity. Bill thought that the electricity was in the rails in the entrance area, so I went over and even put my tongue on the rail – still no electricity. But because I was there, I saw one of the milkers poke a cow in the belly with a stick in order to prod the cow up to the front – another mental note.

"Bill," I said later, "I think there are a few things that we should try. There is never just one thing that is the reason cows are becoming lame." I gave him a few ideas of things we could do, such as trying to shorten the distance that the cows walked. Also in the list was to ban all sticks from the shed. He soon began to see fewer lame cows. Now I always ban sticks. If I see sticks, I know there is a potential problem. It usually means that cows won't come because they are afraid of the stick and have to be "encouraged" by the same stick – a vicious cycle.

I was in South America visiting a farm to see some lame cows. We were working around the corner from the milking area when we heard a shout. "Help, we need a vet!" (In Spanish, of course.) We ran over to where there was a cow bleeding profusely. Someone had poked a little too hard with a stick in the cow's stomach and found a blood vessel. Another reason to ban sticks.

I had learned that when cows get afraid, they act differently, usually by being difficult to handle and refusing to move. Then the people do more things that will make the cows afraid – like using sticks. Maybe we should concentrate on eliminating the things that cows were afraid of and those things that made life difficult for cows. The idea was to audit a farm for all these things.

But there was only one of me, and I was beginning to travel all over New Zealand. A better idea would be to invent a package that farmers could use themselves or that their own vets could use with farmer clients. This would be a way we could help farmers not only solve their lameness problems but also prevent cows getting lame in the first place.

Turns out that Dairy NZ had a similar idea.

Dairy NZ is a group that conducts research and development for dairy farmers. The aim is to find the best ways to farm with dairy cows. Each dairy farmer pays a small levy per kilogram of milk that they produce, and this money is used to fund Dairy NZ and to get the information out to the farmers. Dairy NZ liked the way I was working, and so we got together. For a whole milking season, we worked on producing a programme for farmers which we called Healthy Hoof because that was what we were aiming at. Healthy hooves. Other dairy-producing countries had similar ideas and similar names for their programmes. Healthy Feet in the UK was also in its infancy.

The plan was that when a farmer joined Healthy Hoof, they would receive a folder of information and a visit from a vet to audit their farm and to help them to improve their treatment skills to get those cows that were lame back on their feet as quickly as possible. I trailed a modified audit form or checklist on twenty or so farms in the South Island. This checklist we developed into the Healthy Hoof Farm Audit Form – much briefer than my fourteen pages and with pictures to illustrate what was the ideal farm. My booklet became the basis for handouts for the farmers, and we also produced a field guide to the various types of injuries that you might see on the foot of a lame cow.

The next job was to train vets to be Healthy Hoof providers. I had already designed a course for vets to learn about lameness called "Stamping out Lameness," so we started the training with that. At this course, they learned about lameness and shared ideas about how to teach farmers.

Farmers were also keen to learn about lameness. I was already giving seminars all over New Zealand and had been overseas to Ireland. I had useful information that my research had verified. These seminars were popular, not so much because of the information but maybe because I had lots of stories to tell and videos to show of real-life farms in New Zealand, or maybe because there was a cup of tea and food. The investigations and seminars were taking up more time, and I needed to travel to other towns to help farmers and vets understand cows. Hopefully this would this result in better farming practices and fewer lame cows.

I was starting to need wings. Our trip to Ireland and Slovenia turned out to be the first of many overseas trips. People seemed to enjoy my style and combination of investigation and training as well as the connection to New Zealand and New Zealand farmers. Also, I was now gathering even more stories and experience along with "anecdata" that now confirmed my scientific data results instead of the other way around. After our first trip, it worked out that once or twice a year, we would travel overseas. For the next fifteen years, we spent so much time overseas that when we finally decided to become New Zealand citizens, we had not been present for enough days during the last few years in the home country!

I had started going to the lameness conferences every second year. This opened up more opportunities to visit other countries where there were pasture-based cows and where farmers wanted advice on how to manage the cows. Because there were many factors involved with what might be a risk for a cow and where it might become lame, my portfolio was broadening from just fixing lame cows. It now included the behaviour of cows, the behaviour of milkers, cow flow and dairy facilities, like tracks and sheds.

The next Lameness Conference was to be in Uruguay, and I wanted to continue to speak for the vets discovering that pasture-based cows have somewhat different conditions to handle than the housed cows that are more typical of the Northern Hemisphere. I registered for the conference. I was to give a talk about helping farmers understand cows.

At Massey University, there were students from around the world doing postgraduate studies in dairy cattle medicine and management. There were quite a few from South American countries. One of these was an Argentinian by the name of Gonzalo, who heard that I was planning to go to the Uruguay conference. He had attended one of my annual talks for the Massey veterinary science students.

"When you go to the conference in Uruguay, could you also come to Argentina and give some of your seminars there?" he asked. "I will organise it for you."

At the same time, another New Zealand farmer spoke to me. He was managing some farms on behalf of a New Zealand company in Chile and he wanted some advice on his lameness programme and facilities.

"Is there any chance that one day you could come to Chile?" he asked.

"Well, in actual fact, I am flying past on my way to Uruguay," I replied.

A trip to South America like this sounded fun. Of course, I planned to take Sandra along; well, she decided not to be left behind. In our previous travels, Afghanistan was seriously difficult to get to, Europe was seriously easy, and South America was in between.

We were booked on Aerolineas Argentinas to fly to Buenos Aires, then to Chile and back, then to Uruguay. Shortly before we left, we received a phone call from the travel agent: "Your flight to Buenos Aires has been cancelled, but you can go the day before or the day after." We decided to leave a day earlier in order to connect with our flight to Chile. We were promised a bed and meals in Buenos Aires.

We arrived in Buenos Aires to find ourselves in a sort of limbo – we were a day early, and no one seemed to have told the airport office that we, and about a dozen others, were going to need to be looked after for twenty-four hours. We discovered this when we finally found the office behind a door that looked more like the entrance into a cleaning cupboard than an office. This airport, like almost every airport worldwide, was under renovation. The first time we knocked at the door, we were told that the office staff had all gone off to lunch, which in South America can take quite a while. Our group waited for an hour or so and then almost literally pounced on the first person who arrived back at the office door. After much talking, that person found the relevant person who did know about us. He put us all in taxis to be taken to a hotel for the night. The next day they collected us and took us back to the airport, so we "arrived" on the correct day and at the right time!

The flight from Buenos Aires to Chile was magic – first miles and miles of flat cultivated land and then suddenly the Andes mountains.

"Please fasten your seat belts and remain seated as there may be some turbulence." It certainly was bumpy! The rugged snow-covered peaks seemed to be just outside the windows, almost within reach. Some even seemed to be higher than we were. I was reminded of our flights into and out of Afghanistan flying over the Hindu Kush mountains. Hindu Kush means "Hindu killer," which is probably quite true as any person from "Hindu land" (India) wanting to cross this formidable barrier could very easily perish. I crossed the Hindu Kush several times on horseback, and I can tell you flying is much better fun.

Chile was more efficient than Argentina – at least at the airport. We had no sooner left the mountains behind than we were descending into Santiago. No offices in cupboards here; it was a bright new shiny airport. Renovations complete. We spent the day and night in Santiago, exploring the area where our hotel was situated. It was the first place where I saw a "green" building with plants growing right up the side having been planted in containers at different levels all the way up the building. There was a watering system to keep them green.

From Santiago, we flew south to the lakes area, where the New Zealanders had bought dairy farms, three of them. Chile is an amazing place – long and thin. Flying south, you could see the sea on one side and the mountains on the other. There was a thin green strip, which was Chile, in between. We landed in Osorno and disembarked from the plane, and there in front of us was what looked like Mount Taranaki. It turned out to be a lookalike – Chile's Vulcan Osorno, a "twin" of our mountain. You could have fooled me. In fact, I have tricked many people since then when I show photos in my seminars. Even without the familiar-looking mountain, the countryside looked just like New Zealand. Green paddocks with cows dotted here and there. One major difference was soon visible – hiding among the trees were splashes of bright red – the Chilean firebush. It was in full flower. The long sprays of fiery red flowers look a little like honeysuckle flowers but without the scent.

Vulcan Osorno

Chileans, of course, had been dairy farming for much longer than New Zealand, but most of their experience and any innovation had come from Europe or the United States. Many cows were housed, and if they were outside in paddocks, they were handled by cowboys riding on horses who often seemed to think they were herding beef cows. In the south, we saw the influence of early settlers from Germany evident in the old wooden buildings everywhere. Most of these buildings, unfortunately, were in a very poor state of repair. Every now and again we would see an old restored building which was truly magnificent. We photographed a huge century-old wooden, German-style barn.

The lakes district of southern Chile also had similar problems as Taranaki, including lots of rain. This fell at some times of the year by the tubful. We visited the three New Zealand–owned farms and also a couple of others either owned by their friends or which were possible purchases. Advice for building tracks was sorely needed here as well as some know-how on handling dairy cattle.

On one farm, we met some new South American friends, Francisco and Paulina. Francisco was managing a farm for his brother-in-law. He had previously been working with IBM. As always, when you come to farming with experience from another field, you can be more open to solving problems with lateral thinking. He was experimenting with different glues for the blocks which many of his cows needed for their lame feet.

Having forged a connection to Chile, we flew back again to Argentina where we were met by Gonzalo, who treated us to some really neat Argentinian cultural experiences. We went to a tango show, "Only in Argentina"; visited an old, above-ground cemetery and church; and even went to a soccer game to see the Bocca Juniors play. We arrived very early at the stadium on a bus with other tourists and were shepherded to our place in the stands. Crowds of supporters of the opposing team began to fill an area behind wire and ringed by security personnel. At the opposite end of the field, the home fans were filling another huge stand. Apparently, this arrangement is so that there are no riots. How to play football is something that the South Americans could teach the Kiwis about. We watched and cheered for the locals. There was a lot of singing and jumping up and down in the stands, so much so that we feared that the whole stadium might collapse! At the end of the game, we were again shepherded out of the stands this time into a museum under the seating. We stayed in the museum for some time until the out-of-town supporters had been bussed out of the vicinity. The tourist operators didn't want any of their clients getting caught in a battle between locals and the opposition.

However, I had come to teach the South Americans about dairy cows, so we set off on a whirlwind tour of farms to give seminars on cow behaviour and lameness. This time, the countryside was more like Australia or South Africa, and the trees were also similar – huge jacarandas and casuarinas reminded me of Harare in Zimbabwe. We were definitely in the Southern Hemisphere. We drove on long straight roads for miles. When we arrived at the farms, they often had a guesthouse for visitors, so we would stay on the farm. The houses were very Spanish in style, so the similarity between Australia and South Africa finished there. And with the barbeques. I think there was a tiny bit of bread and maybe a leaf or two of salad, but most of the barbeque was meat in capital letters. And delicious.

After our week of touring in Argentina, it was off to the Lameness Conference in Uruguay, in the beautiful Colonia del Sacramento. This is an old-world town with cobbled streets and tiled roofs, situated on the Platte River, the border between Uruguay and Argentina. Old cars, many in mint condition, were parked by the roadways as if just left there in about 1930 something.

Arriving at the conference was a reunion with many of the same people we had met two years earlier in Slovenia. We had all been hard at work studying lameness and trying to put the picture together better so that we could prevent it. In New Zealand, we had been thinking about our Healthy Hoof programme, but so far it had not begun. We walked the old cobbled lanes and talked about cows. I had been teaching farmers and vets about cow behaviour and characteristics hoping that an understanding of how the cow acted would help farmers be more patient. This was also my topic at the conference.

I was dispelling the two wrong ideas – that a cow is a human and that a cow is a dumb animal. It is not a human; neither is it totally dumb. I had started basing my seminars on the differences between cows and people and where we are similar.

The first big difference I had noticed is that a cow is easily scared, and that is because it is a prey animal. In the wild, if it doesn't look out, it will be dinner for a predator! Because of this fact, the cow is different from humans. It has different eyesight – not as clear as ours but more panoramic. The cow's hearing and smelling is much better. This is because it needs to see, hear, or smell its enemies while they are a long way off so that it can move to protect itself. And a cow can't move very fast. A cow needs fairly flat ground to walk on and preferably not slippery. It needs to keep its head down to look for safe places to tread as I learned while trying to spy on cows through the bottom of a hedge. If it stumbles on one foot, it needs its head low in order to balance. The cow moves more like a truck and trailer than a motorbike. Or a human.

There are also similarities to people – the cow is a social animal – like us. It has herd rules and leaders and followers, like us. It gets lonely and insecure if you leave it alone, maybe like us? And just like people, it has habits and likes routine.

All these traits I had learned by watching cows and farmers. They were all on my "Twelve Characteristics" list. Many farmers instinctively knew them, but somehow they hadn't realised how to use these traits to advantage. Training the cows to have good routines and allowing them to be normal have great advantages. The biggest disadvantage of not allowing the cow to act like a cow was frustrated people who got impatient with the cows and ended up pushing and shoving them. Often the result was lameness from excess pressure on the feet. Remember, a cow is heavy and has relatively small feet to balance and take the weight.

There was now a new category in our lameness conferences – it was called cow behaviour and welfare. That was where I fitted in. I was beginning to get a reputation as someone who could understand cows – or a cow whisperer. I would rather have been called a cow listener.

The big issue in the dairy industry was becoming welfare or cow comfort as it was called. Milk was being marketed as coming from contented cows – but were they really contented? How could they be contented if they were getting lame, or if they were afraid or couldn't behave like the cows that they were?

As the conference wound up in Colonia, we were organising buses to return to the airport near the capital, Montevideo, when a Dutch vet working in Uruguay asked if we would like to see a farm on the way, and in that case, she would drive us to Montevideo. We were delighted to grab the opportunity. So Mette took Sandra and I and another vet to a farm about halfway to Montevideo. We were soon busy snapping photos. Especially the other vet from Australia who was a keen photographer and just about to write a book on cattle. Then I saw a horse and rider bringing in the cows for milking. He was amazing and totally unlike the other South American cowboys I had seen elsewhere on this trip. He was gently handling the cows, and the cows were happily going at their speed. I asked Mette if she would speak to him in Spanish for me and commend his handling of the cows.

"You can tell him yourself – he speaks English – in fact, he has been to New Zealand." She introduced me to Sebastian.

"Whereabouts in New Zealand did you work?" I asked.

"In Taranaki," he replied.

"Oh, that's where I come from, in a town called Inglewood – did you go there?" So he asked the inevitable "do you know" question.

"Do you know a guy named Peter with green hair who plays soccer for Inglewood?" My son! It turns out that whilst in New Zealand learning how to handle cows, he was also playing soccer and teaching his New Zealand friends how to handle the soccer ball. He didn't actually play in the Inglewood team, and needless to say, the local team for which he did play had a winning streak that year. His visit had coincided with a period of hair colour experimentation for one of my sons, which had made him extra memorable.

We returned home after an extended trip away, with hundreds of photos of cows from different farms, different ways of milking cows, and lots of different and beautiful scenery. Sandra used these to make a collection of scrapbooks so that if I went back again in the future, I would remember the things that had impressed me enough to photograph. And it seems that I had also made an impression with Kiwi ideas, as we were invited back quite a few times over several years, involving lots of flying.

Being a flying vet requires patience. There is a lot of waiting around, lining up, and not knowing what is going on. No wonder they sometimes call the economy class the "Cattle class"! Luckily, however, the air crew and hostesses realised that we were slow and needed time to find our seat and stow our bags even if there were some of us that were a bit bossy and required a bit more patience. Generally, flight attendants know how to be patient and polite, not to push and shove us onto the plane. We were starting to get plenty of experience of these patient people over the next little while. How did they teach those flight attendants to be so patient?[1]

My biggest question was turning out to be how to teach patience to stock handlers. I often quote the old adage (which I am sure is not really true) "patience is a virtue sometimes found in women but never in a man." Maybe you can't teach such a thing; it might just have to be caught.

## CHAPTER 17

# New Angles (2008–2010)

ONE DAY, MANY years before the events on this chapter, Alice, then my mother-in-law to be, who was a florist, had quietly whispered to me, "You know that even florist's daughters like to receive flowers," and I had taken her advice – although often the flowers were wild flowers or some blossoms from a friend's garden souvenired on the way home!

Being a florist and married to a nurseryman, one of my mother-in-law's long held dreams had been to visit the Chelsea Flower Show in London. This dream finally came to pass when she was a widow and almost eighty years old. And she shared the experience with me.

My in-laws were world travellers having started out their married life with a big OE to the U.K. and Europe. Years later, as they kept travelling, one of their "tickets to fly" was to do with being a florist and a nurseryman. Even before we were living in New Zealand, they would travel there nearly every year to attend a Teleflower[1] conference, which is how it had come about that Sandra had visited New Zealand as a teenager even passing through Inglewood. So, of course, they continued the yearly visits once we moved to New Zealand to live and started bringing up their grandchildren there. My father-in-law was also a Rotary member and travelled for them to visit various aid projects.

When we lived in Pakistan, they came and visited there. But until I got my "ticket to fly," the Chelsea Flower Show had remained just a dream.

One of the great benefits of my interest in lameness, which is not a subject with many followers, was turning out to be that I got to travel all over the world visiting farms, seeing first-hand what the situations were like in other countries and both spreading and collecting ideas. My "ticket to fly."

I talked to my new friends from the U.K. whom I had met at the lameness conference in Uruguay. We thought that some of the same information about cow behaviour and how to handle cows that I was teaching the outdoors farmers would also be useful for the indoors people.

"We think that you should come to the U.K.," said my U.K. friends.

"Stay with us too," joined in Roger Blowey and his wife, Norma. "Then we can all go together to the next lameness conference in Finland."

So I was invited to come and do a series of seminars in the U.K. Going to the U.K. at that time of year would be the perfect opportunity to take Alice along and also see the Chelsea Flower Show.

Traveling with an elderly person around the world is no small feat; we had to go a bit slower, especially where there were stairs in every hotel and house! However, we could enjoy the sights and visit things we had never thought of.

We started out in London and of course the Flower Show. As Alice was a mobility-restricted person, we had organised a wheelchair for her, which meant that she could rest whenever needed but also meant that people in the displays opened gates to let her in where most people never went. Our photographs now included flowers and gardens, along with the old buildings and tourist sites, such as Buckingham Palace and the Tower of London, which Alice remembered from her OE fifty-five years earlier.

For my mother-in-law, traveling with a vet meant that she went to places that other florists likely never visited.

Leaving London, we began a short seminar tour around the U.K.

and Ireland, stopping off first at the home of Roger and Norma in Gloucestershire. Roger is a little older than me but is in many ways similar to me – always asking questions and with great enthusiasm. We have had the immense privilege of meeting people from all around the world who enrich our experience, and Roger and Norma were some of them. Roger had a vet practice in Gloucester, and he shared many of his ideas with me. I visited his garage where he boiled up his cow foot bones. I was still the new boy on the block, but a friend like Roger was a great encourager. We went to visit some of his client's farms and I gave a seminar for some of his farmers. I chatted lameness with Roger whilst Alice, Sandra, and Norma chatted flowers and other stuff. Several years later, we all met up again, this time in New Zealand at our home and – wouldn't you guess it – followed by another lameness conference!

My parents-in-law had not started out as a florist and a nurseryman but instead as radio engineers. They had met whilst still studying. Alice and Peter on their OE in the U.K. had worked for a short while with Marconi as radio engineers. Whilst there, they had stayed with a family related to Peter. There was a son born to that family during their stay, so Alice had a connection with that family. At the time of our Chelsea Flower Show visit, this son was the only one of those relations surviving. He was living in a village near Gloucester. So taking Alice and some nice fruitcake, we went to visit. This is how we were introduced to David, an ex-accountant who knew everyone! Sitting in his lounge sipping tea from the ancient family tea cups, and surrounded by photos of relations was a little surreal, not to mention stories of how he had suddenly learned that his aunt had left him a dozen houses in her will! The nearest real relation in the room was my wife, who was probably his third or fourth cousin. But David was a bachelor with no children of his own, so he was keen to catch up with what the next generation was doing – as well as to pass on everything that his generation had done.

So much for the relations – from now on, Alice got to tag along with my farm visits. At that time, there were quite a few farmers from New Zealand living in the U.K. influencing how dairy farming was done using pasture and allowing the cows to walk back and forth to the milking shed. Not to mention the various British farmers who had visited New Zealand and picked up lots of ideas.

We headed off north through Wales. When we reached the far north of Wales, we were surprised by a glimpse of how far the New Zealand influence had stretched. Travelling along a narrow road in search of the farm that had asked us to come, following the navigator directions, we turned a last corner.

"Look, a New Zealand–looking dairy farm," exclaimed Sandra. There, as we came over the hill, was a huge rotary milking parlour, looking just like those in New Zealand, except that they had not put a roof over where the cows were riding on the platform. We could clearly see the cows riding the carousel. There was just a covering for the people putting the milking cups on the cows. This set up, we discovered, was to avoid having too much water run off which an extra-large roof would collect and that would have to be got rid of. Imagine our surprise to find out that this parlour was designed and built in Inglewood, New Zealand, right where we lived, and then dismantled and transported to Wales in containers to be re-erected there by the Inglewood team!

The problem on this farm was lameness – that was why they asked us to visit – not to just view the scenery and check out their milking parlour. I had asked them to bring in some lame cows for me to see what type of problems they were seeing, and so there was a group of cows waiting. As I began to treat them, I noticed when I opened up a white-line injury that there was a different sort of smell that many of them seemed to have.

"Look out!"

At that moment, there was a shout from further down the cow yard – a cow had wandered too close to Alice, who was looking on and bumped into her, knocking her to the ground. Lame cows forgotten, we picked her up and dusted her off – no damage done fortunately. I became famous in that area as the visiting vet whose elderly mother-in-law was knocked over by a cow. I was also to become famous for the other piece of advice that I gave to the farm owner here, of which you have already heard – to construct some steps for the cows where they had to go down a particularly steep section of track.

As I travelled around talking about cows and how they behave, I often heard stories that confirmed what I was saying. When I say that most of what I pass on is what farmers have told me – it is true.

"Do you know that your cows recognise you?" The farmers at the seminar nod and immediately think of a story of some time when a cow recognised them. I met two keen young milkers on that U.K. trip who told me a great story. They came from a farm that had two herringbone milking parlours side by side. There were two entrances to each side, and the cows in the large rectangular waiting yard could choose where they liked to go to get milked.

"I milk on the left," said one of the young guys, "and all my favourite cows always come in to be milked on my side in the first two rows."

"I milk the other side, and the 'best cows' – my favourites – always come in first too," added the other guy.

"Well, one day," continued the first young man, "we decided to try an experiment to see what would happen. Guess what it was."

"Don't tell me . . . you swapped sides?"

"Yes!" They decided to swap sides and milk on the opposite side to their usual. The cows, within two weeks, had reorganised themselves and were following their "favourite" milker. I often tell that story when I want people to realise that cows will recognise them, if they are good or bad!

Hearing that story, I wondered to myself: what is the main thing that the cows like about their favourite milker? If you were milker, would they like your personality, your clothes, your smell, or might it be that you like your cows and so they like you. I could tell from the story that the cows knew who was who and obviously some preferred one whilst some preferred the other. I could also tell by the enthusiasm of the two milkers that they really liked their cows. My question was: what were these guys doing that caused the cows to like them?

One farmer thought that he had the answer – he wore the right colour clothes. His friend who occasionally milked for him would always have trouble getting the cows to flow into the milking bails. In frustration, he talked to his friend.

"Try wearing my hoodie – maybe the cows will like that," suggested his friend. And when he borrowed his friend's hoodie to wear, all was well. I did secretly wonder if it was the smell of weed on the hoodie that was making the difference.

Clothes or something about them somehow seemed to be a sort of key. Out on a farm one day, I was trying to get Baby, the cow, to behave for me. Baby was the pet cow of a friend of mine who often had people visit his farm to enjoy his quiet animals. He would let people pat Baby, and she would just stand happily whilst everyone patted her. She would even let children sit up on her back. I wanted her to stand next to me and look like she was talking in my ear, and then Sandra could snap a photograph that I could use for my introduction to a seminar. However, every time I came towards Baby, she would walk away.

Frustrated, I went back to the farmhouse.

"I reckon we could trick Baby," suggested the farmer's wife. "Try these." She held out a pair of used overalls from the washing basket. So I used the clothes trick to get a photograph of that mischievous pet cow. When I donned the overalls and went back to the paddock, Baby became a different cow – and I got my photograph – to which I attached the caption: "Have you herd what I am saying?"

Baby talks to me

Of course, I also hear the opposite stories – where a cow remembers a person who did something they didn't like – and got their revenge later. One farmer who had a rotary platform sheepishly told me how he had been working with a new heifer to help her get used to the milking machine.

"She was being unteachable or maybe just flighty, and I am embarrassed to admit it – I lost my temper. There was a piece of plastic pipe just nearby, and I hit her with it. Not hard, you understand, but enough to give her a fright."

Some weeks later, the farmer was walking around the back of the milking shed just beside the rotary platform when a cow suddenly kicked him.

"This just never happens in my shed." He was shaking his head. A fact that I could easily believe as I often visited that farm where the cows were really quiet and well behaved. It was the same heifer – maybe she was getting her own back!

We were certainly enjoying collecting stories from around the U.K. and Ireland. It was soon time to pack up and leave the UK and head with the British contingent to the Lameness Conference in Finland.

This was summertime in Finland and the first time I had travelled this far north. It was light enough all day and all night to see quite clearly across the lake outside the hotel. I have a photo taken outside our hotel room at 1:00 a.m. What was I doing up at that hour? We had just returned from a boat trip on that lake to a forest lodge where we had been watching a log walking demonstration. Something you might only see in Finland. The logger walks on the floating log and makes it go wherever he wishes – and tries not to fall off! Just for the record, none of the performers fell off, and none of the audience were brave enough to have a try at log walking themselves.

The conference itself was a meeting up of old friends again – not just the ones with whom we had travelled from the U.K. on the same plane. Of course, we were there to discuss lameness, and this time, I really thought that they were just dealing with the Northern Hemisphere's sort of cows that lived in barns. There was some discussion about a type of white-line disease that I had never heard of. The vets seemed to have quite a lot of problems with fixing it, and the lame cow needed several treatments – I concluded that the white line seen in indoor systems must be different from what we see in New Zealand. Better to go home and deal with our own lameness problems.

However, at home, there wasn't much time to think as we were off again to Europe only six months later, this time back to the U.K. to visit the places that we had missed and then to Denmark – the country at the forefront of cow welfare.

I was beginning to get a reputation as a person who somehow knew about how cows thought and behaved and who could tell stories to illustrate the points. And since I came from New Zealand, I was therefore an "overseas expert." In reality, I was just gathering information and ideas from all over the world and sharing them as stories with vets and farmers. I had become the flying vet who could be the interesting speaker for conferences. What most people don't realise is that most of what we all teach is gathered from a big basket of information that we have gleaned from many sources and in my case have been fortunate enough to confirm with research.

Of course, the side benefit of travel is that you can catch up physically with friends from all over the world whom I had met in my travels. This trip I caught up with many families or friends – from my best schoolfriend from Zimbabwe, now working as a civil engineer with my son in the U.K., to the daughter of one of our local Inglewood farmers who had studied and lived in Denmark. Plus vets, farmers, and also a couple of friends from our time in Afghanistan who were now back in Europe and working at an agricultural training school where I gave a talk to the students.

Cow welfare was the hot topic and area of interest all around the globe. I went to a conference for cattle vets in Alice Springs, Central Australia. There I met a person who was keen on the welfare of cows that are so sick or injured that they cannot stand up – we call them "down cows." That is seriously "lame."

Each of the speakers had been asked to give a talk on some new idea or innovation that made life easier for vets and cows. I had given a short talk on an idea of how to lift these "super lame" down cows and carry them to a barn or place where they could be treated, fed, and watered. This was another idea that I had heard from one of my farmers and that I was now sharing with others.

One of the questions I often ask young farm workers in order to see whether they had been observing cows was: does a cow get up by standing on its back legs or front legs first? The answer is that the cow first lifts its rear end and then the front. Completely the opposite to the way we would stand up from an all-fours position. When a cow had difficulties standing the farmer would help her by lifting the back end with what was called hip lifters. Then if the cow was able, she would stand on her front legs.

My lifting method was very simple and used the traditional lifters to lift the back end of the cow and a wide strap, such as is used as a tie down for loads on trucks, to go under the front of the cow. A tractor, fitted with forks at the front, parked behind the cow and with the cow facing forwards. The lifter was attached to the cow with plenty of padding over the hips and then hung from the forks close to the tractor. The strap was passed under the brisket just behind the front legs and the ends tied to forks at the front. The forks were then gently elevated and slight adjustments made so that the cow was about level. Then the whole cow could be lifted straight up off the ground. The tractor could then drive with the cow, right across the farm, if need be, to a good place for her to rest. This was a good use for the various truck tie downs that I had found lying by the side of the road and that I had thought would come in handy one day!

Cow gets a lift

I also got a bit of a lift while at that conference. Alice Springs is in the central Northern Territory of Australia in the middle of a desert. There had just been some rain – rare but resulting in a beautiful crop of grass, so "desert" seemed a bit of a misnomer. Here I fulfilled my dream not of flower shows but of going ballooning. Early one morning, we met the balloon guide, who drove a group of us to the take-off site, where they inflated the balloon, and we all climbed into the basket. What an experience – floating soundlessly over the wide expanse of green desert below, watching the sun rise, and then floating silently down to the landing site for a champagne breakfast. As we drifted along, I wondered if cows enjoyed being lifted and transported effortlessly to a nice warm barn, and breakfast?

Discussing the welfare of these down cows that had to be lifted and carried, sometimes quite a distance, I heard of the cow bath. I knew that water therapy was a treatment used with horses that had done damage to a leg, so why not for cows? I wondered if this could help cows that were "down" because of nerve damage after a difficult calving, which sometimes resulted in paralysed back legs. These cows were really "lame"; they often could not stand at all. Prolonged sitting down caused muscle damage. If the cow could get into a bath of nice warm water and do a bit of aqua aerobics without having to support its weight on its back legs, I thought that this could help.

A bit of research on Google found a cow bath made for really large and heavy cows such as they have indoors. This bath was a big box shape with an opening at the end. The cow couldn't stand and so had to be dragged or rolled into the bath. Then a door closed off the open end and warm water was added. As the water filled up the bath, the cow floated. That was when the dots joined up, and I had the bright idea of not dragging the cow into a bath but lifting it in instead – that way you could have a smaller bath, needing less warm water, and the bath itself could be easily transported using the same method as we used to lift the cow.

My daughter's father-in-law, an ex-farmer and handyman, built me a prototype, and we trialled the water therapy for cows. It was really only useful for the one type of problem where a cow was paralysed due to giving birth to an extra-large calf. Not every cow recovered, but you would know within three days if the cow was going to be able to be saved. Without the bath, there would be up to two weeks of nursing, and even then, the cow may not walk again. The cows appeared to really like the bath, as they happily munched away at the feed that we put in front of them. Think of yourself in a hot tub with a nice glass of something and a good book.

I thought in the end that it was the same as with lameness – prevention is better than cure – and I advise all farmers to aim for their cows to be mated with bulls who tend to have smaller calves. This reduces the problem, and my cow bath had limited use – which is a better outcome.

Fixing lame cows and other problems was like an ambulance at the bottom of the cliff. Everything seemed to point to prevention as better than cure. In the U.K., they were trialling their Healthy Feet programme with this in mind – to keep the feet healthy. They had a group of farmers on the trial, and one of the benefits of being part of the trial was to be able to attend some workshops on handling cows. There the farmers could get a better understanding of how cows operated. Giving the cow behaviour seminars was my job.

The Healthy Feet people also realised that walkways and milking parlours could influence lameness. So we discussed this too, how to improve things so that you didn't get as many lame cows. It was a sort of two-pronged approach. They realised that the more you could get people to enjoy the cows, or at least to appreciate that cows are different to people, the more you would avoid some of the impatience problem. Then if you also made your milking facilities easier for the cows to negotiate, you could avoid impatience as the cows would move more freely. I agreed and enjoyed doing the seminars.

Preventing lameness was turning out to be a jumping-off platform for many areas mostly under the umbrella of welfare. Back in New Zealand, I was thinking about the idea that cows liked people if the people liked them. The Animal Welfare Science Centre at Melbourne University in Australia also had a similar idea – they were working on a programme for people working in the pig industry called ProHand. They felt that if a worker with pigs had a good attitude or opinion of the pigs and actually liked them, they could handle them like "professionals," hence the title "ProHand." The programme was designed to improve this attitude. And the pigs would be better off.

There were some animal behaviourists in the Melbourne group who had been at the last lameness conference, and they thought that the ProHand idea could be modified for dairy workers. They had done some research on Australian dairy farms which had shown that on around half of the farms they visited, dairy cows were chronically afraid of people, and this affected how they reacted to those people. Maybe some training of the people to have a good attitude to cows might make the cows less afraid of the people. More and more the world, both veterinary and people in general, was thinking of the welfare of the cows, not just in terms of whether they were in pain from lameness but also whether they had a good life. More like a gold standard of good rather than simply an absence of bad.

## CHAPTER 18

# Patience Everywhere (2010–)

TRAVELLING WAS FUN especially when Sandra was able to come along. And it seemed that I was communicating. Sandra suggested that the cow flow seminar that we had prepared for a conference in Denmark, which had gone well, might make a good basis for a teaching DVD. So she wrote the script following the seminar outline and added in video that we already had on file. Then I had to make a few extra bits – my worst nightmare – remembering what I had to say and saying it in front of a camera was really difficult. My wife had to have great patience to refilm many sequences dozens of times. I can do a live seminar easily, but to do it according to a script is not my thing – I am an ad lib person. I found a friend who drew some more cartoons and also edited the video. By the end of a year and with this help, we had a saleable DVD titled Cow Flow on the Dairy Farm. This video showed what good cow flow looked like. I thought this could be a great way to teach farm staff about cows, and that way, more farmers would be helped.

That was about the time I met the ProHand people. As behaviourists, both human and animal, they had a different perspective. They thought that if people understood their relationship with cows, then their attitude towards cows would improve, and they would treat the cows better. This could become a good cycle, improving all the time. Instead, many farmers were in what they described as a vicious cycle. If you think cows are dirty and stubborn, you treat them like dumb, dirty, stubborn creatures – which becomes a self-fulfilling prophesy – they behave in stubborn ways and make lots of dirt/dung. So the farmer thinks, *I knew they were like that.* In fact, I had met many farmers who thought that cows were stubborn, just like another four-footed animal – the donkey. It didn't mean that they mistreated the cows; they just didn't understand them. Some of them were in the wrong job or had a poor attitude, but generally they were doing their best.

"Here is someone doing their best," I would say at the beginning of my seminar on how to understand cows, and then I would show a short video clip that I had taken in Ireland.

"Unfortunately, no one taught him about cows, so he didn't really know what to do. Maybe we can help him see what he is doing wrong."

In my travels, I had been in Ireland staying on a farm and watching cows being milked. The farm was managed by an efficient Dutch farmer, and the cows were in excellent condition. However, they seemed to be getting a lot of lameness with many white-line twisting and turning injuries. The person who milked the cows was an immigrant worker from Romania who had never milked cows before. He was very kind and gentle to the cows, but the cows seemed to be afraid of him. With permission, I took some video of him moving the cows into the old herringbone parlour. The milker didn't realise that the cows were quite intelligent and knew what to do, and this resulted in him doing a whole lot of "wrong" things. His face told me "I don't know what these cows are doing."

The real problem I could see in the video was that the floor in the yard and especially up into the milking bails was very slippery, and so the cows didn't want to move fast – it was much safer to go slowly. However, the milker didn't know that and thought that the cows would move quicker if he jumped up from the pit and herded them in. The cows all got a fright when he suddenly appeared and they quickly turned around, some slipping on the concrete, and they moved away from the milker, and the milking bails. So he walked up close behind them and tried to get them to turn around.

The first important thing that he didn't know about cows is that a cow has good panoramic vision because its eyes are on the side of its head. Cows can see things in a wide circle and even behind themselves if they can turn their heads just a little. But if you are behind a cow and can't see their eye or they are too close together to be able to move their head, they can't see you and will try to move further away. Once, for me to use in a seminar, Sandra made an illustration of a cow from behind, and she pasted a large truck sign on the back saying "If you can't see my mirrors, I can't see you." Maybe this should have been on the rears of those Irish cows. They couldn't see, so they just kept on moving away.

All of us humans, including our Romanian milker, have a much narrower field of vision than a cow because we are a predator and have our eyes in front – this narrow field is not a handicap as we can turn our heads around to see what is behind. If the milker here had moved his head around and looked behind, he would have seen what the camera could see – that without him in the way, the cows were moving quietly into the milking position. Maybe he needn't have come out of the pit at all!

Unfortunately, the young man didn't speak English very well, and I had to leave the next day, so I never found out what he was thinking. Maybe the ProHand programme would have found out what he was thinking.

The ProHand idea was for the farmer to do a survey of his attitudes anonymously on a computer – and then do some training about cows and then redo the survey and see if his attitude had improved. They had already written the survey and some of the training when I met them.

"We have seen your DVD on cow flow, and we think it could be good to use for training." They asked if they could use the material in the DVD for the farmers to learn about cows after the initial survey. And then, "Would you trial it with some of your farmers?"

Several farmers with large herds with whom I had worked were interested, so we ran a trial with their staff. They enjoyed the teaching but found it a bit of a struggle sitting at a computer all morning. Maybe farmers prefer to be outside and doing things. They did say that they learned a bit about their attitude to cows. One farmer's wife disagreed with the diagnosis of her attitude and thought that she should have got a better score! Maybe live seminars would work better with her.

I was on farm on one of my seminar tours when I noticed something.

"I hope you all enjoyed your cup of tea," I said as everyone took their seats in the hayshed for the day's seminar. This shed was luxury compared to the one a few days earlier where we had all ended up sitting on upturned formalin containers and the door was rattling in the wind.

"I had trouble resisting the scones too," I continued. "I want to start with a few little questions – that you probably already know the answers to," I said.

"Who can tell me whether the cow's horns are in front of or behind her ears?"

"Neither, my cows don't have horns." A buzz of laughter.

"Well, if the cow did have horns, where would they be?"

"Next question, does a cow stand up from sitting down using its front legs first or the back ones?"

What I realised was that in my seminars I often started out by asking some funny questions about cows to see if people had noticed what cows are like and what they do. Questions like, are the cow's horns in front of or behind its ears? Or does a cow stand up with its front legs first or its back? By getting them to think about cow characteristics, maybe I was doing a similar thing to the ProHand people – getting people to notice cows and think about what they saw.

No time for me to think at home but lots of time sitting on planes – I was off to Europe again – this time to the U.K. again and the Netherlands. All this information about cows meant my new seminars now related not just to the walking cows but also to the ones who were housed. These cows still had people bringing them into a yard for milking and then moving them around in a barn. What we needed was not just an understanding of cows but also of cow flow and how cows act all together. We needed guidelines for moving a whole herd without stress – low stress handling. This was not just my original idea. People had been teaching this for handling beef cattle for a long time. People like Temple Grandin[1] (cow behaviourist) and ideas like the Bud Box (a method of getting cows through a corner of a yard used by Bud Williams[2]) had been around for a long time.

I really enjoyed getting to visit lots of farmers and provoking them to look at their cows. A group called Cow Signals invited me to the Netherlands. One of them had visited me in New Zealand, and so I had met them already. Now they wanted some ideas for their book on grazing cows. They asked me, while I was there, to give some talks at their training. I contacted people in the U.K. and combined this with a visit to England and Wales. After all, who wants to fly around the world for just one job?

I must admit that I had an ulterior motive as by now our civil engineer son had moved to the U.K. and was working on dams there whilst his wife worked in banking. So we were able to combine a visit to them with our seminar tour. Work was during the week, and on the weekends, we visited and went touristing with John and Elaine.

We now had phones for cameras and could take thousands of photos. The catalogue of what we photographed was growing. What you take pictures of depends on what sort of things you are interested in.

So of course, we took photos of dams and reservoirs as well as the usual cows and dairy facilities! Luckily, our interests were a bit wider than that. John's work was in Cambridge, so we visited the university there and looked at all the old buildings and explored places we had heard about or read of. We came across a sign that said "Chesterton Place," so of course we had to have a photo of that to add to the buildings, scenery, gardens, dams, canals, and lame cows.

We were driving down a road on the way to a seminar one day when we spotted an odd-looking collection of white domes. Curiosity got the better of us, and we pulled over and got out of the car to have a better look through the fence. *We will have to ask someone later what that was*, we thought. No need for that! Halfway through the seminar the organisers received a phone call from Internal Security – "Did they have a rental car with such and such a number, and could they speak to the driver who stopped at the radar facility this morning?" I talked to them and reassured them that I wasn't a spy and didn't take photos of radar installations. We continued on, thinking that we had better only photograph genuine tourist stuff.

Although having said that, most of the farms we visited should have been on the tourist trail as well with their beautiful old farmhouses – sometimes well over three hundred years old – as well as modern milking parlours. We stayed in an old castle that had been converted into a modern conference centre. And whilst catching up with some old friends, we walked along a section of Hadrian's wall. Definitely worth photographing. In New Zealand, there is nothing really old – except our house, which was only just over one hundred years old by then.

We found ourselves always comparing ourselves and our countryside with others and where we live. Maybe that is also some of the problem with cattle stockmanship. Everyone is doing it only as they have seen others do it. In South America, they apply beef gaucho–style herding on horseback to herding dairy cows. In Europe, many farm workers are completely new to the job and have no one to collect ideas from, like the Romanian milker – or else they are the fifth or sixth in the line from father to son and have still the same practices that their father taught them when there were only half a dozen cows in the herd. Nobody asked them if they wanted to be a dairy farmer – it was just assumed.

So I tell the story of the day on an earlier trip when I was speaking at a seminar in Austria, which was called "Meet the Real Cow." Beforehand, I was talking to some of the people waiting for us to get started. There were a few who spoke English, but mostly I had to have an interpreter. There was a young guy sitting in the second row wearing a yellow T-shirt with "Patagonia" on the front.

"Do you speak English? I asked. No, he didn't, so the vet I was with translated for me.

"How many cows do you have on your farm?" I said through my translator. He said that he worked on the family farm in Austria, and he just had a few cows which were very hard to handle – and anyway, he hated milking.

After the seminar, we went on our way, and several days later, the vet called me over to see a message that he had received. He translated for me. It was from "Mr Patagonia."

"I got interested in what you were saying at the seminar, and so I decided to try out six or eight of your suggestions. They worked, and now the cows flow into the parlour happily and quickly – and now I like milking – and I like cows." Just as the ProHand theory had predicted.

We moved off from the U.K. and began our little tour in the Netherlands. Starting in the north and working towards the south – to the province of Zeeland – the old one that is! We were now working with the company called Cow Signals, which had originally invited us. They had the innovative idea of looking at the cow and working out things like how healthy it was from what it was doing or signalling. And how happy it was. I was to give some seminars to their consultants about cow behaviour and cow characteristics from the perspective of cows that live in paddocks and not in barns. The consultants were well trained and all great at presentation, so I was a little nervous. They made their information amusing – calling it "infotainment." Entertaining and informative, and therefore attitude changing. Everyone seemed to be going in the same general direction.

At the end of this time in the Netherlands, we went to stay with Jan

Hulsen, the author of the cow signals book, and his family and took some time out for some fun – tasting his homegrown white asparagus and the amazing Dutch cheese from a shop that sold nothing but cheese. It was incredible how much cheese we ate just trying different ones. We also had fun with Jan's pet cows, herding them from a paddock and trying out flight distances and balance points.

During all these travels, I was continuing to find that the thing that people found the most interesting about lameness and cow flow was the collection of stories of what I had seen myself of cows and lameness. And stories that I had heard from farmers. I used these liberally to illustrate my seminars. My wife said that I needed to make things organised and give people simple, catchy, but true headings to make each lesson from the story memorable. The Cow Signals people agreed. "Meet the Real Cow" had been a good start. "Mr Patagonia" had done a fantastic job to remember six or eight things that I had said – I have trouble remembering them myself. The solution according to the great presenters at Cow Signals was to organise the information better. And then it would be memorable. Maybe instead of twelve things to know about the real cow, I should categorise it into just a few groups of things. Maybe five groups, as that is a handful. My cow characteristics, all twelve of them, ended up in just four groups or categories of characteristics: "The Cow," "The Cow and People," "The Herd," and "The Herd and People." Much easier to remember.

Patience, cow signals, cow welfare, cow flow – all these topics in my talks were turning out to be similar things, just different perspectives on handling cows. I thought again of the airline staff on my travels. In all my flying around as a flying vet, I have had the opportunity to watch many airline staff exercise patience when handling people – and getting them to happily go to the right places. For airline staff patience was smiling even when stressed. For travellers, it was knowing that once you were in the system, there was nothing you could do to speed things up – you would get there on time or not, but just amuse yourself for the meantime. Airline staff have been trained to know by observing the passengers what sort of treatment they need. When there is a delay, a person who is anxiously looking around for a place to charge their cell phone needs Wi-Fi, a person sitting on their suitcase reading a magazine needs a comfortable chair. Another person is eating the last chocolate in the dish – they need some more edibles.

Teaching patience was becoming, instead, teaching about observing the cow and getting people to understand how it thinks and even to like cows, reading the signals that the cow is sending. Then they will work out how to work with her and not against her.

Good facilities help, but what if you have old or poor facilities? You need to understand that the cow is having trouble and be patient. Not an easy message to convey but much easier if you have laid the right groundwork.

The question that I was asking was: What is impatience? Is it impatience or ignorance, or poor training? Are you in the wrong job like Mr Patagonia thought he was? Are the cows scared of you like ProHand discovered in Australia? Do they like you? Do you like cows? Do you notice cows – like Cow Signals was teaching? How to pass on what to do and not just give a list of "don'ts"?

Maybe the question to ask was: what is patience – how to measure it – what does it look like? Impatience was easy to see, at least you could see the cows' reaction, the cow signals they were giving, such as bunching up or pushing and shoving other cows. And as always, it is easier to point out what someone is doing incorrectly than to tell them what is the right thing to do. I remembered from my earlier studies the answers farmers had given when I asked why they thought that some farmers had more lameness than others. When I asked why did those other farmers get lame cows, older farmers said, "It's the young guys on bikes." Young farmers said, "It's the old guys with their dogs." What they were doing was pointing out impatience. But I didn't usually ask why they thought that some farmers *didn't* get many lame cows.

By now, you would have realised that eliminating lameness from the dairy industry was a multidisciplinary work. My daughter in her studies had started out as an early-childhood teacher. She told me that you shouldn't say no to children; it is better to say "yes – when . . ." to the right thing. The challenge is to work out what is a good thing to say yes to. I often said to my vet staff it is better to say yes at first but then modify it. For example, if someone asks if you would like a cup of tea, just say "yes" – then, if you are in a rush, put it on credit for another time. I needed some positive memorable guidelines on what patience looked like. Instead of giving a list of don'ts, I needed some dos.

So I started with how to be patient walking the cows from the paddock to the milking parlour. Question – how long does it take to get your cows from the paddock to the shed? How fast does a cow walk? Every farm has a slightly different expectation and idea of how long it takes – depending on the weather, time of year, and so on; maybe there should be a formula.

I was out on a farm still asking questions when I heard one new farmer's innovative answer to how to be patient bringing in the cows. I had visited this farm for many years, and there had always been a lot of lame cows – the tracks were in a terrible condition, but this year there was a new farmer, and so far, I hadn't been called to any lame cows there.

"Why do you think that you have had so few lame cows on this terrible track, when Joe (the previous farmer) had dozens go lame?" I asked.

"Oh, that's easy" – he winked – "I have got this track rated as three roll-your-owns."

"Three roll-your-owns?" I quizzed him.

"Yes, I stop my quad bike three times on the way in with the cows – when I catch up. I roll a cigarette and smoke it, and then we all move on."

I don't advocate smoking cigarettes, but this certainly was a great way to keep yourself back from the cows and to appear patient. But what happens if I don't smoke? How do I become patient or at least seem patient? Three roll-your-owns is just a strategy to keep back from the cows who are going just a bit slower than the motorbike wants to go. Being patient on a bike is easier now with a cell phone to play music or games or check messages and Facebook. Alternatively you could park the bike and use the downtime to clear a drain or get rid of some weeds.

Another strategy could be to go and open the gate, come home and have a cup of tea, or better still, have automatic gate openers. Of course, you only need an automatic gate opener if the gate is shut, but if it is open, how do the cows know when is the right time to come for milking? Probably they can tell by some method which we don't realise. One farmer found out about his cows' "clock." His farm was situated right beside a railway line. Every afternoon at three o'clock, a train passed by, and somehow the cows had learned to leave the paddock when they heard the train. His cows always arrived at the milking shed at around three-fifteen – until the railway company changed the schedule.

Maybe we should have a measure of how far away from the cows you need to be on the track when you are bringing cows in. I used to recommend at least the distance between fence posts or about five metres. One day I was being the farmer on a friend's farm. He had had a motorbike accident and had a foot in plaster. I was getting his cows in to be milked, and I was keeping well behind them, but they were bunching up in front of me.

"Jim, why are the cows bunching up?" I asked.

"That's because they don't know you," answered the farmer patiently as though it was obvious. I found that for me, the stranger, I needed to be at least two fence posts' distance behind in order for the rear cows to relax and stop bunching up.

So now we had information and ideas for how to appear patient on the track, behind the cows. If all the impatience resulting in lame cows occurred on the track, then only the cows at the back of the herd where the herdsperson was would be affected, and we would have solved the lameness problem. However, in my studies of the order that cows walked, we had found that any cow could be affected – even the very front ones. Something must be happening in the milking yards as well.

Maybe a Cow Signals and Temple Grandin idea could be a solution – low-stress handling or, as ProHand put it, professional handling. Or as I and Dairy NZ were finding – have a good protocol.

In the meantime, just as we thought that we were going to be successful, it was time for me to go back to the bottom of the cliff.

# CHAPTER 19

# Enter Infection (2012)

"I HAVE LOTS OF lame cows which don't seem to be getting better," said the caller on the phone. "They are costing me millions. Can you move over here for a year and see what the problem is?" I had answered the phone that afternoon, and the caller had said, "Hi, I am calling from Chile." I recognised the voice as that of the New Zealand manager of a group of farms in Chile. He had moved there himself from New Zealand in order to manage and expand these farms owned mostly by Kiwis.

I had travelled to Chile and other places in South America several times, mostly just teaching about cow flow and how to improve facilities to get better cow flow. I had already done some seminars and visited the Manuka farms several times, when they had wanted some advice on where to put the sheds and how to build the tracks. My visit earlier that year had been especially memorable as when we were standing out in a paddock with several farm managers, the phones had beeped with a volcano eruption warning. The volcano in question was just at the top of the farm we were on at the time. We got some stunning photos of a volcano belching smoke – but later that week, as we went to leave Chile to return home, we were delayed in Santiago, at the airline's expense, for an entire week as ash had drifted into the flight path we would take getting back to New Zealand. We ended up flying a different route, from Santiago to Tahiti and then Sydney and then Auckland to avoid the ash that wasn't clearing.

"I have worked out that these lame cows are costing me millions of dollars," said the Kiwi manager. He was not exaggerating. He was a farm manager who knew what lame cows were costing him and was willing to take some strong action. Many farmers over my time as a vet were unaware or unconvinced as to how much lameness was costing them. The economics of a farm is difficult to work out. My accountant-turned-farmer friend, Colin, had had more of a handle on it than most. Economics and balancing the budget are not a really good motivator for action in the middle of all the other activities that the farmer has going on.

It really is quite complicated. If a cow gets lame when it has just started its milking season, then the loss is much more than if it gets lame just before it is dried off for a rest. And the problem is that many of the cows that get lame usually choose the beginning of the milking season. Think of all the milk that it might have produced if it hadn't got lame. Maybe it won't get pregnant this year either, so that will be another loss. Or maybe you will have to pay for a vet to come along and treat her, or worse still, she may be too lame to recover. Lots of costs, difficult to measure, and difficult to estimate. Then there is the time wasted in drafting out lame cows, treating them and, if they are given antibiotics, keeping the contaminated milk separate. Definitely too complicated to be a good motivator for change.

These are just the monetary costs – but there are lots of other costs that are not counted, such as workers who get overworked because they have to treat lots of lame cows and milk them separately.

And the welfare cost for the cow – misery every day.

Then there is the one cost we don't often think of – the misery for the farmer and the workers who have to watch cows limping along in obvious pain. This often turns out to be the main motivator until there are too many cows lame, and the farmer gets used to it.

The manager in Chile understood all this and was taking action. But a whole year or even six months was impossible for me to be able to squeeze out of my time. There were other things booked, and I had a business to run – and grandchildren to watch. So we settled on a compromise – I would come for six weeks at a time, three times during that year. Once to investigate the situation and teach the staff how to treat lame cows, once to continue to monitor and make sure the action plan was going well, and once to finish up the milking season. I also could combine the visits with other seminars in Chile. Sandra and I planned three extended visits to Chile in that year – 2012.

The farms were working on an outdoors grazing New Zealand type system, so I thought that this should be easy. Obviously, I thought, they would just need to learn how to treat and fix the cows better so that the lame cows would recover quickly. Wrong again!

We started learning Spanish to communicate with the farm staff. Well, Sandra started to learn Spanish, and I attempted to start. The first visit was to be January right after spending Christmas with our grandchildren. There were eleven of them at that time. After the hectic time of getting ready we decided to have a little holiday in Osorno, Chile, before starting work. What a privilege to be able to live and work in so many different countries and cultures! We already had friends in Chile whom we could visit on weekends and holidays.

We were staying in a hotel right in the middle of Osorno, southern Chile. The town is not very giant and has lots of old-looking wooden buildings in it. The second day of our holiday, we rented a car and managed to get about one kilometre down the road before smoke started to pour out from under the bonnet. It seemed to be coming from in the engine, so we stopped, and a tourist from Argentina stopped as well and helped us explain to the rental car lady, in Spanish, what the problem was and where we were sitting on the side of the road. The lady from the rental company came down with a mechanic, and after a bit of fluffing around, they decided that the mechanics at the depot must have spilled some oil on the engine earlier that morning when they cleaned it. So we drove off again. We had planned to visit a farm that we had been to before – just to visit the owner and say hello and enjoy some lunch together.

Felipe, the farm owner, was a civil engineer, and his wife was a schoolteacher. They started out working for the mines in Chile (Lithium) and lived in an indigenous village near where the mine was situated. She taught at the school, and he worked at the mine as an engineer. They then moved to the United States where they lived for five or six years – and their kids went to school and learned to speak English like locals. They must have been very successful as they decided to retire early and buy a farm in order to make it a model of all the good things you can do on a farm. This was the farm where we were visiting that day. Felipe and his wife were very progressive as farm owners. In Chile, farm staff are very low on the pecking order but not on Felipe's farm, where they had much more input into the farm and were valued members of the team. They installed about the second or third rotary shed in Chile. The next project was to build a large house on the farm repurposing the timber from the old German barn that we had photographed on our very first visit to Chile. It seemed that there were not many photos of it from the days before it had been demolished, so we were able to give them a copy of our photo.

Felipe's brother-in-law also wanted some change from the city so he came to be the first manager. In fact, Francisco had been the first person we had met on that farm the first time we had been in Chile. He had been working with IBM so was knowledgeable about computers. He worked out how to use all the Wesphalia software that came with the rotary shed – and by the time we were back on the farm for this visit, he had moved to Osorno, where he was their consultant in Chile. When we first visited the farm, Francisco and his wife, Paulina, were living in a cottage on the farm. While Francisco and I had gone to look at the cows, Sandra had stayed at the cottage with Paulina who spoke only a little English. However, they went for a walk around the garden and found that the names of many plants and trees which they knew in Latin were a point of communication. That had been several years earlier. This time around, we would need more than just a smattering of Latin/Spanish.

Visiting the farm during our little holiday, we found that Felipe's son, also called Felipe, was now managing the farm. He was a sociologist – and ex-champion skier. He had all sorts of ideas on managing the people on the farm – including running personal training for the wives of the workers. He was about to add another dairy farm conversion. His father had another company with engineering projects. He had just finished building a "run of the river" power station in the south of Chile. Our son, John, being a water engineer, was able to explain how it worked. It is a power station that has no dam – just an intake canal that becomes a pipe and carries on level or gently falling until there has been enough drop in the original river, and then it drops through a penstock into a power station. His little power station was generating enough power for a medium-sized town in the south of Chile. He had another one in the planning. He told us that his partner in the engineering business has a daughter who has been to New Zealand and had just landed a job with the New Zealand grazing company, Manuka, to help translate for a New Zealand expert in cow's feet who was arriving this week. Felipe laughed and told him that the New Zealand expert was having lunch with him that day. Chile was turning out to be a small world. So we discovered beforehand that Consuelo was to be our translator. Our long association with Consuelo continued although her job as translator came to an end. We were delighted to be able to attend her wedding in Santiago a few years later.

Our little holiday was soon over and the last evening we were picked up by the vet from Manuka, the company we were to work with off and on over the next several years, and we drove 50 kilometres south to meet up with the Kiwi manager who had invited us to solve his lameness problem and recoup for him the $1.3 million that he figured he was losing. I did suggest that for my pay, I should get a share in the money – that would be a good incentive.

While we were working for Manuka, the company would accommodate us. There was a spare farm cottage in the middle of the farms that we were working on. The company gave us this house as a base to set up house and for Sandra to do the computer work needed. We were going to be really busy, so it was good to have a house nearby to live in. The farm workers were provided with lunch every day, and so were we. No cooking to think of. We explored near the house and found a huge raspberry garden – raspberries for morning tea. The house was a cute little holiday lodge of two storeys. It was entirely made of wood, but the wood was going rotten in places mainly because of poor design – things like flat surfaces where water sat. The interesting thing about it was that it was built around twelve support poles – four on each side and four down the middle. These support poles had been put up first and bolted to the foundation, and then the beams had been bolted to them, and then the rest of the house was sitting on those beams. There were several houses just like this on the property. Our cottage was originally the main house for a campsite on a little creek just nearby, so there was a decent-sized lounge and dining room, and on one end of the house, there was an ablutions block with two lots of two toilets and showers. Plus there were two bathrooms upstairs. We would be really clean.

Home away from home

I joined the farm vet team where I met the young vet, Juan Pablo, who was to be my specific assistant in charge of lameness. We renamed him JP at his request. He spoke a little English but not enough to be able to communicate well at the start. Consuelo filled the gap in language. Juan Pablo improved so much over the year that eventually he didn't need a translator. A few years later, his English was good enough to enable him to come to a lameness conference and present a paper on our work in Chile. My Spanish didn't improve as much as his English, but we got on well and became good friends.

"What size do you wear?" I was looking at a row of gumboots in the storeroom. JP was outfitting us with the farm issue boots and overalls. I had brought along my own vet equipment. Suitably dressed and accompanied by Consuelo and JP, Sandra and I were ready to begin work, looking at each of the farms. The first big job was to treat the lame cows and to get them recovering quickly.

We had the use of a 4WD double-cab ute to get around the farms. As I drove, I had to keep remembering to keep right. Sandra would say, "tight right" or "loose left" depending on the circumstances. However, the upside of this was that we were driving around in the beautiful scenery of Chile in the tenth district with mountains in full view – including the volcano that was still busy erupting and spewing ash. Occasionally there was a bit of ash haze, and one morning the windscreen of the vehicle was covered with a light dusting of ash.

Our first big task in tackling the lameness problem for the company was to be visiting every farm and doing a sort of audit on each rather like the Healthy Hoof programme that we had begun in New Zealand. The daily routine was established in the first week: arrive at the farm, meet the manager and the hoof treater, treat some feet, photograph each one and record the details, get a comprehensive history of the farm, watch and video as the herdspeople brought in the cows and milked them, and then go back to our cottage and download photos and videos and label everything before we forgot what it was. No wonder there were some twelve- and fourteen-hour days.

This was going to take time – no wonder we needed a whole six weeks, to get around all thirty-five farms. We also ran into some cultural barriers. I remembered the same or similar difficulties in Afghanistan and put into practice what I had learned there. Sometimes I think that if I know the answer to a problem, I just need to tell the people and they would fix it. Nothing could be farther from the truth.

I had grey hair, so I was immediately accepted, no problems there.

I could back up the much younger JP if needed. Then we needed to work out who was who on each farm and then to find out the story of each farm – which was different each time. And all that had to be translated and worked on until we thought we knew what they were talking about. Asking questions was difficult as we had to know what was the right question to ask so that nothing was lost in translation. For example, "Where did the cows come from?" could mean where did they come from this morning, i.e., which paddock, or where did they come from before they were on this farm? Then we had to know how to find out the real answer to each question. What usually happened was that when I asked a question, the people felt like this was an examination, and they wanted to get all the answers right. So often they told me what the right answer should be, not necessarily what was really happening there. If you asked them whether all the lame cows had been treated and were they getting better – the obvious answer should be yes, but in actual fact, it was really no. As I was to find out the staff were treating the cows, and doing a good job, but there were so many lame that they had got behind, and even then many were not getting better no matter what they did. But they didn't want to tell us that because that was the "wrong" answer.

So we got to work.

I arrived at the first farm, we lifted the first foot – and immediately I remembered a smell from four years earlier in Wales. I had been a little distracted at the time as a cow had just knocked my elderly mother-in-law over, but I was sure it was the same smell. I had never smelt it in New Zealand. Then I remembered the lameness conference in Finland that we had been to just after that visit to Wales. There they had talked about a sort of white-line disease – called smelly white line. It was outside my experience in New Zealand, so I had sort of zoned out. But now the dots had begun to join up. I got onto the email and then on to Skype and was in contact with my friend Roger in the U.K.. We exchanged several photos and agreed that this condition that I was seeing in Chile was the same thing, an injury infected by something called digital dermatitis. We had the usual New Zealand–style lameness that I was used to, which is to do with track and shed design and maintenance and how the cows are handled, but in Chile, there was an added problem – a nasty mean bug that showed as a dermatitis on the skin of the foot but was also, we were discovering, finding holes under the nail to hide in as well and causing havoc. The "new" cases that we were seeing on the farms were not actually new but old cases that had nearly healed and then got infected under the nail of the foot. Roger had seen it in the U.K., and others were seeing it as well. Right at that time in U.K., there was a discussion going on in the *Vet Record Journal* about these infections as they were relatively new on the horizon. Neither was there any definite information on the effectiveness of the various treatments. So there we were in the south of Chile connected to the rest of the Northern Hemisphere "lameness world" with a giant laboratory to look into this problem. What fun for me, but what a disaster for the cows.

I had to do some quick study on the infection involved called digital dermatitis. Luckily now there was such a thing as Google and the Internet. Digital dermatitis, I found, is an infection that occurs on the skin of the feet of cows, usually at the back in the middle just above the hoof. People had been seeing it in Europe and the USA for some years. It is just a skin infection, a dermatitis, and doesn't smell. We knew that it was seen in Chile but generally not, as far as I knew, in New Zealand. Some vets had noticed that, in many countries, the infection had spread from the skin and was now infecting other injuries. My U.K. friend, Roger Blowey, had found the same digital dermatitis microbes under the wall of the hoof in cases of white-line injury. These cases had a pungent smell and, as I remembered from the lameness conference in Finland, seemed to be very difficult to clear up. That was why some people had even called this condition "non-healing" white line although we hoped this was a misnomer. Roger had found that often the infection got right down to the bone causing the bone to grow extra spikey bumps. Or the infection might eat the bone away. In either case, the hoof was permanently damaged. In severe cases, the best treatment was to amputate the affected claw and let the cow walk on one claw without pain.

This was what I was seeing in Chile.

By the end of our first visit, we knew what we were going to have to deal with, so we packed our little house up for six weeks and returned to New Zealand.

# CHAPTER 20

# Solving the Double Problem (2012–2015)

SIX WEEKS LATER, we were back in Chile. It almost felt like nothing had changed – except the weather. Winter was well and truly on the way, and we were going to really need the gloves, jackets, thermals, and hats that we had brought with us. Every day Juan Pablo and I were outside treating dozens of cows. Each time if it was possible, we saved the foot; otherwise we amputated just the injured claw. Gradually we were getting on top of the problem.

I wanted now to find out if the bones were damaged as Roger had said, so I boiled up some in the kitchen of our cottage. Bad idea. The smell was horrendous. But the photos were great! Not a good trade-off according to Sandra. The bones were definitely damaged. Some were even eaten away, so there was very little healthy bone left. No wonder they needed to be amputated. These bones were going to prove very valuable as I could show farmers and hoof trimmers that what they were treating was going to beat them, and they would lose the cow unless they found the cow before it got really bad and cut all the infection out.

I found that the local people treating the cows were doing an excellent job – just the job had become much more difficult, so harder to get the good quick result that the Kiwi farmers expected. Some re-education was needed for those Kiwis to explain this new problem that they had never met before.

Having visited all the farms and diagnosed the problem, our second job was to devise a clear plan for the way ahead so that things would not get into the same desperate situation again. We needed to make a plan of how to manage lameness in situations where there was secondary infection with digital dermatitis happening. A double problem. In the end we came up with a plan we called the "five-point plan." Point one was to write down what you see and treat, and then you will be able to know what got better and how successful you were. Second, find the lame cows early and treat them well so that the infection has less chance to get away. Those first two points were dealing with what every farmer should be doing everywhere there are dairy farms. The middle points number three and four were what we needed to concentrate on next – the big problem. Point number five was to do with keeping the cows fed properly so the feet would be healthy – another thing that all farmers everywhere do pretty well.

To tackle the big double problem, we needed a twofold attack. Point three: Get rid of the infection, which meant kill the bugs, and, at the same time, point four: try to prevent cows from getting injuries in the first place that could later get infected. The first part was a job for Roger to give advice on, and the second was my department.

The first advice Roger gave was that the whole herd should be foot-bathed – have their feet disinfected every milking. This meant walking through a trough of smelly antiseptic solution on the way out after milking. Sounds easy – but not so. If you were a cow, would you like to do that? Many of the farms had long herringbone parlours with up to forty cows all leaving at once. Imagine having forty cows baulking at a foot bath and holding up the traffic. We had to design something that wouldn't hold up the traffic and that would hold enough water so that if cows dropped dung into the solution or had dirty feet, the bath wouldn't end up too contaminated to be effective.

The ball was back in my court – how to implement this. I had already thought about the problems and difficulties of foot bathing in New Zealand. There is another foot infection that needs a foot bath treatment when it occurs. It is the one called foot rot, where an injury or a stone jammed in between the claws has broken the skin to let a different infectious bug in. When I was designing a foot bath to clear up this infection, I found that cows can get used to any sort of foot bath if it is familiar and there all the time. However, there are some things they don't like. Slippery surfaces such as wet plastic or metal, or slopes are frightening to a cow. Combine that with a smelly solution or a sudden appearance of a portable bath made of metal, and it is a no go. They don't mind stepping over a block wall in the way, but they don't like stepping down into water. With all that in mind, I had recommended that farmers in New Zealand build foot baths on the concrete surface (non-slip) right where the cows must go every milking (fits the normal routine) and with just a square concrete block wall to step over. In fact, you can build the whole bath with concrete blocks on an existing area of concrete. It needed to be large enough to hold a volume of at least one litre per cow so that the cows could all walk through after being milked, and the bath would not have to be changed mid-milking.

Then after milking the foot bath had to be able to be washed out easily or it would become a slurry of infection. So, we put a bung in the corner to let water out. This proved not such a good idea, so we changed that for a sluice gate replacing one of the blocks in the wall.

Next was to work out how much solution to put in so that the antiseptic was the right concentration, and there was sufficient to cover the feet of the walking cows. I came up with a simple formula based on the square area of the bath at a depth of ten centimetres. This design was the basis of each foot bath. We varied the position slightly according to the layout of the milking yards. The company sent a maintenance crew to each farm to build a foot bath designed to fit every situation.

Finally, having built the baths, we tested them with lots of cows – and videoed the cows walking happily through. Some even seemed to enjoy stamping in the puddles. I got Sandra to count how many of them dropped dung in the solution and calculated how much contamination that would make. When all was said and done it made a nice little paper for the next lameness conference in Bristol, U.K., along with a poster on the discovery of "non-healing" white-line injuries in Chile.

That was the first part of solving the problem of infection. The ball was back in Roger's court. Next, Roger said we had to find out where the infection was coming from. We checked the feet of the cows at milking. A sure way to get dirty, getting in the pit with the milkers, keeping out of their way whilst squirting the back feet of the cows standing somewhat above you to be milked. Then getting up close enough with a torch to examine the skin just above the hoof. Sure enough, we found that quite a few had skin lesions that could be spreading to other cows. Hopefully the foot baths would help with preventing more of those as well.

The next question was how would that pass from cow to cow and get into lesions on the foot? Time for me to go back to the Northern Hemisphere experts and read what they had discovered. What they had found was that the bug liked dirty skin and especially skin covered with slurry made from cow dung and urine. Then if the cows walked through that sort of mess the bug could easily spread. It would be like not washing your hands before eating. A lot of muddy slurry was common in large indoor barns – but outdoors? Where was the infection hiding?

We didn't have to look far to see where the dirty feet were coming from, and the possible place of transfer of the infection from cow to cow. It was most likely in the entrance ways to the waiting yard for the cows. The yards were all concrete and kept clean, but the entrance areas through which the cows passed in order to get onto the concrete were gravel and basically became just cess ponds. With about six hundred cows walking through on their way to milking, it was no wonder there was a mess. We also have this mud problem in New Zealand. The cows slow down and get worried if they have to walk through mud as they can't see if there are stones underneath or if they have to walk onto a concrete area which is either slippery or has small stones on it. The result is that they add more dung to the pile.

I had found several solutions that had worked in New Zealand. Sometimes the source of the mud was simply a drainage problem. If this could be solved with something like a nib wall, we were happy, and so were the cows. Another solution for this area was to extend the concrete out onto the entrance and further away from the gate leading into the yard. This put the slowing down area on concrete where the cows might bunch up to get through a somewhat narrower gateway. A bit costly and anyway impossible to do during the milking season.

Another solution was to put some sort of transition material on the walking area before the concrete where the cows begin to slow down and bunch up a bit as they get ready to enter the yard. This would absorb small stones that might drop off the cows' feet and end up on the concrete or in the mud. Then the cows would walk happily over this section and not drop dung to make it muddy.

The main material that we use in New Zealand to transition between gravel and concrete is crushed lime, but there was none available locally in Chile. Then local ingenuity came up with a temporary solution. First, spread sand, and on top of that, spread white synthetic sacking stretched tight. Perfect for a short-term solution.

On the job in Chile

The person with this idea was another friend who was doing similar work to what I was doing but with more of an emphasis on nutrition. His wife, another Paulina, showed Sandra how to cook some of the traditional Chilean milk desserts – delicious. She had written a book with both Spanish and English text full of recipes of how to prepare things like dulce de leche, semolina pudding, and caramel custard. Dulce de leche was my main "downfall." My favourite stocking filler at Christmas for myself and my two younger sons used to be a can of condensed milk to sip slowly whilst watching a movie – probably not the healthiest snack. Dulce de leche is caramelised condensed milk, so no wonder I loved it.

The second part of the problem, my department, or point four, was to prevent the injuries that could get infected. I needed to help the people to handle the cows better so that there was less damage to the feet. Less damage that could become infected. This meant training for all the staff in low-stress handling – or finding the ones who knew how to handle the cows and getting them to show how it was done. Low-stress handling in the two areas of the tracks and in the waiting yards.

In New Zealand, I had worked on what patience or good herding on the tracks looked like. A bit different in Chile – this usually meant leaving the horse at home. Training a person is one thing, but training a horse and rider is another. Sebastian in Uruguay and another rider, also in Uruguay, managed to bring cows in gently whilst on horseback, but often it wasn't the rider; it was the horse. The horse has longer legs and naturally goes faster than cows so has to be reined in. And it doesn't have a cell phone to keep it occupied – or three roll-your-owns to smoke.

That was bringing cows along the walkways. My next task was to pass on what I had learned in New Zealand about getting cows that are waiting in a yard to come up to the milking bails without having to be pushed. We had discovered that if cows are afraid of slippery surfaces or some other part of the facility, they will go slowly, so there will be a strong temptation to jump up out of the pit to push the cows along. The milker I had seen in Ireland had been an example of that. On the farms in Chile, there were several different styles of milking sheds, ranging from an old herringbone shed with just six milking machines on each side to modern New Zealand–style herringbone sheds with forty machines down the centre. Some sheds the cows liked, and some they didn't. We discovered some of the reasons why. There were upsetting things like grates in the entrance, tight corners, and slippery slopes. We checked to see that all the rails were in the right place at the correct height. Sometimes in New Zealand we even check for stray electricity in that pipe work. In most of the sheds on the Chilean farms the cows were rewarded for coming in with a scoop of tasty supplementary food – so there should be no problem encouraging them to come in.

Here, in Chile, I was about to get some video footage of how cows can organise themselves with no people visible. And then some more footage of a milker unknowingly doing all the right things to move some cows. Two valuable clips to show in my seminars on low-stress handling, filmed in Chile with local workers in charge

Despite the supplementary feed available in the bails, in some of the sheds, the cows seemed really reluctant to come up to be milked. So of course the milkers were jumping up out of the pit to get them in. When the milkers came into the yard, they shouted to the cows to get a move on – which the cows interpreted as "Go away, I am angry with you!" (In Spanish, of course.) And so they did. The cows ended up afraid of the milkers. We persuaded the milkers to stay in the pit and let the feed encourage the cows to come in. That was when we got the first video of cows organising themselves and deciding who is the next one in line to go and get milked.

When Sandra was young, her family had a yacht which they sailed on the bays near Sydney. Her father was the captain, her sister was the helmsman, and Sandra was the deckhand. Every now and again this would involve a trip to the top of the mast in the bosun's chair to adjust the rigging or repair something. I am not the sort of person who is happy with heights, just the roof of my house is high enough for me. But Sandra is okay with heights. So it was she who scaled the feed bin ladders with the video camera to get the bird's-eye view video of cows coming to be milked.

The clip which I now show at seminars she took on a sunny afternoon from the top of a feed silo on one of the farms where the milkers had stayed in the pit. It shows cows patiently waiting, standing a little back from the entrance to the forty bails. Then when they hear the front gate open, they begin to move slowly forward, some overtaking others who stand to one side. Then at about cow number thirty in the row, an obviously dominant cow wakes up, bunts one cow in front of her out of the way, and then bunts another waiting one in the back end, "telling" her to go in now, and the dominant one follows. No people are visible.

But what do you do about those last cows who just don't come in? Maybe they aren't hungry, they are lazy, they like being last, or they are waiting for something. In this case, I told the Chilean workers they just need to understand a bit about how a cow keeps herself safe.

Every creature has some strategies to keep itself safe, and the first is to keep your eyes open and focus on what might be dangerous. Then try not to let that dangerous person or thing get too close. We all have a personal safe space. Most of us don't like to have someone so close that we could touch noses. I have experimented with people in queues, waiting to board a plane, for example. If I have my back towards a person, we can be quite close, but if I turn to face them, they tend to back off. Cows are the same. They have a personal safe space or flight zone, and if we get near this, they will try to escape to feel safe again. The question is – which way is safe? The answer is obvious. The direction that will put the unsafe object out of her personal space zone as quickly as possible. If we are in front of a cow, she will go backwards, or if we get too close too fast, she will turn and walk away. If we are to one side, a cow will turn or go forwards depending on where we are standing. If we are behind her, she will turn her head to see where we are, and then, following her head, she will turn and walk away.

Sandra videoed a milker in Chile who instinctively did all this in sequence. Then she created a thought bubble of what the cow might be thinking – if indeed cows think in English! Here is the scenario: In a yard at the end of milking there were three cows left to be brought in. The milker appeared out of the entranceway to the milking bails, talking to the cows. *Hmm*, thinks the closest cow, *that is a human – might be dangerous – but I know this one – he is okay.* The milker walks off to one side in order to pass by the cow. The cow can still see him with one eye but is still facing straight ahead. *Where he just came from looks like a good place to go, he is not in the way, and there is food in there. I think I might go get it.* The milker walks a few steps further going past the cow. *Oh good, I think I will go forward and leave him behind.* The cow behind thinks, *That cow, my friend, must know where she is going, I think I will follow*, and she does. The milker walks past all three cows, but they are already going forward so he doesn't have to go very far before he can follow them himself to get on with the milking. The last cow doesn't even think; she just follows. This second video is my excellent illustration of how in real life you can move a cow or a group of cows.

Returning to New Zealand in between visits to Chile, I was interested to see if, in fact, there was any of that nasty digital dermatitis in New Zealand – so I started looking. I wrote an article in the local farming paper. "Have you seen anything like this?" With a photo below. I received a phone call from a farm in Taranaki not too far away from where we live.

"One cow in my herd has had a recurring odd sort of thing on the back of its foot," said the farmer on the phone. "It looks a little like your picture."

I went to check it out. There were not many cases, and it was just on the skin, but that is how it starts. I quietly began to panic. In the New Zealand system, we already get too much lameness from injuries that could be prevented. What if that infection, which it seemed was already here, began to infect injuries – we would have an epidemic. Just like in Chile.

I got together a few of the other lameness people including some from Dairy NZ, and we formed a "working party." The BDD (bovine digital dermatitis) working party. As a group, we decided that we should start with a survey of farms in Taranaki where we knew there was some digital dermatitis. We would see how widespread it was.

Back to the proposal writing, getting money, and setting up the project. This time I knew more of the ropes, so we managed to get funding and hired a technician to screen a group of Taranaki herds from my area (aka laboratory). Then Sandra entered the data (cow numbers and which foot had the lesion), we took samples to test at a laboratory, and then a PhD student named Aaron did the analysis. I love collecting data, but as you know, collating it and getting the analysis are outside my area – in fact, I know nothing about it at all. So Aaron was a great help. Aaron, whose surname was Yang, had grown up in China and done his first studies there. I don't think I have ever met anyone so enthusiastic. He was willing to give anything a go. Even the dirty practical stuff of visiting cow sheds to check feet for digital dermatitis himself. He was, and still is, in the middle of a love affair with data and its analysis. He would look at the results and think of ways to analyse them and then explain them to Sandra and myself with such enthusiasm and knowledge. We were amazed.

The outcome of this initial survey formed the basis of a paper at the next lameness conference in Chile, which was presented by Aaron. All the experts were there and were stunned by his knowledge of statistics and his speedy (we only had fifteen minutes) presentation during which most of us got lost, and the ones who could follow and ask questions were bowled over. He was also so amusing in his manner and dedication to the correctness of his calculations that he had us all laughing. At the end, we all stood and applauded.

The content of the study was something entirely more serious, however, and now I needed to get the information out to farmers wherever I could, that digital dermatitis was coming, and they had better look out for it – plus it indicated there was even more reason to prevent injury. I soon got the reputation for "bringing" digital dermatitis to New Zealand as very few had seen it before I showed them it was here. Wherever I went it seemed to appear.

Aaron went on to complete a bigger survey of herds all over New Zealand and demonstrated that digital dermatitis clearly is here and will probably stay.

At that same lameness conference in Chile, I was honoured to be asked to give a keynote address. This I titled "The Lame Game." It was the year of a world cup football competition, and we all know that South America is mad on soccer. Sandra managed to extract some video of some highlights from some of the matches and put in some cows walking, and some vets working as well as the players. It was quite a hit. Using my story in Chile as an illustration, I talked about how you need a whole team of people to win the lameness game. People who do all sorts of jobs, from farmers to foot trimmers, to vets and laboratory staff, and even statisticians. All the people involved might not agree on the strategies, but they can all contribute. My finding of the non-healing white line in Chile, which took meeting people in Wales and Finland, checking with experts from all over, and finding good localised solutions with bright ideas from people on the farm, was an excellent illustration. A great team – and the winners hopefully will be the cows.

## CHAPTER 21

# Old House, New House (2012–2016)

ALL THE TRAVELLING I was enjoying was confirming connections in many places around the world. Whilst I was overseas, when I met someone who wanted to visit New Zealand, I always invited them to come to Inglewood and stay with us. And of course, while they were here, they could see some of the amazing Taranaki dairy farms in my "laboratory." At some seminars in Europe, I met an Israeli vet called Chen. His expertise was nutrition.

Of course, when we had met, I had issued my usual invitation, and he also had said when, if ever, we were in Israel, we should visit him and his family. One day, I received an email from Chen, from Israel. He had beaten us to it. In the email, he said that he was coming to New Zealand with his family for a holiday and asked if he would be able to see some farms if he passed through Taranaki. I wrote back immediately and invited him and his family to stay at our house. That will be a problem, he replied – I will have five children with me. Not a problem to us, I wrote back, we have a big house – and all our five children have left home. So they all came to stay and we enjoyed having another language around the house – a biblical one with the young boys addressing their father as "abba." Chen informed us that he was having such a great time that he felt that there was some bigger person looking after him. We assured him that this was true.

The opportunity arose on our next trip to Europe not long after this to visit Chen and his family in Israel. After a seminar trip in Europe, we took a few weeks' holiday before coming home. We managed to visit some friends in Turkey, Chen and family in Israel and our son in China, all on the way home from Europe.

We had been to Turkey briefly a few years earlier in order to go to Iraq and meet up with our daughter and see her work in Kurdistan with the education and inclusion of special-needs children in regular schools. We didn't meet any dairy farmers or see many animals, just one stray cow on the side of the road, near a dam. In this case, one photograph sufficed for both the vet and our son, the dam engineer. This second visit to Turkey was entirely in the city of Istanbul – so no cows at all. We visited with friends who were living there and enjoyed the sights and sounds and tastes of the Middle East. The photographs were old buildings and famous sites. Then it was on to Israel.

Obtaining the relevant visas and permissions to visit Israel, we flew in for our ten-day stay. Chen picked us up at the airport in Tel Aviv, and we drove up to his home in Galilee. Another truly ancient place, but at the same time with modern ideas. Of course, I had to visit some farms, so our touristing was, as was more usual, via dairy farms. Many of these had the Israeli version of what was called compost barns. We visited one large farm with hundreds of cows, and next door was another shed with hundreds of sheep – milking sheep. All on compost bedding. Of course, Israel has a really dry climate so not quite like New Zealand, but I thought that some of the things that they were doing could be brought to New Zealand. I stored this information for the future.

Then we decided to do some typical touristing and went with Chen and his wife to some beautiful places in ancient Israel. What a privilege to be taken to visit a country by a local person. We visited Masada, a fortress near the Dead Sea. The fortress is a natural rocky table mountain with all four sides nearly vertical. The palace on top was built by Herod the Great as a fortress and summer palace, to impress his neighbours, over two thousand years ago. We were interested in how they managed to get water to the top of the mountain, another photo for our water engineer son. This fortress is famous for the desperate siege in the first century AD by the Romans of a group of faithful Jews. Sadly, it ended in the deaths of all the defenders. Still remaining from the time were ancient mosaics and the ramp that the Romans had built in order to end the siege. We didn't use the ramp to get to the fortress and palace but a scenic gondola instead. And of course, as we were nearby the Dead Sea, we had to have a "swim" in the super salty water. Rather difficult to swim and to sink was impossible. Staying upright was more of a problem as we were so buoyant. We had to pinch ourselves to believe that we were actually there.

We happened to be at Chen's house at the beginning of Succoth or the Feast of Tabernacles, when hundreds of Jewish people gather in old Jerusalem. They are remembering the biblical journey of the Jewish people through the desert on the way to the Promised Land. Everyone who is Jewish erects a sort of gazebo in their garden using palm branches for a roof. They decorate it with grapes and pomegranates in much the same way that we might decorate our home or tree for Christmas. Sandra saw some cellophane fold-out pomegranates for sale as decorations. She bought some to take some home to join our Christmas decorations. We had fond memories of pomegranates from our time in Afghanistan, where we had five or six varieties in our garden. We had hung them up to dry in the hallway, and their skins became like leather while the inside remained juicy – to eat months later.

We were amazed that here we were in Jerusalem with hundreds or thousands of Jewish people. We were walking the streets where the stories of the New Testament actually happened, where Jesus walked, and they were celebrating festivals of even greater antiquity from the Old Testament! Teaching about lame cows and ending up in Jerusalem is not what you might expect.

China was another place you might not expect to find a Kiwi vet. Unless he had a son who was a keen rock climber and a teacher of English. On this same trip, we also managed to squeeze in ten days in China. We were mainly in the towns and parks. One day, we hired some little electric scooters very similar in size to my old motor scooter that had faithfully taken me and sometimes Sandra as well back and forth to university. We saw lots of lovely green citrus orchards but no cows. However, we did find a tapestry of cows walking in a paddy field to keep the cow theme going.

We had done lots of moving around the world now. This was about my thirtieth country to visit. Where was home now?

When we first arrived in Inglewood back in the 1970s, we had met a slightly older couple, Alec and Doreen, at church meetings. They had older children while we had only one small baby. They had spent years buying, renovating, and selling houses. So when we had first acquired our old house, Alec helped a lot with ideas and know-how for the renovations. He was the one who was leaning on the old laundry when it fell down. We had quite a few good friends who also helped with ideas and hands on stuff. But the old house remained just that – an old house – draughty and hard to keep warm. We installed gas heating and new carpet, and it became comfortable and a real home for our growing family. When we returned from Pakistan in 1993, we added an extra room and a second bathroom. After all, we had seen houses in Pakistan where every room had its own bathroom – but then every room probably held a whole family.

Shortly after we bought and started work on our old house, Alec and Doreen decided that renovation was not their thing anymore, so they built a new, modern dream home – it even had an ensuite bathroom, which was twenty years before we had got around to it.

For the first ten years or so of our pre-retirement travelling for work, we would come home to the old house, now over one hundred years old and beginning to need some more maintenance. When all our children had left home and moved further afield, I was now without young, fit, and healthy helpers to share the jobs – so I would have to do the work myself before I retired in many years' time, I thought. A friend visiting with us shared his retirement plans. "Before you retire you need to do four things," he said, "get the car you want, travel, work on your relationship, and buy a low-maintenance house." We ticked the first three boxes, but the last one obviously would need attention.

We had certainly been doing a lot of travel. In fact, during our Chile year, we had done so much travel that you could hardly say that we were at home. We had found some friends who needed an interim house. They came and house sat for us almost the entire year. For the short periods that we were home in New Zealand, we were the "flatmates" lodging in the extra bedroom with the ensuite bathroom that we had added when we returned from Pakistan with two teenaged daughters. Whenever we were home in New Zealand during the year of 2012, we looked around for another house in Inglewood to buy. It had to be low maintenance, of course, and warm, as in our old house we were always fighting the damp cold draughts.

One day, flipping through the real estate advertisements during a short stay at home, Sandra noticed that the very dream house that our friend Alec had built over thirty years ago was for sale.

"That's our house," she declared. I remembered that it had lots of windows, so it was sunny but also very cold in the winter and needing a lot of heating to warm up the large lounge area, so I said that we wouldn't like that house. However, Sandra was keen to have a look at it – and you can guess the rest of the story. The heating problem had been solved as the last owners had completely double-glazed the entire house and installed a larger wood fire, so it was now cosy and warm.

So much for any ideas of downsizing ready to retire – the new house had three large bedrooms, two bathrooms, and an office, plus sheds and garage. Virtually none of the stuff we had accumulated over the years got thrown out as there was plenty of storage for all those bits and pieces that could come in handy one day. Things like the wide tie-down straps from trucks that I often pick up off the road and turn to good use in lifting cows. Ready to retire – well, not quite yet. I still had things I wanted to do, places to go, and people to meet. The advantage of still having a large house was that people from all over the world could come and stay, and so I wouldn't have to travel to them.

So we sold the old house, bought the newer one, and promptly left for Chile again but knew that we would return to a warm and cosy low-maintenance home.

Soon after one of our Chile visits, I was in Germany at a mini conference where I met Jeffrey, a lecturer from Kentucky University in the United States, who had come to Germany to talk about compost barns for cows. Jeffery told us that compost barns need a lot of maintenance – and I thought of our old house. He was so enthusiastic that I quickly decided that I needed to learn more about this – and of course I invited him to New Zealand. "But please wait," I said, "until I have organised some local compost barns."

Now I had some new ideas that maybe could help with our feet problem – compost to stand on.

Returning to New Zealand from the conference in Germany, I decided to investigate. In New Zealand, we don't usually house our cows as they do overseas but, in the winter, when the weather is really wet in Taranaki, especially up under the mountain, cows can ruin a whole paddock of grass and make it a mud hole instead of a paddock. The grass then takes a lot more work to maintain and regrow for the next feed for the cows. In order to get around this problem many farmers would let the cows graze till their stomachs were full and then put the cows on a "stand-off pad" where they could stand or sit around and chew their cud. To start with this stand-off pad might simply be a spare unwanted paddock or a gravelled area or even the track itself. However, more and more farmers were using a dedicated area often with a roof, much more comfortable for the cows, and in fact rather like a cosy home for the cows to return to after feeding in the paddock. One manufacturer of these shelters called them "herd homes."

However, the downside of this was that underfoot, it could become messy or, if it was concrete, uncomfortable and a risk for foot problems. In Jeffrey's compost barns, he had told us the bedding or flooring of the entire area was woodchip up to a metre deep. Now, as you can readily imagine, cows standing on woodchip for any length of time would end up creating a stinking bog with all the cow manure and urine produced. The solution to this, said Jeffrey, was constant maintenance, looking after the bedding almost like you would look after a baby. Stir or turn over the bedding regularly, and the mixture becomes warm cosy compost.

Already some of my farmer friends were using woodchip as the bedding in their herd shelters, but the cows only mixed it a little bit as they moved around. After some months, when it became too messy, the farmer would put more chips in on top and, after some time, would have to throw out the whole lot and renew. I thought that with a bit of maintenance, the farmers could not only save material and money but also end up with a more useable compost to apply to paddocks later. And hopefully the cows would love it as much as I liked my newer cosy home.

The United States wasn't the only place in the world using the composting idea. But it might pay to check it out there first.

Our friend Jeffrey, who taught about compost barns, invited us to come to Kentucky to see his barns first-hand and, while I was there, to give a few seminars on how to handle cows. Cow flow and good handling of cows had become my ticket to the world. At the same time, a New Zealand company with farms in Missouri asked me to come and help them as well with lameness. So we set about getting there. Every place has its challenges in getting there.

Our travel agent told us to apply for a visa waiver (meaning we didn't need a real visa).

"Do this about three weeks before you are leaving," she had advised.

We thought that visitors like us from New Zealand would be able to get a visitor's visa easily, but think again, not with our record! Since 2001, things had changed, and borders were getting harder to cross. We were not your usual visitors as we had visited quite a few sensitive countries in the last few years, including Iraq and Afghanistan – bad timing for us. The United States had just two months earlier changed the rules for visitors. In the wake of the 2001 terrorist attacks, they had put extra precautions in place, so we would now need a full visa. Hearing this, the travel agent thought we should give up the trip as these visas usually take three months to process, but we were willing to give it a try. We quickly filled in the paperwork and drove up to the U.S. consulate in Auckland to be interviewed. I think that we were meant to go to the United States as we ended up getting a full visa in a miraculously short time frame. The travel agent was stunned and still calls those visas astounding.

We set off for the States. Everything it seemed was larger than life there. Huge scenery, huge cows, giant wide roads, and rivers and storms. We visited the New Zealand–owned farms first.

Missouri looks flat from horizon to horizon, as far as the eye can see. We stayed with the manager of the Kiwi farms, who took us the first week to visit each farm. We arrived at one shed where we were to give a seminar on lameness and handling cows. As we were getting ready the rain started. Gentle at first. As the seminar progressed it became heavier, and soon we couldn't hear ourselves think, let alone talk. Phones suddenly began to buzz – there was a flash flood warning in the area. So we quickly loaded the equipment into the vehicle and headed for home. Just in time; water was everywhere, across paddocks and roads. It was still below the doors of the giant ute, but soon we couldn't see where the road was. Luckily by then we were just around the corner from home, which fortunately was on a slight rise above the surrounding floods. Apparently storms like this can occur with very little warning. Tornadoes also can strike here – we were near Wizard of Oz territory. We tried out the tornado shelter in the back garden of the house where we were staying, just for fun.

It was fall/autumn in the United States, so there were decorations everywhere, which interested my wife. I was more interested in the interior of cow houses than the decoration of people houses, but the photographs show both pumpkins and cows!

Then we moved on to visit Jeffrey in Kentucky, and our tour of compost barns began. We covered quite a few miles between farms, seeing different styles of farm, from the university farm to small Amish farms. On each farm, the cows looked really happy lying on the compost and chewing their cud. These farmers did a lot of work to keep their compost healthy and dry. Whenever the cows were out of the shed at the milking parlour, the compost was turned over to keep it working. Jeffrey told us that they didn't seem to get any more infection of the foot or even mastitis. They were generally cleaner, maybe because the cows were drier. The cows live permanently in these houses as they do in Europe, and they could get quite damp, but the farmers had installed giant fans to move the air. We had learned in Europe that cows indoors need ventilation anyway as they get quite hot because of the digestion process going on inside. Cows can walk around in temperatures that we would find freezing cold as they have their "heater" inside to keep them warm. In the past, the cowherd would sleep with the cows to keep him warm as well. On the way and at the farms, I picked Jeffrey's brain and those of the farmers to gather all the ideas that I could. After all, I was going to see if some of this system would work in New Zealand.

We did visit another rather different kind of animal house whilst we were there – a floating house – a replica of Noah's ark built in Kentucky to the biblical specifications and truly impressive. No wonder the expression "of biblical proportions" indicates giant size. The ark must have been a sight to see when Noah built it.

The United States wasn't the only place where I saw compost barns on that trip. I also went to Brazil and saw the Brazilian take on them. I must say they were much better smelling – they used the waste coffee bean husks instead of wood shavings – I am not sure if the cows appreciated the particular blend. I did see some problems with the really humid climate and some compost barns that were not working. Having spent some time with Jeffrey, I had a few ideas of what you could do to make them work better that I could pass on.

However, the New Zealand cows were still my priority. I made composting my new project back at home. Several dairy farmers nearby where I lived had herd shelters in which they already used wood shavings as bedding. I managed to persuade them to turn the bedding with a rotary hoe or tines to see if they could get a better result from their bedding. The cost to get rid of the entire barn lot of wood chip and replace with new chip was huge, not counting the work involved. Maybe this could save some money as well as material and be a more useful product in the end.

Now that I had a few farmers turning the bedding I emailed my American friend, Jeffrey, and found that he was already coming to a conference in Auckland. Of course, I invited him to come to Taranaki and stay so that he could see my compost barns. Jeffrey came for a visit and gave some advice and now quite a few of the local farmers are turning their bedding and even finding it economical, as they don't need to change the bedding every year. In fact, some farmers are finding that the bedding lasts even up to four years just by adding a little each year. We have some problems with the damp in New Zealand, which is partly solved by not keeping the cows inside all the time as they do in the United States or Europe.

I ran a field day for other farmers to come and see what we were doing. On the day when the farmers all gathered on the farm, I interviewed the farmer about his experience with his compost barn. He had done the numbers, and they added up to a bit of saving, but the best thing for him was the less stress he felt knowing that in the winter his cows were safe inside on a rainy night. When he had to check on them, they were only a few hundred yards away in a warm cosy house. Peace! Happy cows and happy farmer! They also had less lameness.

## CHAPTER 22

# Data Addiction Carries On (2017–2022)

WHEN WE BOUGHT our new house, we also acquired a glasshouse and a paddock at the back. Shortly after moving in, our daughter and her family joined us while they were looking for a house for themselves. They were given a hen with some chicks who set up house in the old donkey shelter out the back. Pretty soon we were getting eggs, and of course I wanted to know if this was going to be an economical venture. So I wrote down when the eggs were collected, how many, when a new bag of chicken pellets was opened and so on. Before you knew it, I had records of all sorts of things: the rainfall, the number of tomatoes the glass house produced, and so on. I found out that the chickens were not really economical. However, they were free range and therefore healthier and laid eggs with nice orange yolks. Just as with the herd home compost barns, the outcome doesn't have to be just economics.

Housing for animals had now become a bit of a passion. Back in New Zealand again with composting in mind, I decided to do some lame-animal investigating of a different kind. About three kilometres from my new home in Inglewood was a goat farm with a large shed for housing the goats; maybe this could also be a candidate for composting.

Nobody knew much about goat lameness in New Zealand, and I was supposed to be a lameness vet.

I hadn't worked much with goats before – or not goat feet anyway. Soon I had a whole string of questions that I was asking. Déjà vu. Did goats get the same sorts of lameness as cows? Goats in the wild run free over rocks and rough ground, and their feet are usually quite healthy. However, with no rocks to wear them, they grow too long, and soon the goats become a bit lame. The solution to this is to trim the feet several times a year, just as they do for indoor cows and just as you would do for your fingernails. The goat trimmers would surely know all about lame goats.

I started to visit some local goat farms to watch the foot trimmer and catalogue what the feet looked like. I devised a way of naming the foot problems I was seeing, similar to the way we name lesions on the feet of cows. The foot trimmers get paid by how many goat feet they trim, so they work really fast, so fast that I usually had less than two minutes to observe and record information about all four feet – that's just thirty seconds per foot! I spent many days at those goat farms just recording the different lesions that I saw. There must be an easier way to do this, I thought. How much easier it would be if I could just tap a phone to record what I saw. I took Sandra along on a couple of occasions to photograph the feet.

I also observed the goats walking. I was looking for lameness in a similar way to the way we would with cows. In a large herd of cows, it is sometimes difficult to spot a slightly lame cow among all the other cows, so advisors have invented a way of "scoring" cows as they walk past an observer. A non-lame cow is scored as zero lameness. This means that it is walking freely and normally. If the cow is even slightly lame, it walks a little differently. When a person has a limp, we can instantly recognise an abnormal walk. What are we looking for? A slight lift of the whole body to take the weight off the sore foot. A funny posture often leaning towards the non-lame foot. And a shorter step with the sore foot. It turns out that this is similar to what we see in a lame cow. A nodding head, an arched back, and a shorter step. Dairy NZ has a system of scoring to use these indicators. I elected to also use this for goats.

Goats are very inquisitive animals, and I found that this made it rather tricky to score them unless I was quite a distance away and hiding in my vehicle.

I took my photographs and observations to my friend Richard Laven at Massey University vet school. He was really excited.

"No one has ever done this with this many goats before," he enthused. (There were around two thousand goats that I had seen.) "We will write a paper about this so that everyone can get this information, and then we can start finding ways to improve conditions for goats as well as cows." He smiled. So we collaborated to write a paper for a journal.

At the next lameness conference in the United States, he planned to present a small part of the paper where he talked about the "locomotion scoring" of goats that I had done. I was also planning to go to the conference.

"Great idea," I said and promptly forgot about it.

About ten days before the conference, I received an email from Richard.

"I have been refused a visa for the U.S. as I have been to Iran lately, so I won't make the conference. Can you present the paper?"

Of course, I said yes. And then began to panic. I was already about to leave to spend a few days with our son in California on the way to the conference – when would I find time to do this. It was quite some time since I had read the draft of the paper. Plus, I am usually the person who talks about cows, not goats. And I wasn't planning to take my laptop on holiday. However, Sandra managed to find some of my photographs online, and John helped prepare the presentation.

However, back to the goats. I had started thinking about goats because of the idea of composting barns. Goats are usually kept in some sort of housing in New Zealand to keep them disease free. On the floor of the sheds were wood shavings just like in the compost cow barns. The way they kept the flooring dry was to add a new layer every few days. However, the flooring usually remained quite damp and smelly. I wondered if this might be a source of lameness or infection. If the flooring could be kept drier, the goats' feet would be drier, and maybe there would be less lameness.

The major question I then had was – would the same idea of turning over and mixing the bedding give good results for goats. Time to investigate. So there I was at the nearby goat farm collecting samples of the turned bedding to see how dry it was. I had my extra-large garage at my new house, with an old kitchen bench complete with an old microwave to dry the samples. I visited a second-hand shop to obtain some microwave-safe dishes, and my laboratory was complete. No need to use Sandra's kitchen. She was relieved to say the least.

Goats are different social animals to cows. Instead of running away from people they tend to come up close and get curious. Whilst visiting this local goat farm, I found myself being mobbed by a group of friendly goats who wanted to chew my overalls, eat my spade handle or even my ears, and destroy my ammonia meter.

Goat friends

I was about to find out that goats are different from cows in another way; they don't like walking or lying on soft ground and prefer firm surfaces. When we turned the woodchip and made it nice and soft and fluffy, the goats refused to lie on it. We had to flatten it down a bit to their liking before they would lie on the drier bedding.

I found some interesting preliminary results not dissimilar to what I had found with the composting barns for cows. Someone else will no doubt carry out more research as I turned my attention back to what I know best – cows.

During the first ten years of my travelling around New Zealand and overseas doing seminars and investigating lameness problems, I had been the "outside Inglewood" department of Inglewood vets. Now I thought that it was about time that I concentrated on this outside work, so I gradually transferred to working from my home and travelling from there. I now had a lot more time to do what I enjoy, what you would call data collection, at home and from home, especially if you included the eggs and the tomatoes.

At the same time, Dairy NZ had gathered together a group of lameness experts – there were just a few of us – to discuss lameness in New Zealand. They named this group the Lameness Technical Advisory Group – or L-TAG. We were a mixed bunch including Dairy NZ people, foot trimmers, vets, university professors – and me. The first thing that we did was to check all the research that had been published in New Zealand and overseas about lameness. Fortunately, someone else had already done the overseas part, so we only needed to compile the New Zealand part. The first thing that we realised was that we still didn't know the answer to the main question: How big was the problem? How could we hope to get farmers to do something about a problem when they don't know if it is bad or not? We had very little real data, just what I and a few others had collected.

At the lameness conference where I had talked about goat locomotion scoring, there was a lot of talk about video locomotion scoring of cows using artificial intelligence – technology plus. Some of it was now almost to the stage of doing as good a job as human observers when well trained. Untrained observers often do a rather ad hoc job just glancing at the walking herd and missing seeing lame cows. The video camera, even though it may make mistakes, sees everything.

The main problem with locomotion scoring is what to do with

the results. There has to be an advantage or pay back to make it worth spending the time. It seems to be a useless piece of information. It is the same problem that the L-TAG group had found in their review. The score, unless it gives a score to each individual cow, seems a waste of time. It does give a general idea of whether a farmer has just a few lame cows or many that he is not observing. However, if there are lots of lame cows, and the wrong person gets hold of your score, you could be in trouble. We had a lot of discussion about how to use locomotion scores as incentives to do better or as welfare ticks.

Data collection is definitely my favourite occupation, so no wonder it annoyed me when a farmer didn't know how many lame cows he had had, let alone when the problem might have occurred. Now that the cell phone had become everyone's constant companion, I thought that there must be some way to use this for data collection – not for me, of course, as I am rather cell phone illiterate, but for the new generation who do use them.

It seemed that very few, if any, farmers were writing down what they saw when they treated a lame cow – unless it needed antibiotics, and they had to be careful to keep the milk out of the main vat. Some farmers wrote down everything that they saw, but they were a rarity. What most of them wrote was very basic. However, what the lameness group wanted to know was quite a lot of information about which foot was lame and what type of lesion it was, what they treated it with, which cow it was, and so on – quite a bit of writing when you think of it. No wonder it was hard to get people to write it down. And then what did they do with the information? Lose the piece of paper, keep it in the book in their pocket, write it on a whiteboard, or hopefully type it into the computer.

Various valiant attempts had been made to get farmers, vets, or foot trimmers to record notes of what they saw on paper or in a little book. These efforts had mostly failed. Only data fanatics like myself ever recorded any detail. I had a system of my own to name each type of injury or lesion, but this was by no means universal. Names for the injuries and conditions varied from country to country and even from farm to farm.

The year before, I had been visiting Brazil to attend the very first local lameness conference there. The first sessions were dedicated to "what do we call this type of lesion so that we know what we are talking about." In the veterinary world, there was available a chart with names for each type, but what if you saw something different to the picture?

I had initially been invited to Brazil by another New Zealand company selling dairy equipment and also giving advice to farmers. And there were New Zealand style farms in Brazil. I thought that I knew what dairy cows looked like, and I had seen some quite different ones in places like Queensland, Australia, where it is very hot and the cows were related to Indian breeds. I was totally unprepared for what Sandra called the cutest calves with giant ears (Google that and you can see some pictures of them) which grew up into large cows that didn't look at all like dairy cows from the limited perspective of a New Zealand vet.

We travelled around the country with the local people and met farmers who had great ideas and were doing wonderfully well but who knew very little about how to treat lameness. Many did not even have a proper hoof knife. Consequently, the lame cows were very lame and the lesions very complicated. No wonder the local vets didn't know what to name them.

Touristing in Brazil was extremely tasty. We tasted Brazilian cheese bread, beautiful cheese, fruit cheese, and fantastic fruit. One day, we visited a Jersey cattle stud and were treated to a huge feast of watermelon. Everywhere were mango trees. The streets of the capital, Brasilia, were lined with them, just ripening. They had been planted there on purpose to provide fruit for everyone. On a farm one day, we were standing underneath a huge, ancient mango tree admiring the fruit that was ripening high above us. The lady of the farm asked whether we liked mangoes. "Love them," we replied. But how on earth was she going to get one from six metres up above us? We didn't know. She produced a bamboo pole at least that long with a basket on the end. She reached up with it and put it under a ripe mango. A little jiggle and the mango was in the basket and on its journey to our stomachs.

A trip to Brazil would be incomplete without a visit to Iguazu Falls, the "Niagara" of Brazil. So when we had a couple of days off before the conference, we flew up to see the amazing waterfalls. There had been a drought that year, but the falls were still spectacular. There were no cows there to photograph, so we visited a huge dam and power station that straddles the border with Paraguay and photographed ourselves standing on the border. Then we photographed some of the pipes and other parts of the installation for our civil engineer son. Just nearby was a bird sanctuary where we also photographed the photogenic birds in rainbows of colours and in sizes from bee-sized hummingbirds to giant macaws.

In New Zealand, talking with the L-TAG people, we realised that naming all the different types of lesions on the foot of a cow was not going to work; even the typical ones had several names. And although naming everything was a good idea, how was that going to help the farmer? The most useful thing that I wanted to know was whereabouts on the foot it was painful. Then we could fix it. But not only that – we could work out ideas of how it might have happened, and what the risk factors might have been, just as I had done with the cows with white-line injuries on the outside claw of the back foot, while heifers had the same pain but at a different place. Knowing this hopefully we could begin to stop this injury happening to other cows. What I needed to do was find the pain, fix the lesion, the fight the risks. This was to be my new mantra. Find it, fix it, fight it. Right where it hurt. So we came up with the idea of using the "point of pain" as an identifier of the lesion.

It already had seemed obvious that to make it easy to record, we should be using the cell phone. In Chile whilst working with other vets, I had seen that even if a vet had nothing else with him to write data for me, at least he had a cell phone. In fact, he usually had several so that he could tap into whichever network was available. So in our lameness group, we hit on the idea of a cell phone "game" to record lameness events. Dairy NZ found a programmer and told him what we needed, and he created an app that farmers could download onto their phone. They just type in the cow number – the phone already knows the date and time. Tap which foot it is that they have lifted, and then, on the picture that comes up, tap where they have found the point of pain, and the phone does the rest. And you are the winner! The app, called the Healthy Hoof App, even gives you an alert if it thinks you have too many lame cows.

Actually, if we play the game well on our cell phones, we could all be winners. The farmers, because they have one step recording and don't have to think of names for each type of lameness; the vets, because they now know what the farmer's main problem is; and the researchers, as they can begin to see trends and start to get an idea of what the main problems are and when they occur. And the cows are winners too as their lameness problems can be managed better.

For the first time in my career, I can ask my "laboratory" farmers to tell me what lame cows they have had, and with a few taps, they can email me the data, and I can add this to a spreadsheet – well, my wife can – and I have a detailed report and can give targeted advice, such as: do you need to change your style of milking, do you need to fix up your facilities, or both? So now I could concentrate on giving better advice and fine-tune my seminars to fit the need.

The Healthy Hoof App is really useful to me but still needs a bit of work to help farmers realise its use on the farm. Maybe we need to connect to an online friend to play the game with. We could all post results and see who can achieve not the highest score but the lowest lameness.

Every seminar now I was giving at field days for farmers I would demonstrate the app, and some of the farmers would download the app and begin to use it. It is still a wonderful tool waiting to be discovered.

However, more and more of the seminar requests were not focusing directly on lameness but on cow flow and how to work with cows to get them to move happily through the dairy sheds and at the same time keep the workers happy. Herds were getting larger, and the staff often were inexperienced and often immigrants to New Zealand with English as their second language. I needed to keep my seminars easy to understand and use ideas that people could relate to.

In New Zealand many years ago, I think in the 1970s, there was a TV series called *The Herd*. It was aimed at teenagers who were the "Herd." Everyone has been a teenager, and some may now have teenage children, so we all know that "The Herd" is probably a good title for teenagers, at least some of the time. And parenting or managing teenagers could be something that people would relate to. One parent educator in New Zealand, thinking of the same comparison, said that when working with teenaged boys, one needed an electric fence – I immediately saw the connection – although I suspect she may have been thinking of the sort of electric fence topped with razor wire that you see around embassies in Third World countries and not the single wire that is sufficient to keep cows in the paddock.

Cows are individual animals, like teenagers, who have a pecking order, like teenagers, who follow the crowd, like teenagers. Maybe if we got a bit of an idea of this herd mentality, it would help with managing dairy cows – and also help dairy farmers to remember what I was teaching in my seminars. So I called my latest seminar "Herd Mentality" and focused on understanding how the "teenager cows" act in a herd.

I was travelling to do seminars from home base – and suddenly travel became impossible because of the 2020 COVID-19 pandemic. I had to adapt to some more technology – Zoom. I called in another of my sons and Sandra to help me work out how to do online "virtual" seminars. Now I could really do armchair travel to anywhere in the world and be home for lunch, or dinner or even breakfast depending on the time zone of the seminar participants.

In the last few years, working from home has become the usual, so I am no different from anyone else. Having retired from coalface vet work, I have lots of time to collect data and to follow up ideas like goats' feet and composting. Of course, I still have lots of questions unanswered and ideas of possible solutions – we never stop learning. With all the data from the Healthy Hoof app that I am collecting, I have lameness details from not just hundreds of cows but thousands each year. I am working on my questions, but they will have to wait for another book.

In the meantime, farmers still phone me; I still teach vet courses and do seminars for farmers. And spend time collecting more cow data – and counting and eating tomatoes from my glasshouse!

# FOOTNOTES

## Chapter 1

1. Lameness for the layman just means that the cow is having difficulty walking along – limping. It can be a big problem if more than a few cows are limping or lame.
2. Spring refers to the season change from the winter cold to when the weather is warm enough for the grass to grow to feed milking cows. This could be anywhere from the end of June to the beginning of August depending on the local conditions. It is usually before the official start of spring.
3. In New Zealand, most farmers operate on a seasonal dairy system. The cows all calve together, and all dry off together according to the season when there is the most pasture growth to feed the cows.
4. An infection in the udder is called mastitis.
5. Youcanfindthissortofinformationinabookorfromthelnternet, https://www.extension.iastate.edu/dairyteam/files/page/files/FeedingDairyCowsonQualityPasture.pdf, or you can sit and observe cows.

## Chapter 2

1. The Rotolactor was a giant, glass-walled revolving machine that could automatically milk thousands of cows a day at Camden Park Estate in Menangle, south of Sydney, Australia.
2. https://i.stuff.co.nz/business/farming/99362818/milking-machine-creator-recognised-100-years-after-his-invention--dairy-farming
3. Te Ara Encyclopaedia: https://teara.govt.nz/en

4. Norman Lindsay in "The Magic Pudding."

## Chapter 4

1. *Te Moa 100 Years History of the Inglewood Community 1875–1975* by R. W. Brown

## Chapter 9

1. *N.Z. Vet. J.* 37:135–142.

## Chapter 13

1. Behavioural Characteristics of Dairy Cows with lameness in Taranaki, New Zealand. *New Zealand Veterinary Journal* 52(3), 103–108, 2004.

## Chapter 16

1. Electric fences are widely used by dairy farmers all over the world. The electric fence consists of a single wire running across or around the paddock raised above the ground by "standards" or metal, removable, insulated wire holders. These are about three quarters of a metre high with an insulated wire holder at the top. A New Zealander, Bill Gallagher, was the first to use an electric fence for livestock – his horse – and his company now supplies electric fence components, much improved, for dairy farmers.
2. *Pressing the Right Buttons* by Allison Mooney.

## Chapter 17

1. Teleflower was the name of the business started by florists in 1926 to send flowers anywhere in the world. Customers would contact their local Teleflower florist, who would contact another member in the appropriate part of the world who would deliver the flowers. It is now known as Teleflora or Petals.

CPSIA information can be obtained
at www.ICGtesting.com
Printed in the USA
LVHW041601200423
744868LV00010B/326/J

9 781669 880516